TOWARD A CRITICAL THEORY OF STATES

SUNY series in New Political Science
Bradley J. Macdonald, editor

TOWARD A CRITICAL THEORY OF STATES

The Poulantzas-Miliband Debate after Globalization

CLYDE W. BARROW

SUNY PRESS

Cover art from iStockphoto by Getty Images

Published by State University of New York Press, Albany

Printed in the United States of America

For information, contact State University of New York Press, Albany, NY
www.sunypress.edu

Production, Diane Ganeles
Marketing, Kate R. Seburyamo

Library of Congress Cataloging-in-Publication Data

Names: Barrow, Clyde W., author.
Title: Toward a critical theory of states : the Poulantzas-Miliband debate after globalization / Clyde W. Barrow.
Description: Albany : State University of New York Press, 2016. | Series: SUNY series in new political science | Includes bibliographical references and index.
Identifiers: LCCN 2015042432 | ISBN 9781438461793 (hardcover : alk. paper) | e-IBSN 9781438461816 | ISBN 9781438461809 (pbk. : alk. paper)
Subjects: LCSH: State, The—Philosophy. | Nation-state and globalization. | Marxian school of sociology. | Poulantzas, Nicos Ar. | Miliband, Ralph.
Classification: LCC JC11 .B375 2016 | DDC 320.101—dc23 LC record available at http://lccn.loc.gov/2015042432

10 9 8 7 6 5 4 3 2 1

CONTENTS

ACKNOWLEDGMENTS

I owe special thanks to the many individuals who encouraged me to keep writing on state theory even after I thought I had nothing left to say on the topic. In this pursuit, I have often been encouraged by Stanley Aronowitz, Peter Bratsis, Paul Wetherly, Manfred Steger, and Leo Panitch, and by the many students who have taken my seminars in Marxian Political Theory and Critical Theories of the State. I also benefited from many informal discussions and seminar sessions while spending time as a visiting scholar at the Centro de Estudios de Educación Superior, Universidad de Puerto Rico (2010); the Faculty of Social Science, Kassel Universität (2005); and the Institute for Political Science, Philipps-Universität Marburg (2003).

I also gratefully acknowledge the following publishers, who have generously allowed me to reclaim my work without a fee:

Chapter 2: "The Miliband-Poulantzas Debate: An Intellectual History." Pp. 3–52 in Stanley Aronowitz and Peter Bratsis, eds., *Paradigm Lost: Revising State Theory*. Minneapolis: University of Minnesota Press, 2002.

Chapter 3: "Plain Marxists, Sophisticated Marxists, and C. Wright Mills' *The Power Elite*." *Science & Society*, Vol. 71, No. 4 (October 2007): 400–431. Copyright Guilford Press and reprinted with permission of Guilford Press.

Chapter 4: "Ralph Miliband and the Instrumentalist Theory of the State: The (Mis)Construction of an Analytic Concept." Pp. 84–108 in Paul Wetherly, Clyde W. Barrow, and Peter Burnham, eds., *Class, Power, and the State in Capitalist Society: Essays on Ralph Miliband*. London: Palgrave MacMillan, 2007.

Chapter 5: A much abridged version of Chapter 5 appeared in German as "State Theory and the Epistemologies of Structuralism (in German)." Pp. 32–47 in Lars Bretthauer, Alexander Gallas, John Kannankulam, und Ingo Stutzle, eds., *Poulantzas Lesen: Zur Aktualitat Marxistischer Staatstheorie*. Hamburg, Germany: Verlag-Springer, 2006 and in English in Lars Bretthauer, Alexander Gallas, John Kannankulam, und Ingo Stutzle, eds., *Reading Poulantzas* (Pontypool, Wales: Merlin Press, 2011).

Chapter 6: "The Return of the State: Globalization, State Theory, and the New Imperialism," *New Political Science*, Vol. 27, No. 2 (June 2005): 400–430.

ABBREVIATIONS

AIG	American International Group
CMP	Capitalist Mode of Production
CUFTA	Canadian-U.S. Free Trade Agreement
CUNY	City University of New York
EU	European Union
FDI	Foreign Direct Investment
FDIC	Federal Deposit Insurance Corporation
GATT	General Agreement on Tariffs and Trade
GDP	Gross Domestic Product
IMF	International Monetary Fund
ISA	Ideological State Apparatus
LSE	London School of Economics
MFN	Most Favored Nation
MOFA	Majority-Owned Foreign Affiliate
NAFTA	North American Free Trade Agreement
NATO	North Atlantic Treaty Organization
NFIC	National Foreign Investment Commission

NTBs	Non-Tariff Barriers
OECD	Organization for Economic Cooperation and Development
TNE	Transnational Enterprise
UNCTAD	United Nations Conference on Trade and Development
WTO	World Trade Organization

PREFACE

I occasionally think back to my first year of graduate school at the University of California, Los Angeles, when in 1977 the Marxist theory of the state was all the rage among radical scholars. The Poulantzas-Miliband debate had just reached its dénouement with Nicos Poulantzas' (1976) final dismissive reply to Ralph Miliband in the *New Left Review*. At the same time, *Kapitalistate* collectives were springing up on campuses all over the United States and everyone was required to take sides in the debate between Poulantzas and Miliband.

I had entered graduate school under the influence of G. William Domhoff's, *Who Rules America?* (1967) and Charles A. Beard's, *An Economic Interpretation of the Constitution of the United States* (1913). Consequently, I was immediately drawn to Ralph Miliband's *The State in Capitalist Society* (1969), once I had the opportunity to actually read it, but fellow graduate students immediately dismissed my "naive instrumentalism." I decided not to join the recently formed (and short-lived) UCLA *Kapitalistate* collective. Nevertheless, I eventually succumbed to the elegant temptations of Poulantzasian structuralism, while not realizing at the time that my reading of Poulantzas was not quite the same as that of my colleagues, because I came to him backward by reading his last books first and this gave me a distinctively non-Althusserian perspective on structuralist state theory.

Structuralism and instrumentalism sat comfortably side by side in my mind as I first ventured into the topic with my dissertation, which was later published as *Universities and the Capitalist State* (1990). In that book, I employed both a structural and an instrumental analysis, and even combined those theoretical approaches with the new institutional approach to analyze the historical origins of what we now call the corporatization of the modern university. I did not pursue this research strategy because of a preconceived philosophical commitment to theoretical synthesis, but because I found that as a practical matter none of these approaches alone was sufficient to provide an adequate understanding of a state policy that consciously linked together thousands of individual colleges and universities into an integrated "higher education system" that would be responsive to the economic demands of leading corporations and to the political and ideological goals of the state.

In fact, after taking two graduate seminars on structural Marxism, I initially made a vigorous effort to write a history without agents and to develop a structural account of the capitalist university as an ideological state apparatus (ISA). However, I found that once the structural (i.e., political economy) context of the university had been defined (empirically by the way), it was not possible to move the analysis forward except by venturing into the actual historical and institutional development of the modern university and its relationship to actually existing corporations and the U.S. imperial state. This required an account of actually existing universities, professional associations, foundations, government bureaucracies, and judicial decisions and while I used structural concepts to theorize these developments, the actual development of the modern university required that I examine elite decision-making, resource allocations, and even real class struggles (such as intellectuals were able to muster it).

The book was reviewed extensively in education, political science, sociology, and history journals. Structuralists thought I was a structuralist, because I used the term "ideological state apparatus" to conceptualize the corporatization of universities in the United States. Instrumentalists embraced me as one of the last of their kind, especially when I used the term "corporate liberalism" in the subtitle of the book, but I had also ventured into the new institutionalism and even delved into a bit of systems analysis with the caveat that the "university system" and its "systematization" were conceived as a historical project of the U.S. capitalist class and not as an abstract analytical method.

I was actually embarrassed by this apparent jumble of structural, instrumental, new institutional, and systems theory, so I set out to clarify the various approaches to state theory in *Critical Theories of the State* (1993), which appeared just as scholarly interest in state theory was waning in the United States and Europe. In *Critical Theories of the State,* I argued that Marxian state theory had splintered into a matrix of artificially constructed antinomies anchored in competing methodological commitments that fundamentally had nothing per se to do with Marxism. This process of fragmentation had begun with the Poulantzas-Miliband debate.

As I developed this thesis further through a series of articles, I suggested that Marx's classical texts had generated *Gestalt*-like interpretations of the same corpus, where one person's focus on a particular text or passage leads them to see something totally different in Marx than another person, even though both are looking at the "same" textual image. My (1993, 156) conclusion was that the conceptual apparatus available to the Marxian paradigm and the methodological approaches to which that paradigm was wedded made it "highly unlikely that there could be any further theoretical discoveries of a revolutionary nature . . . because the conceptual and methodological antinomies of Marxism establish a bounded matrix of plural, but finite, theoretical options." In other words, there was no such thing as *the* Marxist theory of the state, but we could nevertheless develop theoretically informed analyses of actually existing states.

I thought I was done with state theory after *Critical Theories of the State,* and indeed it seemed as if state theory itself was done by the early 1990s, when most scholars among the original generation of critical state theorists moved on to other topics and even shifted toward other emerging paradigms, such as poststructuralism, postmodernism, and globalization theory. Nevertheless, I was encouraged over the years by the large number of graduate students who approached me at conferences to tell me that *Critical Theories of the State* had been their first introduction to state theory and they appreciated the fact that one could read the book and understand it. Consequently, I have long contemplated a follow-up to *Critical Theories of the State* that would reassess state theory in the context of globalization, while incorporating the most salient insights of poststructuralist and postmodernist theory. However, as I began to work on that book, I could not escape the idea that some final housework on the last generation of state theory was still warranted so that I might learn from the mistakes that could now be avoided and because the basic conceptual apparatus of state theory has not been superseded in the era of globalization.

The chapters in this book are a collection of essays and articles that have been published in earlier versions as journal articles and edited book chapters. They orignally appeared in print in a more or less random order in many different outlets, but as I reviewed the articles, I realized there was a continuity of argument about the past, current, and future condition of state theory that would only became apparent if they were presented in the sequential logic of a single book as opposed to their original chronological (dis)order in a diversity of unrelated outlets. My experience was that potential readers may have seen one or two of the pieces, but missed others and, consequently, the overall trajectory of the argument presented in this book would not be readily evident to readers who had seen only one or two of the chapters in a previous format.

Nevertheless, there are some scholars who may gasp at the idea of the Poulantzas-Miliband debate *again*?! Yet, the truth of the matter is that it is already being widely revisited by both senior and junior scholars who find that they cannot move forward with state theory in the age of globalization except by moving through and past the Poulantzas-Miliband debate in a constructive and synthetic way that eluded the previous generation of state theorists. Moreover, by merely "moving past" the Poulantzas-Miliband debate, as some have recommended, we leave behind much that is valuable in understanding the state, particularly the need to understand the contemporary transformation of the state form and the state apparatuses as part of the new conditions of globalization and transnational capital accumulation (Panitch, 2009, xxiii; Sorensen, 2006). Unfortunately, after the Poulantzas-Miliband debate seemed to break state theory into irreconcilable warring camps, many scholars eventually abandoned the debate as a "sterile and misleading" diversion (Jessop, 1982, xiv) and many of these scholars abandoned state theory for other fields of study.

However, a key turning point in reassessing this view of the Poulantzas-Miliband debate was a special conference on "Poulantzas-Miliband: In Retrospect and Prospect," sponsored by the Graduate School and University Center at the City University of New York (CUNY) on April 24–25, 1997. Stanley Aronowitz and Peter Bratsis, who organized the conference twenty years after the conclusion of the *New Left Review* debate, rekindled interest in Poulantzas and Miliband at a time when both mainstream and radical scholars were asserting the end of the state, or at least, the retreat of the state in the wake of the neo-liberal "Washington Consensus," global trade liberalization under the World Trade Organization, and the burgeoning power of transnational corporations. The CUNY conference brought together more than a hundred scholars and graduate students from throughout North America, South America, and Europe. The anticipation surrounding that conference was palpable, since everyone expected to replay the bitter clash between Poulantzas and Miliband with old warriors and new disciples coming to the battlefield to join arms. A surprising outcome of the conference was that no one came to reenact the old debate, but to talk and learn from each other, and to discuss ways to reestablish state theory in the new era of globalization, while carrying forward the most salient components of the theoretical work bequeathed to us by Poulantzas *and* Miliband. It was agreed that state theory was in need of new work, but that task was to begin with a reassessment of Poulantzas and Miliband, because few of the remaining state theorists at the conference were prepared to entirely discard either of them (see Chapters 1 and 2). Although there were some in attendance who later complained that the conference had a "Poulantzasian bias," it nevertheless began the process of thawing out frozen positions.[1] Many commentators on the Poulantzas-Miliband debate had previously described it as a polemical "caricature" of both authors' works—or as "a dialogue of the deaf"—but revisiting that debate began the process of aiding many state theorists in understanding what went wrong in the debate and to recognize just how far off track state theory went because of it in the ensuing decades (Jessop, 2008a).

A significant outcome of the CUNY conference is that it initiated the process of demonstrating to a new generation of state theorists that the early structural critiques of Miliband had been straw man caricatures of his actual political theory. This initial breakthrough was soon followed by other reassessments of Miliband's work on state theory, including the first biography of Ralph Miliband (Newman, 2002) and a new edition of Miliband's highly acclaimed *Marxism and Politics* (2003). The recasting of Miliband's work from a less polemical, but still critical posture continued to unfold at three "Miliband panels" convened by Paul Wetherly at the "How Class Works" Conference (Stony Brook, New York, 2004), the annual conference of the Political Studies Association (Leeds, 2005), and the 3rd Annual Historical Materialism Conference (London, 2006).[2] The culmination of this process was the publication of "a collection of essays that re-examines central themes in Miliband's work and . . . demonstrate that his writings remain an essential reference point for contemporary work on the state and for related areas of political theory" (Wetherly, Barrow, and Burnham, 2007). By no coincidence, Miliband's *The State in Capitalist Society* was republished in 2009 amid a global financial crisis when ostensibly neo-liberal states-in-retreat were vigorously reasserting their power through dramatic interventions in *national* financial and economic systems in ways that would have been thought virtually impossible only a few weeks earlier and in ways designed primarily to protect capital and financial assets, rather than citizens, workers, and homeowners (Panitch, 2009).

As a part of this ongoing reassessment of Ralph Miliband's *The State in Capitalist Society*, Chapter 3 demonstrates that Poulantzas' original critique of instrumentalism and voluntarism was actually aimed at the "plain Marxism" of C. Wright Mills, whose work had already been superseded by leading Anglo-American Marxists, including Ralph Miliband. During the Poulantzas-Miliband debate, Poulantzas simply extended his previous criticisms of Mills to Miliband without recognizing the extent to which Miliband had learned from Mills' work, but surpassed it in theoretical sophistication. Chapter 4 goes on to demonstrate that the concept of instrumentalism so closely associated with Miliband's theory of the state is not merely an oversimplification and caricature of his political theory, but an artificial and misleading polemical construct superimposed on his historical and empirical analysis of the state in capitalist society (Domhoff, 1990, 42).

In this respect, G. William Domhoff (1987, 295; 1990, 40–44) has argued previously that Miliband's instrumentalism was willfully distorted and misinterpreted for the purely political purpose of exaggerating the theoretical originality of "new" theories of the state that claimed to be "more Marxist" and "more revolutionary" than Miliband's theory, but this entire project rests on the assumption that there is *a* Marxist theory of the state. Thus, Chapter 4 builds on Domhoff's earlier argument by showing that many, if not most, of the criticisms directed at Miliband's political theory during the 1970s state debate were actually straw men created by polemical adversaries, who introduced an analytic construct called "instrumentalism" that Miliband himself never embraced as an accurate conceptualization of his published work. From this perspective, the instrumentalism that so many state theorists have sought to move beyond since the Poulantzas-Miliband debate (1969–1976) is merely a simplistic ideal-type that was steadily, artificially, and often deliberately imposed on Miliband over the course of a polemical encounter that accomplished little more than the ideological fracturing of Marxist state theory.

Despite Poulantzas' apparent triumph in the early state debate, state theorists have also systematically reassessed his theory of the state and, particularly, its relation to Althusserian structuralism. Bob Jessop initiated this reassessment in 1985 with his outstanding intellectual biography of Poulantzas, which provided the first overarching analysis of Poulantzas' entire corpus of work. Jessop (1985, 24) concludes that *Political Power and Social Classes* (1978) was the culmination of a "hybrid Althusserian and Gramscian approach" that should be viewed as a self-contained phase of Poulantzas' theoretical development. He finds far more useful concepts in Poulantzas' later works, such as *Classes in Contemporary Capitalism* (1978) and *State, Power, Socialism* (1981), which effectively salvages a "later Poulantzas" from the wreckage of the Poulantzas-Miliband debate.[3] A decade later, Paul Thomas made an Althusserian move that was also designed to rescue Poulantzas from the grip of Althusserian structuralism by suggesting that Poulantzas had an epiphany after the May Days of 1968. This similarly leads Thomas (1984) to conclude that we should focus on Poulantzas' "mature" theoretical writings after 1968, rather than his early writings, such as *Political Power and Social Classes*.[4]

The development of these themes continued at the 1997 CUNY Conference, which yielded additional essays by Bob Jessop (2002a), Paul Thomas (2002), Stanley Aronowitz and Peter Bratsis (2002) that each articulated some variant of this thesis. The net result of this reassessment of Poulantzas' work within the Anglo-American academy is that his last book, *State, Power, Socialism* (1981) has been elevated to a more prominent status, while *Political Power and Social Classes,* the bête noir of the Poulantzas-Miliband debate, has receded into the background as an early experiment gone bad. This transformation in our understanding of Poulantzas was signaled by Verso's republication of *State, Power, Socialism* (2000) twenty years after its initial English language version. The book was reprinted again in 2014 following the release of a new Poulantzas reader (2008).

Meanwhile, a parallel and related movement has emerged among German scholars over the last decade, who established the *Poulantzas lesen* (Reading Poulantzas) project to reintroduce German scholars to Poulantzas' theoretical work.

Poulantzas' writings were republished in German in 2002, when VSA released a German edition of none other than *State, Power, Socialism* on what would have been Poulantzas' 70th birthday. Its German language release was accompanied by the publication of a companion volume of interpretative and analytical essays, which were first presented at three standing room only Poulantzas panels at the 3rd Annual Historical Materialism Conference in 2006 (as compared to one for Miliband, but also standing room only) (Bretthauer, Gallas, Kannankulam, and Stutzle, 2006; 2010). The Germans' discovery of Poulantzas has paralled that of the Anglo-American discussions by reading Poulantzas backward (i.e., *State, Power, Socialism* first) and, thus, the stated purpose of the Poulantzas lesen project is to challenge the prevailing view that Poulantzas is "a vulgar structuralist."[5]

Chapter 5 of this book builds on that theme and opens a conceptual space within Poulantzas' theorizing for the type of empirical and institutional analysis pursued by Miliband. Thus, in the end, the major objectives of this book are to (1) reconstruct the Poulantzas-Miliband debate in its political and intellectual context and to demonstrate the many ways in which this polemical encounter generated an artificial and misleading polarization of theoretical positions and (2) to identify mechanisms for moving beyond the Poulantzas-Miliband debate in a manner that will allow state theorists to continue their efforts to update and revise state theory in the context of globalization. Chapter 6 attempts to develop the outlines of such an approach by integrating key concepts from both Poulantzas and Miliband to propose a synthetic understanding of the new imperialism,[6] while Chapter 7 suggests that Poulantzas was already thinking along these lines in his final writings on the state.

ONE

Marxism and the Critique of Bourgeois Social Science

> In the Marxist scheme, the "ruling class" of capitalist society is that class which owns and controls the means of production and which is able, by virtue of the economic power thus conferred upon it, to use the state as its instrument for the domination of society.
>
> —Ralph Miliband, 1969

> The state has the particular function of constituting the factor of cohesion between the levels of a social formation. This is precisely the meaning of the Marxist conception of the state as a factor of "order" . . . as the regulating factor of its global equilibrium as a system.
>
> —Nicos Poulantzas, 1968

The publication of Nicos Poulantzas' *Pouvoir Politique et Classes Sociales* (1968) and Ralph Miliband's *The State in Capitalist Society* (1969) initiated a return to the state in political science and sociology after a long hiatus where the concept had been discarded by mainstream social scientists (Almond, 1988; Commninel, 1987; Easton, 1981, 1990; Evans et al., 1985; Pierson, 1996, 78; Therborn, 1987). Similarly, Miliband observes that prior to the publication of his book, Marxists had also "made little notable attempt to confront the question of the state" since Lenin.[1] The one exception to this claim was Poulantzas' *Pouvoir Politique et Classes Sociales*, which Miliband (1969, 6, 7 fn. 1) described favorably as "a major attempt at a theoretical elaboration of the Marxist 'model' of the state." After the publication of Miliband's *The State in Capitalist Society*, Poulantzas (1969, 67) also praised Miliband's book as "extremely substantial" and wrote that "he cannot recommend its reading too highly." However, Poulantzas' praise was qualified by "a few critical comments" that set off a series of exchanges between the two theorists in the *New Left Review* that came to be known as the Poulantzas-Miliband debate (Laclau, 1975; Miliband, 1970, 1973; Poulantzas, 1969, 1976).

When the debate began in 1969, Miliband was already one of the preeminent intellectual figures of the British New Left (Newman, 2002), but by the late-1970s after he moved to the United States his name also appeared on a list of the most prominent political scientists in the United States (Roettger, 1978). Indeed, at the height of his intellectual influence, Miliband was possibly the leading Marxist political scientist in the English-speaking world, primarily due to *The State in Capitalist Society* (Blackburn, 1994, 15).[2] Nicos Poulantzas' reputation as a political theorist was also immediately elevated in France by the publication of *Pouvoir Politique et Classes Sociale*, which appeared only a few days before the May Days of 1968 (Jessop, 1985, 9–25).[3]

However, following his review of Miliband's *The State in Capitalist Society* (1969), Poulantzas' work soon captured worldwide scholarly attention. The scholarly and political interest in his book on state theory quickly resulted in Spanish (1972) and English (1973) language translations and, by the mid-1970s, Goran Therborn (1987, 1230) observes that "Nicos Poulantzas was arguably the most influential living political theorist in the world." In a remarkably short period of time, Poulantzas' book was influencing left-wing academics and political activists throughout Europe, North America, Latin America, and beyond. Bob Jessop (1985, 5–6), who has written the most extensive intellectual biography of Poulantzas argues "it is no exaggeration to claim that Poulantzas remains the single most important and influential Marxist theorist of the state and politics in the post-war period."[4] For even where Poulantzas' contributions have been superseded by more recent work, Poulantzas has often "set the terms of debate" (Jessop, 1985, 5–6; 1991).

Consequently, in his recent foreword to the new edition of *The State in Capitalist Society,* Leo Panitch (2009, xxii) provides a reminder that contemporary state theory continues to build on the framework of the Poulantzas-Miliband debate, while Stuart Hall (2000, viii) insists that the Poulantzas-Miliband debate has become "an obligatory reference point for all subsequent theorizing on the modern capitalist state." James Martin (2008, 1) echoes the view that the Poulantzas-Miliband debate remains "a central reference point for all students of social and political theory." The exchange between Poulantzas and Miliband was paradigmatic and enduring partly because it set in motion a broader "state debate" that eventually fractured Marxist political theory into warring schools of thought (Alford and Friedland, 1985; Barrow, 1993; Carnoy, 1984; Clarke, 1991; Jessop, 1982). While the Poulantzas-Miliband debate echoed widely across the 1970s, it was never confined exclusively to Poulantzas and Miliband. Following their initial exchange in 1969–1970, political theorists and political sociologists around the world quickly lined up around the question of whether Miliband's "instrumentalist" theory of the state or Poulantzas' "structuralist" theory of the state was *the* Marxist theory of the state (Gold et al., 1975a, 1975b; Jessop, 1977).[5]

Background to the Poulantzas-Miliband Debate

The Poulantzas-Miliband debate erupted within a paradoxical historical context defined on the one hand by the political rebellions of 1968–1969 and, on the other hand, by the ideological dominance of a social science preoccupied with the concepts of "pluralism" and "system equilibrium." The two sides of this contradiction were mediated by a student, intellectual, and cultural revolt that revived the study of Marxism in universities throughout the advanced capitalist societies (Ollman, 1982). Not coincidentally, Nicos Poulantzas and Ralph Miliband were public intellectuals who were already engaged in this ideological struggle and both were theoretically committed to "the Marxist tradition," which they considered the main alternative to the dominance of "bourgeois social science." In fact, the two books that precipitated the initial debate appeared within a year of each other and were published at the global apogee (1968–1969) of the domestic and colonial insurrections in and against advanced capitalism.

Biographical Background: The 1960s

Ralph Miliband and Nicos Poulantzas were both expatriates and refugees who fled repressive regimes early in their lives. Miliband, who came from a Polish-Jewish background was actually born in Belgium in 1924.[6] He joined his first socialist youth organization at age 15 and fled to England with his father in 1940 literally on the last boat to leave Belgium before Nazi troops captured Ostend. The following year, Miliband (1993) entered the London School of Economics (LSE) specifically to study with Harold Laski. Laski (1935, 87–88) was a well-established state theorist by this time and had long claimed that "Since the Industrial Revolution the state has been biased in favour of the owners of the instruments of production as against those who have nothing but their labour power to sell."[7] After completing his studies, Miliband began teaching at LSE in the early 1950s and he remained there until 1969 when he moved to Brandeis University to accept the Morris Hillquit Professorship.[8] Miliband eventually left Boston to become a member of the CUNY Graduate Center in New York and he had just retired from CUNY shortly before his death in 1994.

For most of his life, Miliband did not belong to any political party, but he was closely associated with the "left socialists" in the British Labour Party, who sought to steer a path between Leninism and social democracy. Miliband's first book, *Parliamentary Socialism* (1961) was a critique of the British Labour Party and a critique of the electoral and bureaucratic mechanisms that diverted the party from pursuing more radical objectives (Burnham, 2008; Coates and Panitch, 2002). During this time, Miliband was a founding editor of the

New Left Review and a co-founder of the *Socialist Register*. He was also active in the British peace movement, the anti-Vietnam War movement, and numerous other campaigns against social and political oppression. In the 1980s, Miliband was a founder of the Socialist Society, which helped convene several conferences to provide a new voice for socialists in the British Labour Party. However, by the final decade of his life, Miliband (1995) was calling for a new socialist party capable of forging an alliance between organized labor and the new social movements (Allender, 1996).

Nicos Poulantzas was born in Athens in 1936 where he lived through the Nazi occupation and the Greek Civil War. Poulantzas received his baccalaureate from the *Institute Francais* in 1953 and then entered the University of Athens School of Law. Although active in various political movements as a youth, it was not until the early 1960s, after Poulantzas had moved to Paris that he became a card-carrying member of the Greek Communist Party (Jessop, 1985, Chap. 1). Poulantzas was a professor of legal philosophy at the Sorbonne from 1961 to 1964 and he continued teaching at French universities until his death in 1979.[9] By the time Poulantzas published *Pouvoir Politique et Classes Sociale* in 1968, he was already well known in French intellectual circles, primarily through his association with the "existential Marxists" at *Les Tempes Modernes* (Hirsch, 1981; Poster, 1975). However, shortly after joining the editorial board of *Les Tempes Modernes* in 1964, Poulantzas was increasingly influenced by the British Marxists gathering around the *New Left Review* and the works of Antonio Gramsci, but most especially by the structural Marxism of Louis Althusser (Benton, 1984; Elliott, 2009; Lewis, 2005; Montag, 2013).

Intellectual Background: Bourgeois Social Science

Miliband had conceived of writing *The State in Capitalist Society* as early as 1962 (Newman, 2002, 185), but it was not published until 1969 on the cusp of a rising wave of global political upheaval. Miliband acknowledges at a number of points that his own work was building on a subterranean intellectual movement that had been gaining momentum in the United

States after the publication of C. Wright Mills' *The Power Elite* (1956). Miliband's book effectively linked a vast array of disparate economic, political, and ideological left-wing currents into a *theory* that explained why a nominally democratic state was responding more to the economic and political preferences of capitalist elites than to popular mass movements expressing their vehement opposition to existing state policies at home and abroad.[10]

In the late 1960s, the terms of debate in social science and political theory were defined by theories that could not account for the existence, much less the magnitude, of rebellion within the advanced capitalist societies (Gitlin, 1987; Young, 1977). The concept of the state and state power had been replaced in academic sociology and political science by a concept of "the political system" identified with the works of Talcott Parsons and David Easton. Parsons' sociology identified the political system with individual and collective behaviors that provide "a center of integration for all aspects" of the social system.[11] David Easton (1953, 106), who played a major role in consolidating the behavioral revolution in political science, declared that "neither the state nor power is a concept that serves to bring together political research." In urging political scientists to abandon the analysis of the state and power, Easton proposed that scholars examine instead "those interactions through which values are authoritatively allocated for a society." Furthermore, Easton (1953, 21–23) emphasized that to account for the persistence of political systems, one had to assume that they successfully generate two "system outputs": (1) the political system must be able to allocate values for a society (i.e., decision making) and (2) the political system must *induce* most members of society to accept these allocations as binding, at least most of the time (i.e., legitimacy).[12] The bulk of Easton's theoretical and empirical work during the 1950s and 1960s was on the "support inputs" that stabilize and equilibrate political systems.

However, as Miliband (1969, 3) observes, the systems analytic concept of decision making was wedded to the democratic-pluralist view of society that also came to dominate political science and political sociology at the same time.

Pluralist theory views decision making as the outcome of bargaining and conflict between interest groups in society (Dahl, 1958, 1959, 1961; Truman, 1951). Importantly, pluralists argue that key sources of power, such as wealth, force, status, and knowledge are, if not equally distributed, at least widely diffused among a plurality of competing groups in society. This purported pattern of "dispersed inequalities" means that no one group controls a disproportionate share of all key resources, while all groups in society possess some key resources. This pattern of dispersed inequalities insures that no one group dominates the political process all the time (i.e., authoritative decision making), while no group is completely powerless within that process or involuntarily excluded from it. The significance of pluralist theory is that it seemed to explain how the authoritative allocation of values in the political system *induces* most citizens to accept those decisions as legitimate and binding most of the time.

Robert A. Dahl (1965, 137–138), who was possibly the single most important proponent of pluralist theory among the icons of the behavioral revolution, (1965, 137–138) emphasized that pluralist theory assumes:

> . . . that there are a number of loci for arriving at political decisions . . . business men, trade unions, politicians, consumers, farmers, voters and many other aggregates all have an impact on policy outcomes; that none of these aggregates is homogeneous for all purposes; that each of them is highly influential over some scopes but weak over many others; and that the power to reject undesired alternatives is more common than the power to dominate over outcomes directly.

In the view of most mainstream scholars and public officials, the Western consensus on pluralist democracy and managed capitalism—namely, the Keynesian welfare state—was so complete by the early 1960s that politics had seemingly reached "the end of ideology" (Bell, 1960). However, the worldwide political upheavals of 1968–1969 called into question the dominant assumptions of academic social science at precisely the moment when systems theorists, behavioralists, and pluralists were celebrating their triumph at meetings of the social science disciplinary associations. The idea that Western economic and political systems had achieved system equilibrium through pluralist democracy and managed capitalism literally went up in smoke on university campuses and in the streets of those very countries (Singer, 1970; Touraine, 1971; Young, 1977).

In the United States, the long hot summers of the mid-1960s signaled an end to the system equilibrium of a so-called pluralist society. There were urban riots in the African-American sections of many major cities, including Los Angeles (1965), Chicago (1966), and Newark (1967). Only July 28, 1967, while new rioting was underway in Detroit, Michigan, President Lyndon B. Johnson appointed the National Advisory Commission on Civil Disorders to investigate these riots convinced that the underlying cause was external Communist or Soviet subversion designed to distract the United States from its involvement in the Vietnam War. However, when the so-called Kerner Commission[13] presented its findings in 1968, it concluded that urban riots and other forms of violence in major cities were caused by the profound frustration of inner-city African-Americans and a deeply embedded racism in American society. The report's most famous passage warned that the United States was "moving toward two societies, one black, one white—separate and unequal." The Commission marshaled evidence on an array of problems that fell with particular severity on African-Americans, including not only overt racial discrimination, but also chronic poverty, high unemployment, poor schools, inadequate housing, lack of access to health care, and systematic police bias and brutality.

At the same time, the Tet Offensive was already fueling increased domestic and worldwide resistance to American military involvement in South Vietnam, while the Soviet invasion of Czechoslovakia simultaneously plunged Soviet Communism into an ideological crisis that further eroded its declining image as a viable alternative to capitalism. An accelerating nuclear arms race between the United States and the Soviet

Union reinvigorated the antinuclear movement in all of the Western countries. In France, the May Days of 1968 brought an entire nation to a standstill, caused the DeGaulle government to temporarily flee the country, and left the French Communist Party in disgrace after its refusal to assume control of a provisional government. There were increasingly violent confrontations between students and police in the United States, Great Britain, Germany, Italy, and Mexico. In Japan, students joined farmers in violent resistance to the land takings necessary to construct Narita International Airport outside Tokyo. Meanwhile, homespun terrorist groups, such as the Red Army Faction (Germany), the Red Brigades (Italy), and the Weather Underground (U.S.) splintered from these larger movements to launch domestic terrorist campaigns against military, corporate, and government installations, including assassination and kidnapping attempts on government and corporate officials. In the United States, Robert F. Kennedy, a U.S. presidential candidate who opposed the Vietnam War, and Martin Luther King Jr., the preeminent leader of the U.S. civil rights movement, were both assassinated in the same year. Despite their best efforts, the architects of official social science could not avoid confronting the uncomfortable reality of political disequilibrium even in the heartland of the model pluralist society.

In the wake of these events, David Easton (1969, 1051) opened his Presidential Address to the American Political Science Association by declaring that:

> A new revolution is under way in American political science. The last revolution—behavioralism—has scarcely been completed before it has been overtaken by the increasing social and political crises of our time. The weight of these crises is being felt within our discipline in the form of a new conflict in the throes of which we now find ourselves. This new and latent challenge is directed against a developing behavioral orthodoxy. . . .The initial impulse of this revolution is just being felt. Its battle cries are *relevance* and *action*.

Easton's surrender to "the postbehavioral revolution" was symptomatic of a crisis in bourgeois ideology, which was unmasked as such in the wake of historical political events that overtly contravened its basic tenets (Barrow, 2014). In the wake of this crisis, Miliband's *The State in Capitalist Society* pierced the veil of bourgeois ideology with a Marxist analysis of the Western system of power, while Poulantzas offered an alternative conceptual and theoretical framework for understanding the functioning of the state in capitalist societies. Moreover, their intellectual reputations steadily grew until their stature matched that of leading mainstream social scientists, such as David Easton and Gabriel Almond.

However, in this context, what perplexed Miliband (1969, 1) was the fact that even as the state's power and institutional presence was being vastly extended in the advanced capitalist societies—both domestically and internationally—"the remarkable paradox is that the state itself, as a subject of political study, has long been very unfashionable." In this respect, mainstream social science was concealing the sources, structure, and operation of political power, not by what it studied, but by what it ignored for most of the post–World War II era (Lowi, 1992). It is no accident that since that time scholars have persistently lamented the "end of political science," "the tragedy of political science," "the crisis of political science," "the flight from reality" in political science, and the uncertain "future of political science" (Flinders and John, 2013; Monroe, 2005; Ricci, 1984; Seidelman, 1985; Shapiro, 2005; Surkin and Wolfe, 1970).

The crisis of political science as identified by Miliband was that the theory of the state was being ignored by mainstream social science because it implicitly assumed, or more often explicitly asserted, a pluralist theory of the state that was being called into question by real political events. Importantly, Miliband (1969, 2, 3) notes that because "a theory of the state is also a theory of society and of the distribution of power in that society," pluralist assumptions tended "to exclude, by definition, the notion that the state might be a rather special institution, whose main purpose is to defend the predominance in society of a particular class." Consequently, the maintenance of system equilibrium in capitalist societies is in fact the maintenance of economic and political inequality and, therefore, economic exploitation and political oppression.

The ideological power of Miliband's work is that it did not sidestep a direct confrontation with mainstream social science by elaborating an alternative theory as did Poulantzas, but instead Miliband established the necessity for such a theory through an immanent critique of pluralism, systems theory, and even neo-classical economics. Thus, while Ralph Miliband's *The State in Capitalist Society* (1969) was among the most important books to pose an *empirical* challenge to pluralism during this time (Barrow, 1993; Jessop, 1982) at the *theoretical* level it also returned the concept of the state to a prominent role in Anglo-American political science and sociology. In this respect, Miliband's immanent critique of mainstream social science opens the door to Poulantzas' alternative categories of analysis (Almond, 1988; Easton, 1981; Evans et al., 1985; Ross, 1994).

Although Miliband has often been chastised by structuralists for allowing bourgeois social science to set the methodological terms of his analysis, Poulantzas was responding to a parallel intellectual context. Poulantzas (1978a, 19) explicitly derided French political science as "underdeveloped" compared to its Anglo-American counterpart and, consequently, he calls explicit attention to the fact that his own theorizing makes "frequent recourse" to works by British and American authors. These authors include Talcott Parsons, David Easton, Gabriel Almond, David Apter, and Karl Deutsch—a virtual pantheon of the systems analysis and structural-functionalist movements in American social science.[14] As Poulantzas was aware, in Parsonian systems analysis:

> . . . the political component of the social system is a center of integration for all the aspects of this system which analysis can separate, not the sociological scene of a particular class of social phenomena. . . . (Parsons, 1951, 126)

Similarly, although relying more on the structural-functionalism of Robert K. Merton, David Apter (1958) had defined the "political" as a structure with "defined responsibilities for the maintenance of the system of which it is a part." Likewise, Gabriel Almond and James S. Coleman (1960, 12) identified the function of the political system as the crucial "boundary maintenance function" within the overall social system. Importantly, Poulantzas (1978a, 47 fn. 17) cites these works favorably in a section of *Political Power and Social Classes* on "The General Function of the State" as examples of how contemporary political science was "beginning to emphasize the role of the political as the factor of maintenance of a formation's unity." Thus, if Miliband was preoccupied with challenging bourgeois social science within the methodological parameters defined by behavioral methodology and pluralist theory, Poulantzas was also working through a methodological position that is directly traceable to the systems analysis and structural-functionalism of Parsons, Merton, Almond, and Apter. Poulantzas diverges from these thinkers primarily in emphasizing that class struggle is an inherent structural dysfunction (i.e., contradiction) of capitalist societies, which generates an inherent and permanent tendency toward system disequilibrium over the long term.[15] Yet, in this respect, it is ironic that so much of the Poulantzas-Miliband debate came to revolve around the question of *Marxist* methodology when there was nothing peculiarly Marxist about either author's *methodological* approach.[16]

Intellectual Background: The Marxist Tradition

Nevertheless, Miliband and Poulantzas did challenge the dominance of bourgeois social science on both an empirical and conceptual level by drawing on a Marxist tradition that each of them identified with the writings of Marx, Engels, Lenin, and Gramsci. Miliband (1965, 5) argues quite explicitly that "the most important alternative to the pluralist-democratic view of power remains the Marxist one." Miliband (1977, 1) identifies classical Marxism with "the writings of

Marx, Engels, and Lenin and, at a different level, [with] those of some other figures such as Rosa Luxemburg, Gramsci, and Trotsky."

Miliband's (1969, 5) reading of classical Marxism was based on his observation that Marx "never attempted a systematic study of the state." Miliband (1969, 5) was well aware of the fact that "this was one of the tasks which he [Marx] hoped to undertake as part of a vast scheme of work which he had projected in the 1850s but of which volume I of *Capital* was the only fully finished part." Hence, most of Marx's political writings "are for the most part the product of particular historical episodes and specific circumstances; and what there is of theoretical exploration of politics . . . is mostly unsystematic and fragmentary, and often part of other work" (Miliband, 1977, 1–2). Miliband identifies the *political* writings of classical Marxism primarily with Marx's *Eighteenth Brumaire of Louis Bonaparte* and the *Civil War in France* and with Lenin's *What is to Be Done?*, and *State and Revolution*. Significantly, although references to the state in different types of society constantly recur in almost all of Marx's writings, Miliband (1977, 5) concludes in the final analysis that:

> . . . as far as capitalist societies are concerned, his [Marx's] main view of the state throughout is summarised in the famous formulation of the *Communist Manifesto*: "The executive of the modern state is but a committee for managing the affairs of the whole bourgeoisie."

Miliband (1977, 5) claims that this thesis "reappears again and again in the work of both Marx and Engels; and despite the refinements and qualifications they occasionally introduce in their discussion of the state . . . they never departed from the view that in capitalist society the state was above all the coercive instrument of a ruling class, itself defined in terms of its ownership and control of the means of production."[17] Miliband (1969, 6) considered Lenin's *State and Revolution* to be merely "a restatement and an elaboration of the main view of the state" found in the *Communist Manifesto,* while after Lenin "the only major Marxist contribution to the theory of the state has been that of Antonio Gramsci."[18]

Miliband identifies the chief deficiency of contemporary Marxist political theory as the fact that nearly all Marxists have been content to assert the thesis articulated in the *Communist Manifesto* as more or less self-evident. Thus, for Miliband, the primary objective in renewing state theory was "to confront the question of the state in the light of the concrete socio-economic *and* political *and* cultural reality of actual capitalist societies." Miliband suggests that Marx provided a conceptual foundation for the socioeconomic analysis of capitalist societies, Lenin provided guidance for a political analysis, and Gramsci supplied the conceptual apparatus for a cultural and ideological analysis of capitalist societies. Hence, Miliband was convinced that the central thesis and conceptual structure of Marxist political theory was effectively in place and that what Marxism needed was empirical and historical analysis to give concrete content to this thesis and its theoretical concepts. The intended purpose of *The State in Capitalist Society* (1969, 7) was "to make a contribution to remedying that deficiency."

Poulantzas' (1978a, 1, 42) *Political Power and Social Classes* also claims to draw on the classical texts of Marx, Engels, Lenin, and Gramsci and "to provide a systematic political theory by elucidating implicit ideas and axioms in their practical writings." However, it will come as no surprise that Poulantzas' epistemological attitude toward these texts was far more complex and problematic than Miliband's position. In *Political Power and Social Classes,* Poulantzas cites Louis Althusser's work as the basis for his claim that Marxism consists of two united but distinct disciplines called dialectical materialism and historical materialism. According to Poulantzas (1978a, 11), dialectical materialism (i.e., Marxist philosophy) "has as its particular object the production of knowledge; that is the structure and functioning of thought" (see also, Althusser, 1969). Marxist philosophy is essentially a process of reading the classic texts rigorously *to produce the concepts necessary to an understanding of history and society* and, for this reason,

Poulantzas (1978a, 11) emphasizes that the raw materials of political theory are "the texts of the Marxist classics." Althusserian structuralists viewed the historical development of Marx's thought as exemplary of this process and to that extent they emphasized a distinction between the young Marx and the mature Marx. For Althusserians, Marx did not become a "Marxist" until he wrote *The German Ideology,* which constituted his "epistemological break" with bourgeois categories of thought, although Marx's thought does not reach full maturity until the publication of *Capital* (Therborn, 1976).

Thus, while Miliband places Marx's and Engels' *Communist Manifesto* at the center of Marxist political theory, Poulantzas (1978a, 20) identifies *Capital* as "the major theoretical work of Marxism" (see also, Althusser and Balibar, 1977). Nevertheless, Poulantzas' (1978a, 21) reading of *Capital* leads to the parallel conclusion that while providing "a systematic theoretical treatment of the economic region" of the capitalist mode of production [CMP], there is "no systematic theory of ideology . . . to be found in *Capital* . . . nor is there a theory of politics in it." Hence, with respect to political theory, Poulantzas (1978a, 18) understood that an Althusserian epistemology had to deal with two problems from the outset: (1) problems related to the "raw material" of theoretical production and (2) problems concerning the status of what texts among the Marxist classics count as "political."

The chief difficulty in designating *Capital* as the central theoretical work of Marxism is that it is an unfinished work. It contains no theory of social class, no theory of the state, no theory of transition from one mode of production to another and, yet, it explicitly intends to address those issues. The known gap between what Marx intended in *Capital* and what Marx accomplished before his death leaves a text that is rife with lacunae, omissions, and stated intentions that are never fulfilled in fact. Hence, Marxist philosophers, particularly Althusserian structuralists, are faced with the task of not only clarifying the existing text, but of completing the existing text. For Althusserians, Engels' role as editor of the final volumes of *Capital,* and his role in explicating various ideas in *Anti-Duhring* and the *Origins of the Family, Private Property and the State* provide exemplary models of the type of intellectual production involved in completing the central text. Therefore, Poulantzas concludes that to produce a theory of the capitalist state, it is not only necessary to "Read Capital," but to "Write Capital" (or at least its political equivalent). Interestingly, Poulantzas concurs with Miliband that after Engels, it was Lenin and Gramsci who did the most to advance this task.

Unfortunately, as Poulantzas observes, these Marxist classics do not specifically discuss politics and the state at the same level of theoretical *systematicity* as one finds in Marx's *Capital*. Thus, Poulantzas (1978a, 19) emphasizes that:

> . . . in order to use the texts of the Marxist classics as a source of information, particularly on the capitalist state, it has been necessary to complete them and to subject them to a particular critical treatment. Because of the non-systematic character of these texts, the information contained in them sometimes appears incomplete or even inexact. . . .

Consequently, for Poulantzas, the concepts required for a theory of the capitalist state are merely *implicit* in the texts of the Marxist classics. Importantly, in sorting out the issue of which classic texts count as political, Poulantzas (1978a, 21) distinguishes between those theoretical texts which "deal with political science in its abstract-formal form, i.e., the state in general, class struggle in general, the capitalist state in general" and "the political texts in the strict sense of the term." Among the former, Poulantzas includes Marx's *Critique of the Gotha Program* and *The Civil War in France*; Engels' *Anti-Duhring*; Lenin's *State and Revolution*, and Gramsci's *Notes on Machiavelli*. It is interesting that Poulantzas never clearly defines "the political texts in the strict sense of the term," although his subsequent citations indicate that they include Marx's *The Poverty of Philosophy;* Engels' *Origins of the Family, Private Property and the State*; Lenin's *What is to be Done?*; Gramsci's *Prison Notebooks;* and numerous pamphlets by Lenin and personal letters by Marx. It is remarkable that the one prominent classic not included on this list is the

Communist Manifesto; the one work that Miliband considered key to a Marxist theory of the state.

Yet, not only did Miliband and Poulantzas see two different Marxes, their different epistemological conceptions of how one engages in Marxian social science is further clarified by contrasting Miliband's preoccupation with fact gathering to Poulantzas' insistence on concept production. According to Poulantzas, historical materialism is the actual "science of history" constructed through the use and application of Marxist categories of knowledge derived through dialectical materialism. More specifically, Poulantzas (1978a, 11) suggests that historical materialism "has as its object the concept of history, through the study of the various modes of production and social formations, their structure, constitution and functioning, and the forms of transition from one social formation to another." In other words, if dialectical materialism (i.e., Marxist philosophy) is responsible for producing these concepts through a reading of the Marxian canon, historical materialism (i.e., general theory) is responsible for defining these concepts so they become the basis of so-called regional and particular theories (Balibar, 2014, 146).

For Poulantzas, regional theory is the study of the elemental structures and practices whose specific combinations constitute a mode of production and a social formation.[19] Particular theories consist of theories of particular combinations, for example, a theory of the slave mode of production, the feudal mode of production, or the capitalist mode of production. For Poulantzas, (1978a, 16) it is particular theories that allow one to understand and explain "real, concrete, singular objects" such as France at a given moment in its political development. Thus, as he understood it, Poulantzas was concerned with producing a regional theory of the capitalist state; namely, the production of the concept of the political superstructure in the capitalist mode of production.

Significantly, therefore, Poulantzas claims that dialectical and historical materialism do not involve the study of facts (i.e., real concrete singulars), but the study of "abstract-formal objects" (i.e., concepts). Poulantzas acknowledges that abstract-formal objects (e.g., the capitalist mode of production or the capitalist state) "do not exist in the strong sense of the word, but they are the condition of knowledge of real-concrete objects." In other words, there is no such thing ontologically as "the capitalist state," but it is this category of knowledge that makes it possible for us to know and understand an actually existing capitalist state (i.e., a real concrete singular). Consequently, the methodological role of the "real concrete" in a Poulantzasian (1978, 24) political theory is merely: (1) to illustrate and exemplify the regional theory or (2) to provide raw material for producing the specific concepts which make concrete knowledge possible.

It is perhaps a controversial claim, but this epistemological position places Althusserian structuralism squarely within the 1950s and 1960s tradition of transcendental and analytic political philosophy. The method of textual analysis and its epistemological underpinnings are again not uniquely Marxian, because one can find the same types of arguments being made in mainstream political philosophy by Leo Strauss and Joseph Cropsey, among others.[20] The idea that political "science" (or political philosophy) is concerned with reasoning about concepts in a timeless present is certainly not limited by the requirement that one accept a particular set of texts as the basis of one's interpretive canon. It may seem astounding to suggest that Leo Strauss the conservative and Louis Althusser the Marxist share the same epistemological ground in political philosophy, but as early as 1974 Jacques Ranciere (2011, 77), a student collaborator of Althusser's, suggested that "'ultra-left-Platonism would be an appropriate name" for Althusser's epistemological claims.[21] Etienne Balibar (1994, 160), who collaborated with Althusser on *Reading Capital,* has also documented that Althusser's references to different kinds and levels of knowledge, as well as his concept of an epistemological break, are "fundamentally Platonic" and owe more to the works of Gaston Bachelard than to Marx (Arditi, 2006, 185). More recently, Warren Montag (2013, 3) has concluded that "Althusser reduced human experience, feeling, and decision to anonymous structures so abstracted from what is genuinely human that they resemble Platonic forms."

Thus, viewed within the larger postwar context of academic political theory, the only thing uniquely Marxian about the Althusserian epistemology was its choice of a sacred canon: the Marxist tradition, rather than the classical tradition (e.g., Plato or Aristotle), or the liberal tradition (e.g., Hobbes, Locke, Rousseau), but *the epistemology* of textual analysis and concept production is identical to the dominant mainstream of American political philosophy. In this respect, the Poulantzas-Miliband debate merely reproduced within Marxism the very same empiricist-textualist dichotomy—the antinomies of bourgeois thought—that had divided mainstream political science since the early 1950s (Ashcraft, 1980; Lukacs, 1971, 110–149). However, the methodological dichotomy at the center of the Poulantzas-Miliband debate, including the radical divergence in the two theorist's definition of Marx's "political writings" (i.e., the canon) is essential to understanding their different concepts of the state, state power, and the role of the state in a capitalist social formation.

TWO

The Poulantzas-Miliband Debate

The Poulantzas-Miliband debate was technically a series of polemical exchanges between Nicos Poulantzas and Ralph Miliband in the *New Left Review* that began in 1969 and ended in 1976 (Laclau, 1975; Miliband, 1970, 1973; Poulantzas, 1969, 1976). The debate was initiated by Poulantzas in a review of Miliband's *The State in Capitalist Society* (1969) shortly after the publication of his own *Pouvoir Politique et Classes Sociales* (1968), which had been published in French but was therefore inaccessible to most Anglo-American scholars.[1] The debate initially focused on questions of definition, such as how to identify the capitalist class and the basis of its political power, how to define the state and its relation to the capitalist class, and the sources and exercise of state power. However, the exchange quickly shifted focus and devolved into a methodological debate about the comparative importance of structure and agency in explanations of political behavior and state policy. This false dichotomy surfaced in many different forms and was posed by Poulantzas as a series of problems—the problem of the subject, the problem of method, the problem of state cohesion, and the problem of ideological apparatuses.

Miliband's Theory of the State

The most succinct summary of Ralph Miliband's (1969, 23) theory of the state is that: "In the Marxist scheme, the 'ruling class' of capitalist society is that class which owns and controls the means of production and which is able, by virtue of the economic power thus conferred upon it, to use the state as its instrument for the domination of society."[2]

In empirical terms, Miliband identifies the corporation as the initial reference point for defining the capitalist class, that is, the class that owns and controls the means of production. In the United States, for example, the bulk of capitalist economic activity, whether measured in terms of assets, profits, employment, investment, market shares, or research and development expenditures, is concentrated in the 50 largest financial institutions and the 500 largest nonfinancial corporations (Baran and Sweezy, 1966; Edwards et al., 1978, Chap. 4; Mason, 1964, Chap. 1; Means, 1939). Thus, members of the capitalist class are identified as those persons who perform the managerial and ownership functions of those corporations. The capitalist class is an overlapping economic network of authority based on institutional position (i.e., management) and property relations (i.e., ownership) (Mintz, 1989; Zeitlin, 1974, 1977, 1989).[3] The wealthy families who own large blocks of corporate stock and the high ranking managers of those same corporations are usually estimated to compose no more than 0.5% to 1% of the total U.S. population (Domhoff, 1978, 4).

Social Class and Political Practice

In making this claim, Miliband was directly challenging the pluralist theory of liberal democrats who were arguing that references to "*a* capitalist class" are empirically meaningless, because corporate power is diffuse and competitive, and the representation of business interests is fragmented among divergent interest groups and/or checked by countervailing centers of social, economic, and political power. Miliband's empirical documentation captured the attention of behavioral social scientists, because it questioned the assertions of political theories that claimed to be "empirical" (e.g., Dahl, 1959; Galbraith, 1952; Truman, 1951). Moreover, in challenging these theories, Miliband was also debunking a widely held ideological belief, especially in the United States, that capitalist societies were more or less classless, pluralistic, egalitarian, and democratic (Barrow, 1993, Chap. 1). Thus, as bizarre as it may seem in retrospect, it was theoretically important within the Anglo-American intellectual context to reestablish the simple empirical fact that a capitalist class does exist and that numerous mechanisms can be identified which facilitate the economic cohesion of capitalists *as a class* (Miliband, 1969, 23).[4]

However, assuming that one can document the existence of an economically dominant capitalist class, Miliband (1969, 54) contends that in conceptualizing the state most Marxists had failed "to note the obvious but fundamental fact that this [capitalist] class is involved in a *relationship* with the state, which cannot be *assumed* in the political conditions which are typical of advanced capitalism," (i.e., political democracy). Instead, if Marxist theory is to effectively challenge the claims of bourgeois social science, then the relationship between states and the capitalist class "has to be *determined*" with historical and empirical precision (Miliband, 1969, 55). Miliband emphasizes that in documenting this relationship the claim put forward by a Marxist theory of the state entails a heavy empirical burden for the political theorist. This burden derives from the fact that Marxists do not merely assert that the capitalist class exercises substantial power, or even that it exercises more power than other classes, but insists that the capitalist class "exercises a decisive degree of political power" *and* that "its ownership and control of crucially important areas of economic life also insures its control of the means of political decision making in the particular environment of advanced capitalism" (Miliband, 1969, 48).[5]

WHAT IS THE STATE?

However, determining the magnitude of the relationship between a capitalist class and the state not only requires a clear definition of the capitalist class, but an equally clear designation of "the means of political decision-making" that constitute the state. Miliband (1969, 50, 48, 49) observes paradoxically that the state "is a nebulous entity," because the state "is not a thing, that it does not, as such, exist." Instead, the state, as Miliband conceives it, is merely an analytic reference point that "stands for . . . a number of particular institutions which, together, constitute its reality, and which interact as parts of what may be called the state system." For Miliband (1969, 49–53), the state system is actually composed of five "elements" that are each identified with a cluster of particular institutions:

1. The governmental apparatus which consists of elected legislative and executive authorities at the national level, which make state policy.
2. The administrative apparatus, consisting of the civil service bureaucracy, public corporations, central banks, regulatory commissions, which regulate economic, social, cultural, and other activities.
3. The coercive apparatus, consisting of the military, paramilitary, police, and intelligence agencies, which together are concerned with the deployment and management of violence.
4. The judicial apparatus, which includes courts, the legal profession, jails and prisons, and other components of the criminal justice system.
5. The subcentral governments, such as States, Provinces, or Departments; counties, municipal governments, and special districts.

According to Miliband (1969, 54): "These are the institutions—the government [executive], the administration, the military and the police, the judicial branch, sub-central government, and parliamentary assemblies—which make up the 'the state', and whose interrelationship shapes the form of the state system." Miliband's emphasis on the state system as a set of *interrelationships* between particular institutions warrants special attention, because he has often been accused of reducing the state to a mere "tool in the hands of the ruling class." Yet, contrary to these assertions, Miliband offers an important qualification that belies this metaphorical straw man.

Miliband (1969, 49) chastises liberal pluralists and left-wing activists for the mistaken belief that "the assumption of governmental power is equivalent to the acquisition of state power." Although it is a simple distinction, Miliband's association with the British Labour Party made him acutely aware that an understanding of the distinction between government and the state can have significant consequences for political strategy and political tactics. Miliband understands that the accession to governmental power at various points in the twentieth century by liberal, labor, and social democratic *governments* was accompanied generally by a simultaneous failure to conquer *state power* in its diverse forms and places within the state system. The fact that a socialist government might control the parliamentary and executive branches of government, whether by election or revolution, does not automatically entail its control of the military, the police, the intelligence agencies, the civil service, the legal system, the subnational governments, the schools and universities, regulatory agencies, public corporations, and so on. As Miliband (1969, 50) notes: ". . . the fact that the government does speak in the name of the state and is formally *invested* with state power, does not mean that it effectively *controls* that power."

WHAT IS STATE POWER?

Consequently, it is theoretically important to Miliband to know who actually controls state power at any given time. One of the most direct indicators of ruling-class domination is the degree to which members of the capitalist class *control* the state apparatus through interlocking positions in the governmental, administrative, coercive and other apparatuses. Miliband (1969, 54) emphasizes that:

> It is these institutions in which "state power" lies, and it is through them that this power is wielded in its

different manifestations by the people who occupy the leading positions in each of these institutions.

For this reason, Miliband attaches considerable importance to the social composition of the state elite. The class composition of a state elite creates "a strong presumption . . . as to its general outlook, ideological dispositions and political bias" and, thus, one way to measure the degree of *potential* class domination is to quantify the extent to which members of a particular class have disproportionately colonized command posts within the state apparatuses (Miliband, 1969, 55). In the eyes of critics, Miliband's theory of the state is considered synonymous with the concept of institutional colonization. This misrepresentation of Miliband's analysis has wildly exaggerated his empirical claims about the direct domination of the state apparatuses by members of the capitalist class.

Despite the importance of institutional colonization to Miliband's (1969, 55) analysis, his empirical claims about the degree to which capitalists colonize the state apparatus were always circumscribed by his recognition that capitalists have not "assumed the major share of *government*" in most advanced capitalist democracies.[6] For that reason, Miliband (1969, 59) argues that capitalists "are not, properly speaking, a 'governing' class, comparable to pre-industrial, aristocratic and landowning classes."[7] Indeed, a fact completely ignored by Miliband's (1969, 55) critics is that he quotes Karl Kautsky to the effect that "the capitalist class reigns but does not govern."[8] The colonization of key command posts in selected state apparatuses is merely one weapon, albeit an important one, in the larger arsenal of ruling class domination. What Miliband (1969, 56, 48) actually claims is that capitalists are "well represented in the political executive and in other parts of the state system" and that their occupation of these key command posts enables them to exercise *decisive influence over public policy*.[9]

The fact that finance capitalists usually control the executive branch of government and the administrative-regulatory apparatuses is considered particularly important, under normal circumstances, for both historical and theoretical reasons.

In historical terms, the political development of the modern state system has been marked mainly by the growth of its regulatory, administrative, and coercive institutions over the course of the last century. As these institutions have grown in size, numbers, and technical complexity, the state's various subsystems have achieved greater autonomy from government in their operations. The growth of independent administrative and regulatory subsystems within the state has occurred as governments, especially legislatures, have found it increasingly difficult to maintain any central direction over the many components of the state system. The historical result is that the preponderance of state power has shifted from the legislative to the executive branch of government and to independent administrative or regulatory agencies.

This development is theoretically important partly because the very basis of state power is concentrated in those institutions (i.e., administration, coercion, knowledge) and because it is those institutions that the capitalist class has colonized most successfully. Thus, the actual degree of state power that capitalists achieve by colonizing executive, administrative, and regulatory command posts has been magnified by the asymmetrical power structure within the contemporary state system, (e.g., in the United States by the imperial presidency and the emergence of independent regulatory agencies). This asymmetrical distribution of state power within the contemporary state form provides capitalists with strategic locations inside the state system from which to initiate, modify, and veto a broad range of policy proposals.[10] Miliband recognizes that a potential weakness of this more limited claim is the fact that capitalists usually colonize only the top command posts of government and administration. The colonization process is clearly unable to explain the operational unity of the entire state system and, therefore, one must be able to identify the mechanism that leads a number of relatively autonomous and divergent state subsystems to operate *as if* they were a single entity called *the* state.[11]

Indeed, the loose connection of lower level career administrators to the state elite is indicated by Miliband's description of them as servants *of* the state. In fact, these servants are frequently conceptualized as a separate professional-managerial class composed of lower and middle level career *state managers* (Ehrenreich and Ehrenreich, 1977).[12] Miliband (1969, 119) observes that:

> The general pattern must be taken to be one in which these men [i.e. state managers] do play an important part in the process of governmental decision-making, and therefore constitute a considerable force in the configuration of political power in their societies.

Likewise, a problem of systemic unity derives from the disparate organization of the contemporary state apparatus. To the extent that the state system is viewed as a web of decentered institutions, one must account for how the state elite and state managers are able to maintain some overarching interinstitutional cohesion that is "capitalist" in its content. Miliband has attempted to explain the coherence of the state system by suggesting that its operational unity is partly ideological. He argues that most state elites, including those who are not members of the capitalist class, "accept as beyond question the capitalist context in which they operate." In Miliband's (1969, 72, 75) account, the ideological commitments of state elites and state managers are of "absolutely fundamental importance in shaping their attitudes, policies and actions in regard to specific issues and problems with which they are confronted." The result of their underlying ideological unity is that "the politics of advanced capitalism have been about different conceptions of how to run the *same* economic and social system."

Miliband (1969, 75) certainly recognizes that state elites and state managers in the various apparatuses, whether members of the capitalist class or not "wish, without a doubt, to pursue many ends, personal as well as public." However, the underlying ideological unity of state elites and state managers means that "all other ends are conditioned by, and pass through the prism of, their acceptance of and commitment to the existing economic system." Thus, in an observation that seems to anticipate Claus Offe's (1975; 1984, 126) "dependency principle," Miliband (1969, 75) observes that:

> . . . it is easy to understand why governments should wish to help business in every possible way. . . . For if the national interest is in fact inextricably bound up with the fortunes of capitalist enterprise, apparent partiality towards it is not really partiality at all. On the contrary, in serving the interests of business and in helping capitalist enterprise to thrive, governments are really fulfilling their exalted role as guardians of the good of all.

Otherwise, as Miliband describes it, the modern state system in capitalist societies is a vast and sprawling network of political institutions loosely coordinated, if at all, through mechanisms that provide a tenuous cohesion at best. Importantly, for Miliband, the diffuseness of the state system in capitalist societies also means that the conquest of state power is never an all or nothing proposition, because it is—in the Gramscian phrase—a war of fixed position, waged on many fronts, in many trenches, with shifting lines of battle, where victories and successes occur side by side on the same day. The conquest of state power is never absolute; it is never uncontested; and it is never complete, because it is an on-going and contingent *political* struggle.[13] Hence, Miliband's concept of the state requires an analysis and understanding of state power that always refers to particular historical circumstances and to institutional configurations that may vary widely from one capitalist society to another, and where over time class hegemony may shift in one direction or another within the same society. Indeed, Miliband (1969, 77) is quite explicit in pointing out that state elites "have in fact been compelled over the years to act against *some* property rights, to erode *some* managerial prerogatives, to help redress *somewhat* the balance between capital and labour, between property and those who are subject to it."

Poulantzas' Theory of the State

Nicos Poulantzas was relatively unknown to Anglo-American scholars until he initiated the Poulantzas-Miliband debate with his review of *The State in Capitalist Society* in late 1969

(Buchanan, 2010, 381). When Poulantzas informed readers that his critique of Miliband derived from epistemological positions presented more fully in his *Pouvoir Politique et Classes Sociales* (1968), the debate itself stimulated a demand for Poulantzas' book, which was finally published in English in 1973.[14]

SOCIAL CLASS AND POLITICAL PRACTICE

In *Political Power and Social Classes*, Poulantzas (1978a, 1–22) claims that every mode of production can be understood theoretically in terms of the functional interrelations between its economic, political, and ideological levels.[15] Each level in a mode of production consists of *structures*, which tend to reproduce and stabilize the mode of production and *class practices*, which generate conflicts and contradictions within the mode of production (Poulantzas, 1978a, 37, 86). A structure consists of one or more institutions that fulfill specific economic, political, or ideological functions necessary to sustain a particular mode of production. For instance, the economic structure of a capitalist society is constituted primarily by the social relations of production as defined in Marx's *Capital*.[16] The political structures of a mode of production consist of the institutionalized power of the state (Poulantzas, 1978a, 42).The ideological structures of a mode of production refer both to the subjective consciousness of individual social actors and to the collective thought-systems that exist in a given society (Poulantzas, 1978a, 28–34; Therborn, 1980, 2). A stable social formation—that is, a social system in equilibrium—is one where the structures at each level function together as an integrated system to maintain and extend the dominant relations of production and, hence, the ability of a dominant class to appropriate surplus value from a subordinate laboring class.

However, Poulantzas emphasizes that the normal functioning of structures within the capitalist mode of production generates contradictory *class practices* that simultaneously destabilize the conditions of ruling class domination. In *Political Power and Social Classes*, Poulantzas (1978a, 41) explains class practices as the effects of: (1) structural dislocations generated by class struggle and (2) the uneven development of structures between and within the levels of a social formation.[17] In direct contrast to what he calls the "historicist conception" of class practice, Poulantzas (1978a, 66) argues that "relations of production as a structure are not social classes . . . capital and wage-labour are not, of course, the empirical realities of 'capitalists' and 'labourers'." Instead, for Poulantzas (1978a, 66), the relations of production:

> . . . consist of *specific forms of combination* of the agents of production and the means of production. This structure of relations of production "determines the places and functions occupied and adopted by the agents of production, who are never anything more than the occupants of these places, in so far as they are supports of these functions."

Thus, Poulantzas can never regard the main tasks of Marxist political theory as empirical or historical, because such analyses in his framework confuse the agents of production (i.e., groups of individuals) with the structural-functional relations that determine social class. Individuals "support" and "carry out" various functions within temporal history, but these functions are in no way dependent upon particular individuals or groups of individuals. Hence, even before the publication of Miliband's *The State in Capitalist Society*, Poulantzas (1978a, 62) was dismissing the historicist conception of class practice as one that:

> . . . leads ultimately to the establishment of an ideological relation between individuals/agents-of-production ("men") and social classes; this relation is given a theoretical foundation in the status of the subject. Agents of production are perceived as agents/producers, as subjects which create structures; and social classes are perceived as the subjects of history.

Poulantzas (1978a, 62) finds the historicist conception of class practice theoretically flawed because it "fails to recognize two essential facts: firstly, that the agents of production, for example the wage-earning labourer and the capitalist, as 'personifications' of Wage-Labour and Capital, are considered by Marx as the *supports* or *bearers* of an ensemble of structures; secondly, that social classes are never *theoretically* conceived by Marx as the genetic origin of structures." Consequently, Poulantzas (1978a, 67–68) contends that "*social class is a concept which shows the effects of the ensemble of structures, of the matrix of a mode of production or of a social formation on the agents which constitute its supports.*" Social classes are *structural effects,* which mediate between structures (e.g., relations of production) and class practices (e.g., trade unionism). Indeed, according to Poulantzas (1978a, 86), "social classes are conceivable only in terms of class practices" and it is these practices which determine agency, not vice versa.[18]

Importantly, Poulantzas (1978a, 86) views the identification of specific class practices as synonymous with the concept of "contradiction" because "class practices can be analysed only as conflicting practices in the field of class struggle . . . for example, the contradiction between those practices which aim at the realization of profit and those which aim at the increase of wages." In other words, it is impossible to understand the structural place of working class practices that aim to increase wages without taking into consideration how such aims contradict capitalist class practices that aim to realize higher and higher profits. In this example, capitalist and proletarian class practices are each produced as the contradictory structural effect of relations of production on the agents of production (who merely carry out and support these practices within the capitalist system). Certainly, one can find explicit textual support for this claim in Marx's *Capital* and such a reading is perfectly consistent with the theoretical status accorded to that work by Poulantzas and other structuralists.[19]

Yet, the importance of class practices in mediating between structure and history in Poulantzas' political theory raises some difficult and immanent epistemological issues. This is because Poulantzas (1978a, 41) equates "the political" with class practices and, thus, he defines the specific object of politics as "the 'present moment' (as Lenin said), i.e., the *nodal point where the contradictions* of the various levels of a formation *are condensed* in the complex relations governed by over-determination and by their dislocation and uneven development." The epistemological difficulty for Poulantzas (1978a, 37) is that if the specific object of the political is the present moment, then "the problem of the political and politics is linked to the problem of history."

As noted earlier, Poulantzas argues that the "the problems of the general Marxist theory of the state and of the political class struggle" are addressed in a group of "political texts" by Marx, Engels, and Lenin that complement one's reading of *Capital*. Interestingly, the critical text forging an explicit theoretical nexus between structure and history is the *Communist Manifesto;* namely, the single most significant text that Poulantzas does *not* include on his list of "Marxian classics" in political theory. Yet, at a crucial point in the development of his argument, Poulantzas (1978a, 37) introduces two propositions from the *Communist Manifesto* to provide a theoretical nexus between class practices and history: "(a) 'Every class struggle is a political struggle', and (b) 'The class struggle is the motive force of history'."

Poulantzas never mentions that passage on the state emphasized so heavily by Miliband, but he does recognize that it is "possible to make a historicist reading" of the *Communist Manifesto*. In fact, to preempt such a reading, Poulantzas engages in a running polemic against "Marxist historicism" throughout *Political Power and Social Classes* and, after publication of *The State in Capitalist Society*, Poulantzas immediately identified Miliband as an exemplar of Marxist historicism. Significantly, Poulantzas (1978, 37–38) never challenges Miliband's "first reading" of the *Communist Manifesto*, as such, but instead questions *the effects* of such a reading on political practice as leading "to the ideological invariant voluntarism/economism and to the various forms of revisionism, reformism, spontaneism, etc." Yet, as if to compound the difficulty, Poulantzas (1978, 39), like Miliband, turns to Gramsci in addressing questions of the political only to find that Gramsci's views are "often tainted by the historicism of Croce and Labriola."[20]

WHAT IS THE STATE?

The contradictory effects of class practices on the equilibrium of the capitalist system means that immanent crisis tendencies are always disrupting the functional stability of the capitalist mode of production. Thus, the basic structure of the capitalist mode of production generates contradictory class practices, dislocations, and crisis tendencies, and it this inexorable disruption of the capitalist system that necessitates a separate structure to specifically maintain, monitor, and restore its equilibrium as a system. Although Poulantzas (1978, 45) modifies structural-functionalism by introducing class practices as a disequilibrating mechanism, nevertheless, he was clearly indebted to mainstream American functionalists and systems theorists insofar as he argues that the general function of the state in the capitalist mode of production is to serve as "*the regulating factor of its global equilibrium as a system.*"[21]

In particular, Poulantzas identifies three ensembles of class practices that require regulation by the state in order to maintain and restore the equilibrium of the capitalist system. First, Poulantzas argues contrary to the mythology of neo-classical economic theory, that the economic level of the capitalist mode of production has never "formed a hermetically sealed level, capable of self-production and possessing its own 'laws' of internal functioning." Rather, the economic level of the capitalist mode of production is only *relatively* autonomous from the political and ideological levels, but given this relative autonomy, Poulantzas (1978, 45) concludes that structural "equilibrium is never *given* by the economic as such, but is maintained by the state." To this extent, the state fulfills a general maintenance function "*by constituting the factor of cohesion between the levels of a social formation*" (Poulantzas 1978a, 44).[22]

Consequently, Poulantzas (1980, 17) identifies a second ensemble of class practices, constituted by the fact that "*the political field of the State* (as well as the sphere of ideology) *has always, in different forms, been present in the constitution and reproduction of the relations of production.*" Capitalist relations of production do not appear *ex nihilo* in history, nor do they reproduce themselves on a day-to-day basis without struggle and resistance on the part of subordinate classes whose labor is exploited by the capitalist class. Hence, in maintaining the cohesion of the levels of a social formation, Poulantzas (1978a, 52) observes that "the function of the state primarily concerns the economic level, and particularly the labour process, the productivity of labour."[23] This claim appears numerous times in *Political Power and Social Classes* and the claim is reiterated in both *Classes in Contemporary Capitalism* and *State, Power, Socialism*.[24]

Despite the evident importance of this function, Poulantzas (1978a, 53) also notes that "this function of the state as organizer of the labour process is only one aspect of its economic function." The state also establishes and enforces the rules which organize capitalist exchanges (property and contract law, enforcement, punishment) and it functions to organize labor through its role of education, teaching, and so on. Finally, Poulantzas calls attention to an ensemble of class practices which occur "at the strictly political level" of the capitalist mode of production. Poulantzas (1978a, 53) identifies the strictly political function of the state with "the maintenance of political order in political class conflict." By maintaining political order, by punishing disorder, and by monitoring political "subversion," the state represses revolution and revolt and, thereby, maintains conditions of exploitation under the neutral guise of "law and order."

The operational objectives of state policy are realized through three "modalities of the state function." The modalities of the state function identify the structural levels in which the *effects of state policies* are realized: (1) the technico-economic function at the economic level, (2) the political function at the level of class struggle, and (3) the ideological function at the cultural level. Regardless of the level at which the state's modalities are effected, however, Poulantzas contends that the state function is always oriented "with particular reference to the productivity of labor."[25]

The modalities of the state function are always implemented through three functional subsystems of the state: the judicial subsystem, the ideological subsystem, and the political subsystem. Poulantzas (1978a, 50, 53) argues that in capitalist societies the judicial subsystem is constituted as a set of rules, which facilitate market exchanges by providing a "framework of cohesion in which commercial encounters can take place," (e.g., property and contract law, fair business practices). The state's ideological subsystem functions primarily through public educational institutions, while the strictly political subsystem consists of institutions engaged in "the maintenance of political order in political class conflict" (e.g., electoral laws, the party system, police, bureaucracy).[26] The state's modalities each constitute *political* functions insofar as their operational objective is the maintenance and stabilization of a society in which the capitalist class is the dominant and exploitative class. As Poulantzas (1978a, 54) notes:

> . . . the state's economic or ideological functions correspond to the political interests of the dominant class and constitute political functions, not simply in those cases where there is a direct and obvious relation between (a) the organization of labour and education and (b) the political domination of a class, but also where the object of these functions is the maintenance of the unity of the formation, inside which this class is the politically dominant class. It is to the extent that the prime object of these functions is the maintenance of this unity that they [i.e., the functions and their modalities] correspond to the political interests of the dominant class.

It should be emphasized as a point of considerable theoretical significance that *structures* (i.e., the levels of the capitalist mode of production) are not reducible to the economic, political, or ideological *institutions* that compose them.[27] On this point, David Gold, Clarence Lo, and Erik Olin Wright (1975,

36 fn.) observe that for Poulantzas the concept of "structure does *not* refer to the concrete social institutions that make up a society, but rather to the *systematic functional interrelationships among these institutions*." Hence, Poulantzas' structural analysis always emphasized "the *functional relationship* of various institutions to the process of surplus-value production and appropriation,"[28] whereas Miliband tends to emphasize the empirical organization, operation, and control of particular institutions.

WHAT IS STATE POWER?

The differences between Miliband and Poulantzas concerning the importance of institutions initially appear to be much more than a mere difference in emphasis or theoretical focus. Miliband and Poulantzas each articulate competing concepts of state power that are linked inextricably to their methodological differences. Whereas Miliband articulates an institutionalist conception of power, anchored by the methodological (Weberian) assumptions of power structure research, Poulantzas articulates a functionalist conception of power anchored by the methodological (Parsonian) assumptions of systems analysis and structural functionalism. Notably, and in direct contrast to Miliband, Poulantzas draws a sharp *analytic* distinction between the concepts of state power and the state apparatus (Therborn, 1978, 148).

Poulantzas (1978a, 104) defines *state power* as the capacity of a social class to realize its objective interests through the state apparatus. Bob Jessop (1982, 221) lends greater specificity to this idea by observing that within this framework "state power is capitalist to the extent that it creates, maintains, or restores the conditions required for capital accumulation in a given situation and it is non-capitalist to the extent these conditions are not realised." In this respect, the objective *effects* of state policies on capital accumulation and the class structure are the main objective indicators of state power.[29] On the other hand, the state apparatus is identified with two relations that are analytically (though not functionally) distinct from state power. Poulantzas (1978a, 116) defines the state apparatus as:

"(a) The place of the state in the ensemble of the structures of a social formation," that is, the state's functions and "(b) The *personnel of the state,* the ranks of the administration, bureaucracy, army, etc." The state apparatus is thus a unity of the effects of state power (i.e., policies) *and* the network of institutions and personnel through which the state function is executed.[30]

The *functional* unity between state power and the state apparatus in emphasized by Poulantzas (1978a, 115 fn. 24) with the observation "that structure *is not the simple principle of organization which is exterior to* the institution: the structure is present in an allusive and inverted form in the institution itself." For Poulantzas (1978a, 115), the concept of the state apparatus intrinsically includes the functions executed through state institutions and by state personnel. Hence, in direct contrast to Miliband, Poulantzas insists that "the institutions of the state, do not, strictly speaking, have any power. Institutions, considered from the point of view of power, can be related only to *social classes which hold power*."[31] State institutions are political arenas for the exercise of class power and exist as such only by virtue of their functional role in the capitalist mode of production (Poulantzas, 1978a, 115).[32]

The First Exchange: The Problem of Method

From the outset of their critical exchange, Poulantzas focused the debate on "the problem of method" in Marxist political theory. As a result, and as I have suggested earlier, even though the Poulantzas-Miliband debate has generally been viewed as a contest between instrumentalist and structuralist theories of the state, it was actually more about methodology than about state theory. Notably, Poulantzas praises Miliband for methodically attacking bourgeois conceptions of the state and political power by rigorously deploying a formidable array of empirical data to challenge the dogmatic assertions of pluralist theory. Poulantzas (1969, 69) acknowledges that Miliband's empirical methodological approach had enabled him to "radically demolish" bourgeois ideologies of the State and to provide Marxists "with a positive knowledge that these ideologies have never been able to produce." For Poulantzas (1969, 73), this means that Miliband's work functions as an ideology critique and that its political value is its ideological effect in demystifying the claims of bourgeois social science.[33]

However, as an ideology critique that demystifies bourgeois conceptions of the state and political power, it does not thereby elaborate a Marxist theory of the state. Ideology critique does not go far enough in challenging the dominance of bourgeois conceptions because, in Poulantzas' view, it is never sufficient to juxtapose empirical facts against theoretical concepts. The concepts themselves must be attacked at a philosophical and theoretical level with other "concepts situated in a different problematic." Instead of merely demystifying bourgeois ideology from within its own problematic, Poulantzas (1969, 69) insists that it is necessary to *displace* that epistemological terrain and Poulantzas claims that "Miliband appears to omit this first step."[34] Poulantzas is not content with an analysis that empirically demystifies the concept of a plural elite, for example; he insists that one must reject the very concepts of bourgeois social science and replace them with "the scientific concepts of Marxist theory." This is because empirical facts only become "concrete" by having a new theoretical meaning conferred on them by their place within a radical theory constituted as an epistemological break with bourgeois social science.

Poulantzas insists that epistemology and theory construction must precede ideology critique for two reasons. First, ideology critique employs the theoretical concepts of an ideological adversary and, in using these concepts, Poulantzas (1969, 70) is certain that "one legitimizes them and permits their persistence." Hence, even the limited objectives of an ideology critique are vitiated by a self-defeating exercise that strengthens one's adversary. Second, Poulantzas is concerned about the risk of being "unconsciously and surreptitiously contaminated by the very epistemological principles of the adversary." Although Poulantzas *initially* agrees that Miliband's methodological procedures have not taken him too far down that path, Poulantzas does caution that "Miliband sometimes allows himself to be unduly influenced by the methodological principles of the adversary," that is, bourgeois social scientists. Poulantzas identifies several specific instances where he believes that Miliband's methodology led him astray theoretically: (1) the problem of the subject, (2) the problem of state cohesion, (3) the problem of ideological apparatuses. If this series of so-called problematics shaped the direction of Marxist political theory for the next decade, it is the Poulantzas-Miliband debate which defined the frontiers and boundaries of those explorations.

THE PROBLEM OF THE SUBJECT

Poulantzas (1969, 70–71) defines the problem of the subject as "a problematic of *social actors*, of individuals as the origin of *social action*." If individuals or groups of individuals are considered as social actors, then Poulantzas argues that theoretical research is diverted from "the study of the objective co-ordinates that determine the distribution of agents into social classes and the contradictions between these classes . . . to the search for *finalist* explanations founded on the *motivations of conduct* of the individual actors." Poulantzas claims that Miliband's empirical and institutional analysis of states in capitalist societies "constantly gives the impression" that "social classes or 'groups' are in some way reducible to *inter-personal relations*, that the State is reducible to inter-personal relations of the members of the diverse 'groups' that constitute the State apparatus, and finally that the relation between social classes and the State is itself reducible to inter-personal relations of 'individuals' composing social groups and 'individuals' composing the State apparatus." Consequently, Poulantzas chastises Miliband for offering explanations of corporate behavior, the state elite, and state managers that are "founded on the *motivations of conduct* of the individual actors." Poulantzas contends that this method of analysis vitiates Miliband's ideology critique to the extent that he fails to comprehend "social classes and the State as *objective structures*, and their relations as an *objective system of regular connections*, a structure and a system whose agents, 'men', are in the words of Marx, 'bearers' of it." Otherwise, Poulantzas is concerned that "to transpose this problematic of the subject into Marxism is in the end to admit the epistemological principles of the adversary." Interestingly, in an earlier essay, also published in the *New Left Review*, Poulantzas (1967) argues that the problem of the subject is a theoretical error endemic to Anglo-American Marxism in general and so in many ways his critique of Miliband merely serves to illuminate his assessment of a widespread theoretical shortcoming within the Anglo-American left.

THE PROBLEM OF STATE COHESION

According to Poulantzas, this same problem of the subject resurfaces in Miliband's treatment of the state bureaucracy, the army, regulatory agencies, and other personnel of the state system. The problem appears in the fact that Miliband places so much emphasis on the role of ideology in linking these agents to the capitalist class and the top state elite, because this explanatory mechanism suggests that the criterion for membership in a particular class is the shared motivations and subjective orientations of a group of individuals. Hence, Poulantzas (1969, 73) concludes that Miliband "seems to reduce the role of the State to the conduct and 'behavior' of the members of the State apparatus." Poulantzas (1969, 71), of course, insists that Marx's criterion for the designation of class boundaries is "the objective place in production and the ownership of the means of production." Instead, Poulantzas (1969, 73) proposes that civil servants, military officers, regulators, and other state managers are "a specific *social category*—not a class. This means that, although the members of the State apparatus belong, by their class origin to different classes, they function according to a specific internal unity." A social category's "internal unity derives from its actualization of the objective role of the State" (Poulantzas, 1969, 74). Therefore, Poulantzas (1969, 73) claims in a now legendary passage that:

> . . . the *direct* participation of members of the capitalist class in the State apparatus and in the government, even where it exists, is not the important side of the

> matter. The relation between the bourgeois class and the State is an *objective relation*. This means that if the *function* of the state in a determinate social formation and the *interests* of the dominant class in this formation coincide, it is by reason of the system itself: the direct participation of members of the ruling class in the state apparatus is not the *cause* but the *effect*, and moreover a chance and contingent one, of this objective coincidence.

Although Poulantzas insists that the state as a whole, as an objective system of power, is relatively autonomous from the dominant class, the state's *internal unity* requires that we not view its individual apparatuses and personnel as relatively autonomous. Rather, it is the general function of the state that gives cohesion and unity to the apparatuses and personnel and which make it possible to refer both to *a* state and to the *capitalist* state. However, from Poulantzas' perspective, Miliband relies on factors "exterior" to the state itself and, therefore, he lacks a theoretical capacity to *conceptualize the necessary unity and cohesion of the state*. In contrast, Poulantzas (1969, 77) insists that "the State in the classic Marxist sense of the term, possesses a very rigorous internal unity which directly governs the relation between the diverse branches of the apparatus."

THE PROBLEM OF IDEOLOGICAL APPARATUSES

Poulantzas was not inclined to dismiss ideology altogether, but instead he proposes to reconceptualize its production and distribution within a Marxist theory of the state. Poulantzas (1969, 76–77) was quite correct to point out that "the classic Marxist tradition of the theory of the State is principally concerned to show *the repressive role of the State*, in the strong sense of organized physical repression." On the other hand, ideology had been dismissed as epiphenomenal (rather than constitutive) of social and political relations, mainly because ideology had been equated "with ideas, customs or morals without seeing that ideology can be embodied, in the strong sense, in *institutions*: institutions which then, by the very process of institutionalization, belong to the system of the State." Poulantzas proposes that the realm of ideology be brought inside the state by reconceptualizing the state as a dual matrix of apparatuses that either perform repressive functions or ideological functions.[35] Poulantzas defines the state ideological apparatuses to include churches, political parties, trade unions, schools and universities, the press, television, radio, and even the family.

In this manner, Poulantzas (1969, 68) seeks to widen the potential range of revolutionary activities in capitalist society, because he maintains that "the principal objective of revolutionary action is *State power* and the necessary precondition of any socialist revolution is the destruction of the bourgeois State apparatus." As Poulantzas (1969, 78) observes: ". . . according to Marxist-Leninist theory, a socialist revolution does not signify only a shift in *State power*, but it must equally *'break,'* that is to say radically change, the State apparatus" and, hence, "the advent of socialist society cannot be achieved . . . whilst maintaining the State ideological apparatuses intact." However, Poulantzas does issue a powerful warning to contemporary culture critics with his conclusion that "the 'destruction' of the ideological apparatuses has *its precondition* in the 'destruction' of the State repressive apparatus which maintains it." Consequently, Poulantzas deems it an "illusory error" to believe that cultural revolution can occur without directly confronting the state repressive apparatus, or as he puts it, to consider "the 'destruction' of the university in capitalist societies, for instance" as a revolutionary activity. Culture is not what supports the repressive apparatus; it is the repressive apparatus that supports and promotes the dominant culture. In other words, revolutions occur on a political and not a cultural battlefield.[36]

THE PROBLEM OF METHOD II

Miliband responded to Poulantzas' critique on most points, although he was convinced that many of Poulantzas' quibbles with his work were trivial and unwarranted. Miliband did not expend a great deal of energy replying to every minor criticism, but instead chose to address only those general points which seemed of particular importance to understanding the nature and role of the state in capitalist society. Miliband readily acceded to Poulantzas' postulate that a precondition of any scientific approach to the concrete is to make explicit the epistemological principles of its own treatment of the concrete. The point, however, is that from Miliband's (1970b, 54) perspective he did "quite explicitly give an outline of the Marxist theory of the state."

In defending this claim, Miliband refers us back to that famous passage in the *Communist Manifesto* only to reiterate his previous position that once stated it is only possible to elucidate that concept further "in empirical terms."[37] Thus, Miliband concludes from within his epistemological framework that Poulantzas, Louis Althusser, and their collaborators are "so profoundly concerned with the elaboration of an appropriate 'problematic' and with the avoidance of any contamination with opposed 'problematics', as to lose sight of the absolute necessity of empirical enquiry, and of the empirical demonstration of the falsity of these opposed and apologetic 'problematics'." As a wry gesture to the Poulantzasian interpretation of the Marxist classics, which emphasized the centrality of *Capital*, Miliband argues that as a methodological text *Capital* stresses "the importance of empirical validation (or invalidation)," while noting that Marx "spent many years of his life in precisely such an undertaking."[38]

THE PROBLEM OF THE SUBJECT II

Miliband also fundamentally rejects Poulantzas' indictment of his work as one contaminated by the problem of the subject. Quite the contrary, Miliband was convinced that Poulantzas greatly under-estimates the extent to which he did take account of the objective relations which affect and shape the role of the state. Indeed, Miliband describes Poulantzas' methodology as "structural super-determinism" and concludes that it is Poulantzas' one-sidedness which makes it impossible for him to recognize Miliband's treatment of objective structural factors and which also leads Poulantzas to go much too far in dismissing the nature of the state elite as irrelevant to an understanding of concrete differences between states and state policies in different capitalist societies. Instead, Miliband (1970b, 57) takes Poulantzas to task for his *exclusive* stress on objective relations which implies "that what the state does is in every particular and at all times is *wholly* determined by these 'objective relations': in other words, that the structural constraints of the system are so absolutely compelling as to turn those who run the state into the merest functionaries and executants of policies imposed upon them by 'the system'."[39]

THE PROBLEM OF STATE COHESION II

Miliband's defense of the role of the state elite, and his rejection of structural factors as absolutely determining allowed him to highlight another significant difference with Poulantzas. Whereas Poulantzas criticized Miliband for not being able to conceptualize state cohesion adequately, Miliband's very point was to emphasize the tenuous unity and tendencies toward disaggregation of the state apparatuses. Miliband's (1970b, 57) analysis is designed to demonstrate that "the state elite is involved in a far more complex relationship with 'the system' and with society as a whole than Poulantzas' scheme allows; and that at least to a certain but definite and important extent that relationship is shaped by the kind of factors," which Poulantzas dismisses as irrelevant; namely, ideology, individual motivations, the fragmentation and disunity of the state apparatuses. In other words, Miliband did not fail to conceptualize state cohesion adequately, but was drawing the *empirical conclusion* that such unity does not exist for states in advanced capitalist societies.

THE PROBLEM OF IDEOLOGICAL APPARATUSES II

Finally, Miliband simply rejects outright Poulantzas' assertion about the neglect of ideology by Marxist political theory. First, Miliband points out that he devoted two chapters of *The State in Capitalist Society* to "the institutions which are the purveyors of ideology" and thus adopts exactly the method of analysis proposed by Poulantzas. Second, however, Miliband rejects Poulantzas' suggestion that these institutions be conceptualized as part of the state apparatus. Precisely because ideological institutions are increasingly linked to and buttressed by the state, Miliband insists that it is important not to blur the fact that in bourgeois democracies they are not generally part of the state, but part of a wider political or ideological system. Certainly, Miliband agrees that ideological institutions *are* increasingly subject to a process of "statization" and he concedes that their statization "is likely to be enhanced by the fact that the state must, in the conditions of permanent crisis of advanced capitalism, assume ever greater responsibility for political indoctrination and mystification." Nevertheless, Miliband (1970b, 59) draws the empirical conclusion that such a process has not gone far enough to permit the conceptualization of such institutions as part of the state, because most of them continue to "perform their ideological functions outside it" (e.g., private schools and universities, churches, the mass media).

The Second Exchange: The Problem of Method Again (1973)

Miliband continued his rejoinder in 1973 following the publication in English of Poulantzas' *Political Power and Social Classes*, which he viewed as "an opportunity to continue with the discussion" begun three years earlier. Miliband's essay again focused on the problem of method, although as a review of Poulantzas' book, Miliband shifted the emphasis from a defense of his own position to a critique of Althusserian structuralism. The availability of a sound English language translation of Poulantzas' book confirmed Miliband's (1973, 83–84) apprehension that the book is "obscurely written for any reader who has not become familiar through painful initiation with the particular linguistic code and mode of exposition of the Althusserian school to which Poulantzas relates." Consequently, in his second rejoinder, Miliband frequently complains of Poulantzas' opaqueness and proposes that instead of describing his method as structural super-determinism, it would be more appropriate to call it structuralist abstractionism. In fact, Miliband provides numerous examples of oxymoronic terminology, self-contradictory phraseology, and completely opaque scholasticism. While a genre of structural abstractionism might make for great art, or even great literature, Miliband did not think it made very good political theory.

First, although Miliband concedes that "poor exposition" is a secondary defect he suggested that the abstractness of contemporary Marxist theory was paradoxical given its claim to be a science of working class revolution. The most prominent Marxist theorists seem to compete with one another as to who can write at a level of abstraction so opaque that it is never likely to be accessible to anyone but a few highly educated and specialized professional academicians. In contrast, contemporary liberal and conservative political theorists routinely write "academic" works that are easily accessible to an educated lay audience and this in no way jeopardizes the intellectual integrity of the work. In this respect, if one is to judge the functional value of Marxist social science by its *objective effects* at the political and ideological levels, then Miliband (1973, 84) suggests that the sooner the problem of excessive abstraction "is remedied, the more likely it is that a Marxist tradition of political analysis will now be encouraged to take root." At some point, the value and role of Marxist political theory must be judged against its effects on the political, that is, in promoting and facilitating socialism as opposed to its current preoccupation with establishing academic legitimacy within the dominant ideological institutions.

Second, as Miliband (1973, 84–85, 91) begins to recognize at this point, Poulantzas' main concern was not to provide a theory of the capitalist state (at least not as Miliband understands that concept), but "to provide a 'reading' of texts from Marx and Engels, and also from Lenin, on the state and politics." As Miliband notes, "such a 'reading', in the Althusserian sense, is, of course, not a presentation or a collation of texts; nor is it commentary on them or even an attempt at interpretation, though it is partly the latter." Instead, an Althusserian reading of the classic texts—which Miliband confesses makes him "a bit uneasy"—involves a complementation of the original texts. To his credit, Miliband did not follow the path of much contemporary literary/political theory by engaging Poulantzas and the structuralists in a debate over "methods of textual interpretation." Instead, he simply returns directly to the original texts as a basis for asking himself how well Poulantzas conducted his interpretive exercise and "whether the 'deciphering' has produced an accurate message." Miliband concludes on the basis of his own reading "that much of Poulantzas' 'reading' constitutes a serious misrepresentation of Marx and Engels and also of the actual reality he is attempting to portray." To put it bluntly, Miliband does not consider Poulantzas' reading of Marx very rigorous and, unfortunately, "care and scruple in textual quotation are not simply matters of scholarship: they also involve large political issues."

In fact, a close reading of Poulantzas (1978a) suggests that he never did a close "symptomatic" reading of the Marxian classics, but instead relied heavily (at least initially) on the conclusions of Althusser and his followers. At nearly every major turn, Poulantzas uses vague and general references to support his major claims; for example: on the construction of general theory, Poulantzas (1978a, 12) bolsters his position with "Marx demonstrated in the Introduction of 1857"; on the concept of overdetermination, Poulantzas (1978a, 17) articulates a concept "as expounded by Marx in *Capital*"; on the autonomy of the levels, Poulantzas (1978a, 29) claims that "Marx demonstrated this in *Capital*"; on the autonomy of the political, Poulantzas (1978a, 30) insists that this claim is verified "In the *Grundrisse* and in passages concerning the feudal mode of production in *Capital*." Yet, Poulantzas never makes a specific citation to support these claims, among many others.

This peculiarity is now far more interesting theoretically, since Louis Althusser (1993, 165–66) admitted that his "philosophical knowledge of texts was rather limited . . . a bit about Hegel, and finally a few passages of Marx." Althusser describes his real method of learning philosophy as "hearsay . . . gleaning certain phrases in passing from my friends, and lastly from the seminar papers and essays of my own students." Similarly, Hall (2000, vii) notes that Poulantzas informed him during an interview that "it was virtually impossible in the early days even to acquire the classical texts of Marx and Engels, and he came to Marxism largely through French philosophy."

In contrast, Miliband (1973, 85) advances his own reading of Marx by noting "that the basic theme of the [Poulantzas] book, its central problematic, is absolutely right." This theme, as Miliband understands it, is to reaffirm "that the political realm is not, in classical Marxism, the mere reflection of the economic realm, and that in relation to the state, the notion of the latter's 'relative autonomy' is central." However, in a significant and lengthy footnote that is generally ignored, Miliband (1973, 85 fn. 4) again returns to his original text to argue that Poulantzas' central theme is already fully contained in:

> . . . the most familiar of all the Marxist formulations on the state, that which is to be found in the *Communist Manifesto*, where Marx and Engels assert that "the modern State is but a committee for managing the common affairs of the whole bourgeoisie" . . . what they are saying is that "the modern state is but a committee for managing the *common* affairs of the *whole* bourgeoisie": the notion of common affairs assumes the existence of particular ones; and the notion of the whole bourgeoisie implies the existence of separate elements which make up that whole. This being the case, there is an obvious need for an institution of the kind they refer to, namely the state; and the state *cannot* meet this need without enjoying a certain degree of autonomy. In other words, the notion of autonomy is embedded in the definition itself, is an intrinsic part of it.

Thus, there is no need for a symptomatic reading of Marx and no reason to complement the Marxian classics, because the requisite theory and concepts are already sufficient to proceed with an analysis of the capitalist state.[40] Moreover, the real problem with Poulantzasian structuralism for Miliband is that it fails to achieve its stated purpose. Poulantzas claims to develop a theory of the capitalist state and, yet, Miliband (1974, 84) complains "the book hardly contains any reference at all to an actual capitalist state anywhere" primarily because Poulantzas has "an absurdly exaggerated fear of empiricist contamination." From this perspective, Poulantzas' "'structural super-determinism' makes him *assume* what has to be *explained* about the relationship of the state to classes in the capitalist mode of production" and, hence, he sees no need for serious empirical or historical investigations. Thus, "the real trouble," as Miliband puts it, is that Poulantzas' *approach* to the questions raised in their first exchange is what "prevents him from providing a satisfactory answer to them." Thus, Miliband (1973, 89, 85–86) laments that "the world of 'structures' and 'levels' which he [Poulantzas] inhabits has so few points of contact with historical or contemporary reality that it cuts him off from any possibility of achieving what he describes as 'the political analysis of a concrete conjuncture'."

THE PROBLEM OF STATE POWER

Miliband illustrates his methodological claim by contrasting their conceptions of state power. Poulantzas argues that state institutions, as such, do not have any power, but must be related only to social classes which hold power. However, Miliband (1973, 87) observes that if the state does not have any independent source of power, "this, *inter alia,* is to deprive the state of any kind of autonomy at all" and, for all practical matters, conceptualizes the state out of existence in everything but name only. Thus, aside from being a self-contradictory and self-defeating theoretical position, Miliband insists that one has to make a distinction between class power and state power, not only because it is necessary to conceptualize the state as relatively autonomous, but because it is also necessary to recognizing that while state power may be the main and ultimate means of maintaining ruling class domination, it is not the only form of class power as Poulantzas' formulation implies. Miliband's point is that state power is not the only form, nor the only site, of ruling class domination. This is another reason why Miliband again rejects Poulantzas' suggestion that institutions such as churches, the educational system, political parties, the press, radio, television, publishing, the family, and so on, should all be brought within the realm of state theory as components of an ideological state apparatus. Indeed, Miliband (1973, 87, 88 fn. 16) scoffs at the suggestion as carrying "to caricatural forms the confusion between different forms of class domination and, to repeat, makes impossible a serious analysis of the relation of the state to society, and of state power to class power."

THE THIRD EXCHANGE: STALEMATE (1976)

Poulantzas did not reply immediately to Miliband's scathing critique, but following the English language publication of *Fascism and Dictatorship* (1974) and *Classes in Contemporary Capitalism* (1975), he decided that "the moment has come to continue the debate." In fact, Poulantzas' polemical strategy was to end the debate by shifting the terms of the debate from a direct confrontation over the problems of method and theory to an ideological divergence between contaminated Marxism and real Marxism. The third exchange essentially ended the debate—at least as a personal exchange between Miliband and Poulantzas—although by this time Poulantzas (1976a, 63–64) recognized that "a good many others, in Europe, the United States, Latin America, and elsewhere, have joined in, in articles and books." By this time, Poulantzas (1976a, 63–64) was acutely aware that the differences between Miliband and himself were being conceptualized by other scholars, "especially in England and the United States, as a controversy between 'instrumentalism' and 'structuralism'." Poulantzas dismissed these terms "as an utterly mistaken way of situating the discussion." As a matter of fact, Poulantzas complains that the only reason he decided to continue the discussion is "that certain authors, especially in the United States, have perceived the debate between Miliband and myself as a supposed debate between instrumentalism and structuralism, thus posing a false dilemma."[41] Consequently, Poulantzas hoped in one last salvo to clarify what he considered to be the "real" conflict as one between materialism and idealism or between Marxist social science and bourgeois ideology (i.e., contaminated Marxism).

THE PROBLEM OF METHOD III

Poulantzas (1976a, 76) curtly dismisses Miliband's comments on the difficulty of his terminology and on the lack of concrete analysis as evidence that their approaches are "situated on disparate [epistemological] terrains." Poulantzas held firm to his claim that it is only possible to "carry on a far-reaching debate with the aid of a precise language, and . . . from within their respective problematics, to attach precise definitions to the concepts, terms or notions they are using." In Poulantzas' view, there was no point in continuing the debate further because Miliband's writings "are marked by the absence of any theoretical problematic" and allegedly it is the absence of an explicit problematic that accounts for Miliband's repeated criticisms of Poulantzas' work for its lack of concrete analysis. Hence, Poulantzas writes that "on the subject of Miliband's own work, I have nothing to add to what I wrote in my original review of his book." From Poulantzas' perspective, Miliband was not engaged in theory construction or in the production of new concepts capable of displacing his own epistemological position. Quite simply, Poulantzas and Miliband do not agree on how to read the Marxian classics, on what constitutes a concept, on what counts as a theory or as theory construction, or even on what counts as a concrete analysis and most of these divergences are anchored in the fundamental assumptions of competing social science methodologies.

Poulantzas (1976a, 76) is certainly aware of this fact and, for this reason, he explicitly rejects the ambitions of Anglo-American authors hoping to escape the dichotomy by finding a compromise between instrumentalism and structuralism or a synthesis of the two perspectives. Poulantzas understood from the beginning that the real debate was about the problem of method. More to the point, however, in his last essay of the debate, Poulantzas seeks to conflate the categories of methodology and ideology to create a new dichotomy between materialism (Marxism) and idealism (bourgeois ideology).

Poulantzas begins to introduce this new distinction in his reply to Miliband's comments on "structural abstractionism." Poulantzas was evidently irritated by Miliband's reproach concerning the lack of concrete analyses or references to concrete historical and empirical facts in his writings. First, Poulantzas (1976a, 65) did not consider the reproach justified because he insists that "constant and precise references to the state of the class struggle and to the historical transformations of the State are abundantly present in *Political Power*." However, once Poulantzas cites his discussions of the absolutist State, historical models of bourgeois revolution, and the forms of the capitalist State, it is clear that Poulantzas' notion of concrete analysis is a usage peculiar to structuralist epistemology and it is certainly not what Miliband means by concrete analysis (e.g., a historical and empirical analysis of Thatcher regime policies in the 1980s).

Furthermore, Poulantzas emphasizes that the difference between him and Miliband over the meaning of the concrete goes back to their "respective approaches to 'concrete facts'." For Poulantzas, as noted earlier, an isolated fact is an abstraction that only becomes concrete when it is given meaning "with the aid of a theoretical apparatus constantly employed throughout the length of the text." Thus, Poulantzas concludes that without an explicit theoretical problematic, "one can pile up as many concrete analyses as one likes, they will prove nothing whatsoever." What Miliband calls a lack of concrete analysis, Poulantzas (1976a, 65) embraces as eschewing "the demagogy of the 'palpitating fact', of 'common sense', and the 'illusions of the evident'." Indeed, Poulantzas returns to an old theme when he berates Miliband for succumbing to "the demagogy of common sense" and, for good measure, sideswipes "the dominant 'Anglo-Saxon culture' as a whole" as the source of this epistemological error. Poulantzas (1976a, 67–68) can scarcely conceal his disdain for "English readers" who steeped in the demagogy of common sense and empiricism are unable to grasp what he acknowledges was "sometimes needlessly difficult language." In the final analysis, Poulantzas is only willing to concede that he shared "an over-rigid epistemological position" with Althusser at the time. Lest anyone think that such an admission carried with it some hope of a reconciliation or a synthesis, Poulantzas (1976a, 66–67) again reiterates that "I naturally maintain my essential difference with Miliband, one that is irreducible, theoretically."[42]

For Poulantzas, this irreducible theoretical break was the distinction between real materialist Marxism and contaminated Marxism. Although Miliband and other plain Marxists generally reject any description of their position as instrumentalism, it is still not widely acknowledged that Poulantzas also came to reject the structuralist label by 1976. Poulantzas was apparently stung by Miliband's references to his structural super-determinism and structural abstractionism. However, in the last exchange, Poulantzas turns these concepts against Miliband by suggesting that such terms have been used historically to criticize Marxists for not granting "sufficient importance to the role of concrete individuals and creative persons; to human freedom and action; to free will and to Man's capacity for choice; to the 'project' as against 'necessity' (hence Miliband's term, 'super-determinism'); and so on and so forth." Poulantzas (1976a, 70) retaliates with the observation that Miliband's use of the term structuralism thus "falls within the humanist and historicist problematic, indeed within a traditional problematic of bourgeois subjectivist idealism such as has frequently influenced Marxism, namely the problematic of the subject." To the extent that Poulantzas always located Miliband's work within the problematic of the subject, this reference is a scarcely concealed effort to push Miliband completely off the terrain of Marxist political theory. In fact, Poulantzas (1976a, 70) ends the discussion with a rejoinder that:

> I would like to state quite clearly that I have no intention of replying to this [charge of structuralism]. I consider that everything there is to say on this subject has

> already been said, and that all those who have not yet understood, or who have yet to be convinced . . . are certainly not going to be convinced by the few lines I could possibly add here on this subject. I shall, therefore, merely repeat that the term structuralism applied in this sense to *Political Power* is nothing more, in the final analysis, than a reiteration in modern terms of the kind of objections that bourgeois idealism has always opposed to Marxism of whatever stripe.

Finally, Poulantzas concludes the debate by returning to the issue of whether one must draw a distinction between class power and state power. Poulantzas (1976a, 73) dismisses Miliband's argument that state institutions must be viewed as repositories of independent power (i.e., coercion) to have autonomy as nothing but a blatant "appeal to common sense." Rather than responding directly to the theoretical argument, Poulantzas again attempts to drive an ideological wedge between himself and Miliband by insisting that Miliband's conception of state power is "an old and persistent conception of bourgeois social science and politics." As if to make his point one last time, Poulantzas (1976, 76) dismisses the entirety of the debate with Miliband by concluding that after all is said and done: "all that remains is a polemical catch-phrase pure and simple, masking a factual and empirical critique."

THREE

Plain Marxists and Sophisticated Marxists

In his book *The Marxists* (1962), American sociologist C. Wright Mills drew an ironic distinction between "plain marxism" and "sophisticated marxism" that not only foreshadowed the next decade's state theory debate, but unintentionally set the stage for many of the misrepresentations that eventually characterized that debate. Consequently, it is no coincidence that renewed interest in Poulantzas and Miliband has also generated "a small but pronounced revival" of scholarly interest in the works of C. Wright Mills after a period when Marxist state theorists rejected his work as that of a vulgar "voluntarist" (Aronowitz, 2003). There are also political reasons for the renewed interest in Mills' exposé of the American power elite, which he described as a tightly knit and venal coalition of the corporate rich, military warlords, and a servile political directorate.

The direct seizure of American national government by upper-class scions that was orchestrated during the Reagan/Bush Administrations (1980–1992) under the rubric of populist rhetoric seemed to expose itself in the Bush II Administration (2000–2008) (Edsall, 1984). A stolen election (2000), corporate corruption scandals (Enron, MCI), a global financial collapse

(2007–2009), and an unpopular war of occupation (Iraq)—all rationalized with bald-faced lying—have made Mills' (1956, 343) claim that "the higher immorality is a systematic feature of the American elite" seem remarkably timely (Wolfe, 1999). Hence, the idea of the power elite once again resonates with scholars and ordinary citizens even as middle-class complacency with it all makes Mills' description of Americans as ideologically "inactionary" seem frighteningly accurate (Mills, 1951, 327).[1] As a result, four of Mills' most important books have been republished in the last few years, each with a new introduction by a prominent scholar, and his daughters have published a collection of his personal letters, including his FBI file, for the first time. This small if pronounced return to Mills seems to have culminated in a three volume reassessment of his work edited by Stanley Aronowitz (2004), which also catalyzed a 2006 panel of the American Political Science Association devoted specifically to *The Power Elite*. More recently, Aronowitz (2012) has published a reassessment of "C. Wright Mills and the Making of Political Intellectuals."

While the revival of interest in C. Wright Mills has emerged in tandem with renewed interest in the Poulantzas-Miliband debate, it is not yet recognized that these two intellectual currents actually intersect in C. Wright Mills' *The Power Elite*, which was actually the main object of Nicos Poulantzas' criticism when he first identified "instrumentalism" and "historicism" as the intellectual sources of a "distorted Marxism." In *Pouvoir Politique et Classes Sociale* (1968), it was actually C. Wright Mills who was on the receiving end of Poulantzas' methodological polemic as Ralph Miliband's *The State in Capitalist Society* (1969) had not even been published when the original French version of Poulantzas' book was released in 1968. Yet, equally interesting, and also evidently forgotten is that there was an earlier encounter between Marxists and *The Power Elite* during the 1950s, when Marxists such as Paul M. Sweezy and Herbert Aptheker took Mills to task, but in ways that yielded a wholly different and far more constructive outcome. The first encounter between Mills and the Marxists was a lively engagement that yielded constructive advances in political theory and, indeed, Miliband's *The State in Capitalist*

Society was at least partially the outcome of that first encounter. On the other hand, during the 1970s, Poulantzas replayed his earlier polemic against "voluntarism" and "instrumentalism" by inserting Miliband into the debate as if he were Mills' identical theoretical twin. In this respect, Poulantzas and the structural Marxists failed to recognize that Anglo-American Marxists, such as Miliband, had already moved beyond Mills, first, by incorporating his many empirical advances into a theoretical analysis but, second, by criticizing Mills for lacking a theory of political economy and, therefore, ironically for failing to incorporate "structural" factors into his analysis of the power elite (Barrow, 2007).

The Power Elite and Marxism

It is hardly a revelation to point out that the central concept in C. Wright Mills' *The Power Elite* is a concept of "the power elite," rather than a "ruling" or "capitalist class." However, it has always been a source of consternation for Marxists that Mills elaborated this concept by starting from the Weberian position that societies consist of *analytically* distinct and autonomous economic, political, social, and cultural orders (Weber, 1946). Rather than asserting that an inherent relationship exists between any of these orders, Mills argued that any such claim was a hypothesis until such time, and to such a *degree*, as it could be demonstrated as the *conclusion* of empirical sociological research. A second source of concern for Marxists was Mills' claim that institutions (and not classes directly) organize power in society by vesting certain positions, and the individuals occupying those positions, with the authority to make decisions about how to deploy the key resources mobilized by that institution.

For instance, as an economic institution, the modern corporation vests its board of directors and executive officers with the authority to allocate and determine the use of any economic resources that the corporation owns or controls. Likewise, government vests specific public offices with the authority to employ administrative coercion or police force against anyone who fails to comply with the law. Similarly, as cultural institutions, schools and universities certify specific individuals as possessing expertise in particular fields of knowledge. In this sense, the individuals who occupy positions of institutional authority in a society control different types of power: economic power, political power, and ideological power and it is the authority to make institutionally binding decisions that makes an individual powerful. Thus, power can be imputed to particular groups of individuals to the degree that they occupy the decision-making positions of the organizations that control wealth, force, status, and knowledge in a particular society. A power structure consists of a patterned distribution of resources that is organized by the major institutions of a particular society (Barrow, 1993, 13–16).[2]

Thus, Mills claimed that:

> The power elite is composed of men . . . in positions to make decisions having major consequences . . . they are in command of the major hierarchies and organizations of modern society. They rule the big corporations. They run the machinery of the state and claim its prerogatives. They direct the military establishment. They occupy the strategic command posts of the social structure, in which are now centered the effective means of the power and the wealth and the celebrity which they enjoy. (Mills, 1956, 3–4)

However, Mills also emphasized that:

> Behind such men and behind the events of history, linking the two, are the major institutions of modern society. These hierarchies of state and corporation and army constitute *the means of power*; as such they are now of a consequence not before equaled in human history—and at their summits, there are now those command posts of modern society, which offer us the sociological key to an understanding of the role of the higher circles in America. (Mills, 1956, 5)[3]

Like many other liberals, the economist Robert Lekachman (1957, 270) was critical of *The Power Elite,* because he thought it contained too many "Marxist and Hobsonite echoes." Indeed, he was not alone in wondering how Mills' conception of a power elite controlling *the means of power* differed from Paul Sweezy's (1942, 243) earlier declaration that the state is "an instrument in the hands of the ruling class for enforcing and guaranteeing the stability of the class structure itself." However, C. Wright Mills was actually quite explicit about his perceived differences with the Marxists on two counts.

First, in what is now a famous passage from *The Power Elite,* Mills rejected the term "ruling class" as an axiomatic statement that assumes what needs to be proven through empirical research. Mills (1956, fn. 277) claimed that:

> "Ruling class" is a badly loaded phrase. "Class" is an economic term; "rule" is a political one. The phrase, "ruling class" thus contains the theory that an economic class rules politically. That short-cut theory may or may not at times be true, but we do not want to carry that one rather simple theory about in the terms that we use to define our problems; we wish to state the theories explicitly, using terms of more precise and unilateral meaning. Specifically, the phrase "ruling class," in its common political connotations, does not allow enough autonomy to the political order and its agents, and it says nothing about the military as such. It should be clear to the reader by now that we do not accept as adequate the simple view that high economic men unilaterally make all decisions of national consequences. We hold that such a simple view of "economic determinism" must be elaborated by "political determinism" and "military determinism"; that the higher agents of each of these three domains now often have a noticeable degree of autonomy; and that only in the often intricate ways of coalition do they make up and carry through the most important decisions. Those are the major reasons we prefer "power elite" to "ruling class" as a characterizing phrase for

> the higher circles when we consider them in terms of power.

Thus, Mills argues that theoretically the economic, political, and military domains are each the source of an independent form of power, while empirically he was not convinced that the degree of cohesion and interlock among the three elites, or their subordination to economic elites, was sufficient to justify calling this power elite a ruling class, much less a ruling capitalist class. In a word, he (1956, 277) claims that "the simple Marxian view makes the big economic man the *real* holder of power; the simple liberal view makes the big political man the chief of the power system; and there are some who would view the warlords as virtual dictators." Mills rejected each of these theoretical positions in defining a radical position between liberalism and Marxism. Yet, in responding directly to Lekachman's comment, Mills (1957, 581) wrote:

> Let me say explicitly: I happen never to have been what is called "a Marxist," but I believe Karl Marx is one of the most astute students of society modern civilization has produced; his work is now essential equipment of any adequately trained social scientist as well as of any properly educated person. Those who say they hear Marxian echoes in my work are saying that I have trained myself well.

Second, while Mills never articulated, nor declared adherence to a particular economic theory, it is clear that he did not subscribe to Marxian economics and that, accordingly, he did not embrace its theory of surplus value and exploitation as a basis for explaining class struggle.[4] In fact, Mills' concept of power renders "the masses" powerless almost by fiat, since power is a function of occupying the command posts of the major institutions that control key resources. This is why early in his career Mills (1948) was hopeful that the "new men of power"—labor leaders at the commanding heights of large industrial unions—would become a progressive counter-elite in American society.[5] However, when this expectation proved false, and the new men of power became secondary actors in the lower tier of the dominant power structure, what other sources of popular power were left in American society? In *White Collar*, Mills (1951, 328) had already written off the American middle classes as being "distracted from and inattentive to political concerns of any kind. They are strangers to politics. They are not radical, not liberal, not conservative, not reactionary; they are inactionary; they are out of it. If we accept the Greek's definition of the idiot as a privatized man, then we must conclude that the U.S. citizenry is now largely composed of idiots." Yet, paradoxically, in a chapter of *The Power Elite* on "Mass Society," where Mills (1956, 300) dismisses pluralist theory "as a set of images out of a fairy tale," he simultaneously concludes that "the Marxian doctrine of class struggle . . . certainly is now, closer to reality than any assumed harmony of interests."

Marxism and *The Power Elite*

While C. Wright Mills' *The Power Elite* was harshly criticized by mainstream sociologists and political scientists in the United States, his book was embraced in Marxist and socialist circles primarily for strategic and political purposes. *The Power Elite* directly challenged the dominance of pluralist theory in sociology and political science (Truman, 1951) and it also captured the attention of the mainstream mass media, which celebrated Mills as the new *l'enfant terrible* of American social science. Consequently, while Marxists were critical of Mills' work from a theoretical perspective, it was accorded a great deal of respect on the left well into the 1960s, because it opened an ideological space that allowed empirically and historically oriented Marxists to reenter a political discourse that had excluded them in the United States for at least two decades.

For example, in a review in *Commonweal*, Michael Harrington proclaimed Mills "the most imaginative and brilliant of all the sociologists writing from American universities" (quoted in Aptheker, 1960, 9). Herbert Aptheker (1960, 9), a member of the National Committee of the U.S. Communist Party, affirmed Harrington's sentiment as "a judgment which does not seem to me to be excessive." Aptheker considered *The Power Elite* to be the *magnum opus* of America's most brilliant sociologist. These views were echoed from across the Atlantic by Ralph Miliband (1962, 16), who proclaimed C. Wright Mills "the most interesting and controversial sociologist writing in the United States." Miliband (1962, 16) praised *The Power Elite* as "a rich and intricate book. . . . There is room for debate about much of its detail. But I don't think there is much room for serious debate about the book's general thesis."

Paul Sweezy's (1968, 118) review of *The Power Elite* in the *Monthly Review* (September, 1956) also exuded praise for the book with his declaration that he could not "pretend even to list all the book's many excellencies." Sweezy (1968, 132) concluded that "We should be grateful for such a good book." Even though Mills was not a Marxist, Sweezy informed his readers that "Mills considers himself a socialist" and that was good enough for him (Cf. Miliband, 1964a, 77). Indeed, Sweezy (1968, 117) declaimed that "the greatest merit of *The Power Elite* is that it boldly breaks the tabu which respectable intellectual society has imposed on any serious discussion of how and by whom America is ruled . . . currently fashionable theories of the dispersal of power among many groups and interests [pluralism] have been bluntly challenged as flimsy apologetics."

In addition to breaking through the ideological mystique of pluralism, Sweezy identified three other major accomplishments of *The Power Elite*. First, the book was infused with "numerous flashes of insight and happy formulations" (Sweezy, 1968, 118), particularly "his damning description" of postwar intellectuals and his recognition that class consciousness is now "most apparent in the upper class," rather than the working class. Second, Sweezy (1968, 119) praised Mills for having assembled and analyzed an impressive array of empirical data to support his main arguments, because it was his empirical research that had the potential to explode "some of the more popular and persistent myths about the rich and the powerful in America today." Finally, and for the reasons already noted, Sweezy (1968, 119) was not the least bit concerned about Mills' lack of Marxist terminology, but instead praised him for speaking "with the voice of an authentic American radicalism." Sweezy (1968, 122) observed that "Mills' theory is open to serious criticism. But he has the very great merit of bringing the real issues into the open and discussing them in a way that anyone can understand."

However, Sweezy's admiration for *The Power Elite* was not without qualification. He criticized Mills on two points that became standard markers in defining Marxists' relationship to Mills and their distance from him. First, Sweezy chided Mills (1968, 121) for not framing his discussion of the power elite's higher immorality "in a context of exploitation, an indictment which Mills conspicuously fails to elaborate in any thorough or systematic way." By viewing the corporate rich merely as decision makers occupying the command posts of corporations, Mills described their higher immorality as if it were the personal failing of corrupt and incompetent individuals, rather than a characteristic to be explained as part of the *capitalist* economic system. Without a theory of capitalist development, Sweezy (1968, 131) was concerned that Mills "goes much too far in the direction of what I may call 'historical voluntarism'." However, unlike Poulantzas a generation later, Sweezy does not offer up a rigid structuralism, but suggests that "What Mills could and should have argued in this connection is that the roles [of the power elite] are *not* like those of a theatrical performance, completely mapped out and rigidly determined in advance. The actors have a *range of choice* which is set by the nature and laws of the social structure under which they live."[6]

Whether Marxist or otherwise, Sweezy argued that Mills needed a theory of exploitation to explain the power elites' behavior and its relation to the masses. Sweezy (1968, 121) mused that "Mills' weaknesses in this connection are characteristically American," but for this same reason he identified this problem as instructive on "the possibility and requirements of an effective American radical propaganda." Sweezy's main argument was that Mills' book could just as easily be read in the same way that individuals follow celebrity gossip and the lifestyles of the rich and famous in various mass media. A mere statement of the facts would not spark outrage, much less political action. Americans are not shocked by the mere existence of spectacular wealth. They are not surprised by the excesses of celebrities or by the corruption of the powerful. In fact, they may well be *entertained* by it, or encouraged to buy an extra lottery ticket, on the faint hope that they too will become a Megamillions or Powerball winner, which is after all the epitome of modern day finance capitalism (Strange, 1986). Despite his impressive research, Sweezy did not believe that any of the facts revealed by Mills would speak for themselves, because they only find their meaning in the theoretical discovery that all this spectacle, excess, and corruption comes at that *their* expense; in other words, in a theory of exploitation that explains the spectacle of the higher immorality as a relation of exploitation between the very rich and the working masses.

Thus, Sweezy (1968, 121) argued that mere denunciations of wealth will "fall on deaf ears" with the American public unless the accumulation and possession of great wealth is linked to a process of exploitation that can be replaced by alternative economic arrangements that have "more of it [i.e., wealth] to offer the great majority of them [i.e., the public] than has the present system of waste and plunder." The purpose of Sweezy's criticism was not to denounce Mills for not being a Marxist, nor to devalue his intellectual contribution, but to suggest a way to move his analysis a step forward theoretically and in a way that would further enhance its value as an ideology critique. It was fine with Sweezy if Mills did not embrace Marxian economics, but the problem was that Mills did not offer a theoretical alternative.[7] Mills rejected Marxian economics, neo-classical economics, Keynesian economics, and institutional economics, but he never identified an alternative political economy in which to situate his sociological and cultural critique of the power elite.

Sweezy offered a second observation about *The Power Elite* that quickly became the single most common theoretical criticism by critics of all persuasions. Sweezy developed an immanent critique of *The Power Elite* based on Mills' own empirical findings. He argued that Mills' hypothesis regarding the autonomy of the three domains of power had actually occluded his ability to see the facts as Mills presented them throughout his book. Sweezy (1968, 124) argues that Mills:

> adduces a wealth of material on our class system, showing how the local units of the upper class are made up of propertied families and how these local units are welded together into a wholly self-conscious national class. He shows the "power elite" is overwhelmingly (and increasingly) recruited from the upper levels of the class system, how the same families contribute indifferently to the economic, military, and political "elites," and how the same individuals move easily and almost imperceptibly back and forth from one to another of these "elites." When it comes to "The Political Directorate" (chapter 10), he demonstrates that the notion of a specifically political elite is in reality a myth, that the crucial positions in government and politics are increasingly held by what he calls "political outsiders," and that these outsiders are in fact members or errand boys of the corporate rich.

Sweezy (1968, 125) goes on to argue that "on his own showing the 'political directorate' is largely an appendage of the corporate rich," and even with respect to the alleged ascendancy of the warlords, he notes that:

> the military has swelled enormously in size and power, but it is precisely then that it has ceased to be a separate domain. The civilian higher circles have moved into commanding military positions, and the top brass has been accepted into the higher circles. What happens in such times is that the "power elite" becomes militarized in the sense that it has to concern itself with military problems, it requires military skills, and it must inculcate in the underlying population greater respect for military virtues and personnel.

Thus, Sweezy (1968, 129) concludes that "the facts simply won't fit Mills' theory of three (or two) sectional elites coming together to form an overall power elite. What we have in the United States is a *ruling class* with its roots deeply sunk in the 'apparatus of appropriation' which is the corporate system." Consequently, Sweezy (1968, 127) points out that even though Mills' analysis was "strongly influenced by a straightforward class theory," he did not consistently explore the implications of his empirical findings, which would have taken him closer to a Marxian position (Cf. Balbus, 1971).

Similarly, Tom Bottomore was another of the many critics who claimed that Mills' own research findings revealed that most members of the power elite were in fact drawn from a socially recognized upper class. Bottomore (1966, 33–34) observes that Mills starts with the hypothesis that he will leave open the question of whether the power elite represents a class that rules through the elites, but when he returns to this theoretical problem late in the book, "it is only to reject the Marxist idea of a ruling class. . . . In short, the question is never seriously discussed, and this is a curious failing."[8] Robert Lynd (1968, 107) identifies Mills' failure to engage this discussion as "the colossal loose-end of *The Power Elite*." Lynd was not alone in his assessment for it is a criticism that reappears again and again in reviews of the book by scholars of every ideological persuasion.[9]

Herbert Aptheker draws out a number of additional issues stemming from Mills not having a theory of capitalist development and he illustrates how this lacuna limited Mills' ability to conceptualize both the power elite and subaltern classes. Aptheker reiterates all of Sweezy's arguments in his analysis of *The Power Elite*, but he goes further than Sweezy in criticizing the limitations of Mills' analysis. Although Aptheker (1960, 34) chastised Mills for not including Lenin among the authors that every educated person should read, his substantive point was that Mills' conception of the economic elite as an amalgam of the "very rich" and the "corporate rich" failed to capture the emerging role of *finance capital* and financial groups as the emerging vanguard of the capitalist class. The "economic elite" was more than an aggregation of rich families and corporate executives, but was itself structured internally by developments in the *capitalist* economy.[10]

Aptheker (1960, 20) chided Mills not just for failing to interpret his empirical findings correctly, but for ignoring "the central depository of power—the financial overlords." Mills was unable to recognize finance capitalists as the overlords of the power elite, precisely because his analysis was not structured by any concept of political *economy*. He saw corporations, but not capitalism; corporate elites, but not a capitalist class. Not surprisingly, Aptheker's critique was theoretically grounded in Lenin's *Imperialism: The Highest Stage of Capitalism* and, indirectly, in Rudolf Hilferding's *Finance Capital: The Latest Stage of Capitalism*. Thus, Aptheker (1960, 35) attributed Mills' theoretical blind spot to his "neglect of Lenin," but he also took Mills to task for failing to even acknowledge the significant work of contemporary Marxist scholars, such as Victor Perlo (1950) and Paul Sweezy (1953, Chaps. 9, 12), who had published empirical research on American imperialism and the American ruling class, respectively.

However, even putting this ideological quibble aside, Aptheker was amazed that Mills could have missed an already substantial body of empirical literature on financial groups and monopoly capital that owed nothing to Marxism. As early as 1939, the National Resources Committee had published *The Structure of the American Economy* (Means, 1939), which used a rigorous power structure methodology to document that the U.S. economy was dominated by eight major "financial groups" (three national and five regional). This government report was based partly on research conducted by Paul Sweezy (1953, Chap. 12), which identified a network of financial groups that each consisted of several large industrial corporations under common control with the locus of power usually being an investment or commercial bank or a great family fortune (Cf. Baran and Sweezy, 1966, 17).[11] The internal structure of each financial group was dominated by one or more financial institutions, which sat atop each group and organized it through interlocking directors, loans, bond and securities underwriting, lines of credit, and so on. (Barrow, 1993, 18–21; Mintz and Schwarz, 1985). This idea was picked up again in 1941 and received a great deal of publicity during the highly publicized hearings of the Temporary National Economic Committee.[12] Moreover, even during the time that Mills was conducting research for *The Power Elite,* the U.S. House Committee on the Judiciary released a highly publicized *Study of Monopoly Power* (1951–1952) and two reports on *Bank Mergers and Concentration of Banking Facilities* (1952, 1955).[13]

Aptheker's point was that the concept of "finance capital" as an organizing principle of the capitalist economy was by no means inherently "Marxist" and that Mills had other more populist or even empirical paths to that concept. However, according to Aptheker (1960, 34), Mills was simply blind to the "intensification of the domination of the sinews of capitalism by the banking collosi and to the mounting merger movement among the banks themselves." Hence, Mills had missed a key factor of class cohesion within the economic elite. In contrast, Aptheker (1960, 35) argues that finance capital "is the apex of power today in the United States, and its absence from Mills' *Power Elite* seriously hurts the book's validity from the viewpoint of sheer description as well as basic definition" (Cf., Zeitlin, 1977, Chaps. 1–5; 1980, Chaps. 2–4).

For Aptheker, there were several additional problems that emanated from this theoretical and empirical lacuna. The orthodox Marxist-Leninist analysis saw finance capital as the engine of a new "epoch of imperialism" (Perlo, 1957), which was defined primarily by the *internationalization of American capital* (Aptheker, 1960, 36). In other words, the power elite was no longer simply an "American" power elite, but one with interests, connections, *and structural limitations* related to its export of capital. Aptheker contends that Mills' failure to analyze the economic underpinnings of imperial expansion seriously weakened his ability to understand the "military ascendancy" of the warlords or to grasp the structural and institutional basis of the power elite's foreign policy. Instead, Mills tended to present the power elite's new foreign adventures as a cynical form of Beardian "diversion" to entertain and distract the masses, rather than part of the process of capitalist development (see Barrow, 1997). Whether one shared a

Marxist viewpoint or not, the importance of this theoretical linkage was that it allowed Aptheker to elaborate the political, as opposed to the methodological, significance of Sweezy's complaint about Mills' "historical voluntarism."

Aptheker (1960, 19) also chastised Mills for depicting "the power elite as, in fact, and despite some qualification, all-powerful" and thus depicting the masses of people as generally powerless. Aptheker was concerned that Mills had constructed an exaggerated image of the power elite's omnipotence, precisely because he does not incorporate "class" and "class conflict" into his theoretical apparatus. In some ways, Mills reproduces the power elite's own worst delusions about the magnitude of its power, while simultaneously undercutting those delusions with satirical observations about its incompetence and mediocrity. However, Aptheker does not merely offer up the concept of "class conflict" as an ideological epithet for dismissing Mills. He elaborates how an empirical and historical analysis of class conflict would have allowed Mills to see the *limitations and contradictions* of power in the higher circles.

Aptheker (1960, 24–25) argues that:

> between the will of that elite and its capabilities of implementing that will stands public opinion, including American public opinion. This public opinion is not simply shaped by the elite, and this public opinion does affect what the elite tries to do and what it does and how it does what it does. Moreover, in whole areas of life—as in wages and working conditions, housing and education, the battle against Jim Crow and against war—the desires and power of the masses do exert great influence, manifested in buses that stop running and in atomic bombs that, though loaded aboard planes that are alerted to take off, never are dropped in war.

Aptheker was theoretically more attuned to the subterranean movements within American society that at the time were invisible to Mills. Even in 1956, there was a small anti-nuclear movement and a peace movement. There was a burgeoning civil rights movement that was expanding into a poor peoples' movement. There were still progressives, and even socialists and communists, in American trade unions. In sum, it was Aptheker's (1960, 20) contention that Mills had overstated the success of "the elite's effort to make all Americans morally as corrupt as the elite themselves." There were poor people, African-Americans, and ordinary middle-class Americans who struggled day-to-day to make a living and who did not share the power elite's war-mongering ways or its self-absorption with conspicuous consumption. In this sense, Mills' conception of a power elite dominating "the masses" obscured the fact that there were not just very rich people in America, but poor and very poor people in America (Aptheker, 1960, 12). It was not enough to challenge Louis Hartz's (1955) America as a middle-class thesis by demonstrating the existence of "the very rich," because this critique still ignored the fact that the United States had an underclass of the poor and very poor and that much of this underclass was racialized and gendered (Harrington, 1962).

Moreover, Aptheker's theoretical lens also made him far more attentive to the liberation struggles in what was then called the "Third World." Here, too, Aptheker (1960, 27) argues that Mills' inability to recognize the significance of the internationalization of capital as the economic basis of American foreign policy meant that Mills could not see that American public opinion was important, but also that world public opinion, splits among the imperialist partners, and divisions in the opinions of the American elite were also potent forces in constraining the power elite. These factors had all played a role in staying the hand of Mills' "Military Ascendancy." In sum, the main point for Aptheker (1960, 29) was "that the elite are by no means omnipotent, and the masses of people in our country are neither powerless nor apathetic."

Finally, Aptheker suggests that the absence of a theory of capitalist development in Mills' work generates an additional blind spot concerning the role of the U.S. South in American political and economic development. Aptheker's contention was that race and neo-conservatism had a deeper basis in historical class development than Mills recognized in his analysis of the 1950s "conservative mood." Aptheker (1960, 11) suggests that Mills would have arrived at different conclusions had he recognized that "there was a relative, not absolute, absence of feudal forms and institutions here—they were, for example, important in upstate New York and in Maryland—and that there was a prefeudal form in our history, chattel slavery, which played a decisive role in American development through the Civil War, just as some of its survivals exert so decisive an influence upon present-day American life." This was not just a historical quibble, but an omission with profound theoretical implications.

First, this lacuna in Mills' analysis creates a blind spot to the question of race in America. Aptheker (1960, 11–12) laments "Mills' consistent ignoring of the Negro question in all his writings." Hence, he misses what was already becoming an important structural base for progressive political action in the United States. Second, this lacuna also leads Mills to ignore the structural basis of traditional conservatism in America—strongly located in the South, but extended more generally throughout the rural and suburban hinterlands of white America. Aptheker observes presciently that what Mills dismissed as a short-term "conservative mood" actually had a deep historical basis in the American social structure—one that was tied historically to race and region—and that would not abate with a changing political mood. Thus, while Mills states that "there can be no conservative ideology of the classic type" in America, Aptheker (1960, 16) identifies this claim as a significant error "stemming from Mills' complete ignoring of Southern life and history and the realities of a kind of industrial feudalism in U.S. development." Indeed, this is a serious omission for a sociologist of knowledge so deeply influenced by Karl Mannheim.

Finally, Aptheker (1960, 14 fn.) criticizes Mills generally for failing to cite "American Marxist writers, though their work anticipates and expands much of his own." Despite Mills' "bare and very brief allusions" to Marx and Marxism in *The Power Elite*, Aptheker (1960, 15) was hopeful that "perhaps in a future work Mills will yet face up fully to the challenge of Marxism by testing its propositions against American reality as he sees it today." In this respect, a significant feature of Aptheker's critique is a genuine effort to engage Mills theoretically based on a discussion of empirical and historical facts—whether by reinterpretation or omission—rather than through conceptual one-upmanship based on ideological prescriptions or party doctrine. One simply does not find the types of ideological epithets—"distorted Marxism," "semi-Marxism," or "would-be Marxism"—that became so common in the Poulantzas-Miliband debate and its aftermath in the 1970s. Sweezy's and Aptheker's criticisms are meant to build on and extend Mills' work, rather than dismiss it as part of some sterile abstract jargon-laded polemic.

What Is Marxism?

The result of the encounter between C. Wright Mills and Anglo-American Marxists was that real theoretical progress occurred over the next decade as an intellectual "New Left" emerged in the discursive space between liberal-social democratic pragmatism and Communist orthodoxy (Jamison and Eyerman, 1994). Mills did not immediately accept the theoretical implications of Marxist criticism, but it did lead him to reevaluate Marx and Marxism as is evident in his last book *The Marxists* (1962). Mills' rejoinder to the Marxists was interesting not so much because he disavowed being a Marxist, but because he raised the issue that would loom large in the state debate of the 1970s: What is a "Marxist"?

Mills identified three intellectual types of Marxism: Vulgar Marxism, Sophisticated Marxism, and Plain Marxism. Mills (1962, 96) had little to say about Vulgar Marxism,[14] but he observed that Sophisticated Marxists:

> . . . are mainly concerned with marxism as a model of society and with the theories developed with the aid of this model. Empirical exceptions to theories are relegated to subsidiary importance: new theories are

> made up to account for these exceptions in such a way as to avoid revision of the general model. These theories are then read back into the texts of Marx. . . . But there comes a time when the supplementary hypotheses become so bulky, the deviant facts so overwhelming, that the whole theory or even model becomes clumsy. At that point marxism becomes "sophisticated" in a useless and obscurantist sense.[15]

Mills' definition of Sophisticated Marxism is somewhat ambiguous, but he appears to suggest that Marx constructed a "model" of capitalist society that can generate different political theories at various times and in different capitalist geographies to account for both new developments and specific conjunctures in particular capitalist societies.[16] He also suggests that Sophisticated Marxists, because of their political commitment to an official party line, or a particular type of political action, often make the mistake of reducing Marx's model of capitalism to historically specific theories that are ensconced in party doctrine or that justify preconceived courses of political action. Thus, for Mills, Sophisticated Marxism was typically constrained in its theorizing by an official party line,[17] and in contrast to Plain Marxists, were unable to make the necessary theoretical adjustments required by changing times and circumstances.

Since Mills never belonged to any political party—indeed, he probably never even voted—it was the Plain Marxists that were more interesting to Mills. Mills defined a Plain Marxist as someone who works "in Marx's own tradition," whether in agreement or disagreement with him. A Plain Marxist is someone who understands:

> Marx, and many later marxists as well, to be firmly a part of the classic tradition of sociological thinking. They treat Marx like any great nineteenth century figure, in a scholarly way; they treat each later phase of marxism as historically specific. They are generally agreed . . . that his general model and his ways

> of thinking are central to their own intellectual history and remain relevant to their attempts to grasp present-day social worlds. (Mills, 1962, 96)

Mills includes a highly eclectic group within this intellectual type, including Joan Robinson, Isaac Deutscher, William Morris, Antonio Gramsci, Rosa Luxemburg, G.D.H. Cole, Georg Lukacs, Christopher Cauldwell, Jean-Paul Sartre, John Strachey, George Sorel, E.P. Thompson, Leszek Kolakowski, William A. Williams, Paul Sweezy, and Erich Fromm. One might conclude, given Mills' earlier reply to Lekachman, that if he did not include himself in this group, he was at least hovering around its edges. Who knows where this ongoing engagement might have led if not for Mills' untimely death at the age of forty-five? Indeed, Irving Howe (1963), one of Mills' former friends, observes that while "Mills was not a convert to Communism," he was turning toward the type of Plain Marxism "which in America is expressed by Paul Sweezy's *Monthly Review*" (Horowitz, 1983; Cf. Miliband, 1964; Zeitlin, 1989, 47).[18]

Indeed, after publishing *The Power Elite,* Mills began moving in Marxist intellectual circles. In 1957, he traveled outside the United States for the first time in his life, where he visited the London School of Economics and met Ralph Miliband (Miliband, 1962, 18). Subsequently, Mills traveled to Poland, where he met Adam Schaff and Lezek Kolakowski. He made two trips to the Soviet Union in 1960 and 1961 and visited Cuba in 1960 to gather materials for his book *Listen Yanqui!* According to Miliband (1962, 20, 18), Mills "did not think of himself as a 'Marxist'" even late in his career, but his encounters with Marxist theory, dissident Marxists, and actually existing socialism "left him intensely interested and pondering, 'ambiguous', as he put it, about much of Soviet society. . . . He was still 'working on' Communism and the Soviet bloc when he died: his last book, *The Marxists,* published shortly after his death, is the last testimony to the rare honesty he brought to that effort." At a minimum, Mills' travels made him enthusiastic about the Cuban Revolution and about the prospects of democratic political reform in the Eastern European bloc. He was convinced, if incorrectly, that dissident and liberal intellectuals in Hungary, Poland, Czechoslovakia, and Russia would eventually triumph in advancing democratic socialism.

In this respect, it is also worth pointing out that Mills' rejection of the working class as an agent of social transformation is sometimes overstated by quoting a few select phrases from *White Collar* (1951) and his famous essay on "The New Left" (1960). Although it is well known that Mills (1963, 256) rejected the "labor metaphysic" inherited from "Victorian Marxism," and came to view the "the cultural apparatus, the intellectuals—as a possible, immediate, radical agency of change," scholars often neglect to mention that in making this proclamation he also qualified his claim by saying: "Forget Victorian Marxism except whenever you need it; and read Lenin again (be careful)—Rosa Luxemburg, too" (1963, 259). At the same time, he wrote: "Of course we can't 'write off the working class'. But we must *study* all that, and freshly. Where labor exists as an agency, of course we must work with it, but we must not retreat [sic] it as The Necessary Lever" of structural historical change (1963, 256). There is no question that Mills was pessimistic about the prospects of structural change in the advanced capitalist societies, but in 1960 when he (1963, 259) declared "We are beginning to move again," it was his view that a "young intelligentsia" might be the new agent of historic change in both capitalist and Communist societies.

It was this *concluding* point that provided the starting point for a new generation of power structure research, such as G. William Domhoff's *Who Rules America?* (1967), which argued that the power elite was merely the leading arm of a cohesive ruling class. Mills opened the intellectual space for a New Left in the United States and became a hero to many of the young intellectuals of the 1960s. The Marxist critique of Mills also laid the foundation for subsequent work by many plain Marxists, such as Michael Harrington (1962), who documented "the other America" alluded to by Herbert Aptheker. Similarly, Eugene Genovese unraveled the political economy of slavery and its enduring impact on Southern society, while Ralph Miliband's *The State in Capitalist Society* (1969) was "dedicated to the memory of C. Wright Mills."

Sophisticated Marxists and *The Power Elite*

It is not surprising that Miliband became the target of "sophisticated" Marxist structuralists in the 1970s, but their critique of Plain Marxism—or "historicism" and "voluntarism" in structuralist jargon—was originally directed at C. Wright Mills. Nicos Poulantzas' *Pouvoir Politique et Classes Sociale* (1968) was written and published prior to the release of Miliband's *The State in Capitalist Society* (1969) and, consequently, it is C. Wright Mills' *The Power Elite* that is actually the focus of Poulantzas' critique of the "instrumentalist" conception of the state. However, Poulantzas' main point of contention with Mills was not his empirical analysis, but the fact that Mills would not abandon his Weberian attachment to the *analytical* separation of the economic and the political. It was a methodological critique of where to begin the analysis of political power, rather than a discussion of political power in capitalist societies.

For example, in a chapter on "The Concept of Power," Poulantzas (1978, 103) cites Mills' *The Power Elite* as the exemplar of what he calls "semi-Marxist theories of *political elites* and *political class.*" His main criticism is directed at Mills' "badly loaded phrase" comment, because it allegedly leads to the conclusion that "the groups which take part in political (i.e. power) relations *differ, in their theoretical status,* from economic social classes, whose existence is elsewhere acknowledged." Mills' power structure approach starts with the separation of the economic and the political, which is a separation that Poulantzas rejects as a bourgeois myth from the outset. Hence, Poulantzas (1978, 103, 104) criticizes Mills for acknowledging "the parallel existence of economic social classes in a distorted Marxian sense, according to which the economic 'class situation' does not call for relations of power," and hence, "the failures of this school of thought become obvious in the confusions which result when it tries to establish relations between these 'economic classes' and the 'political groups'." Although phrased in structuralist terminology, this criticism is not essentially different from the one leveled by Sweezy and Aptheker.

In fact, Poulantzas (1978, 320) cites Sweezy's earlier critique favorably, because he agreed that Mills' empirical findings "end up by acknowledging the unity of the political elites" and thus suggest theoretical "conclusions diametrically opposed to those which they originally envisaged." Like Sweezy and Aptheker before him, Poulantzas was convinced that Mills' empirical findings should have led him to reconceptualize his starting point by adopting a Marxist theoretical position. Poulantzas argues that Mills was unable to make this shift, because his rejection of the concept of a ruling class as "a badly loaded phrase" was based on a "distorted Marxist conception of the dominant class." Unfortunately, what Poulantzas failed to see is that the masses do not *start from* a sophisticated Marxist position, but can be moved in that direction by "palpitating facts."

However, the empirical basis on which Sweezy had developed an immanent critique of Mills is a critical research strategy that Poulantzas found unacceptable, because it requires one to arrive at the conclusion of a ruling class, rather than adopt it as a starting axiom. Moreover, Poulantzas rejected as "historicist" and "subjectivist" any research that attempted to draw empirical relationships between the three domains through network analysis, personal and family relationships, common class origins, educational preparation, and so on. Indeed, Poulantzas dismisses Mills' empirical method of power structure analysis as "fantastical" and "mysterious." In what would be a preview of the Poulantzas-Miliband debate, Poulantzas (1978, 326) explicitly criticizes C. Wright Mills' *The Power Elite*, and all similar theories, for seeing:

> an empirical concentration of all political functions in the hands of the economically-politically dominant class and their practical exercise by the members of that class themselves. For instance, the feudal class exercised control over the functions of political government, of public administration, of the military,

> etc., but this is effectively not the case for bourgeoisie. And so, on this theory it is necessary theoretically to explain this dislocation by recourse to a conception which locates the basis of political power in the very existence of the state apparatus and which, by confusing *state power* with *state apparatus*, attributes to the bureaucracy its own political power . . . these theories see the conception of a state functioning as a mere tool for the domination of the dominant class.[19]

Although it is true that Mills had an overly voluntaristic conception of political power, and never explicitly identifies any mechanisms of structural constraint on political power, Sweezy and Aptheker had already made this point more effectively. Moreover, contrary to Poulantzas' claims during the Poulantzas-Miliband debate, and as I have documented elsewhere at greater length (Barrow, 2007), Miliband largely corrected this problem in *The State in Capitalist Society*. Yet, Poulantzas (1978, 330) further claims that a "major defect" of Mills' *The Power Elite*, and similar works, is that "they do not provide any *explanation* of the foundation of political power. In addition, they acknowledge a plurality of sources for political power but can offer no explanation of their relations." However, it is not that Mills fails to offer a conception of power (i.e., the command posts of decision making), it is that Poulantzas rejects the idea of institutions and organizations as repositories of power and therefore rejects the idea of multiple sources of power.

It is certainly true that power is a structured relationship between classes, rather than merely an attribute of institutions or organizations, but as later structuralists (and also Miliband) recognized, the structural power of capital is its ability to make decisions about capital investment and disinvestment and they would not have that power if they did not occupy the command posts of financial and industrial corporations. Structural mechanisms such as disinvestment and capital strikes are not automatic and impersonal market forces, but decisions made by economic elites occupying the top command posts of financial and nonfinancial corporations. When "the market" responds to an unfavorable business climate, it is signaling a series of decisions made by those in positions of economic power.

Finally, Poulantzas (1978, 117) also claims that Mills' analysis relies on "the conception of *zero-sum* power. On this theory, any class or social group *thus has as much power as another does not have,* and any reduction of the power of a given group is directly translated into an increase in the power of another groups and so on." This is a "closed systems" argument adopted from Talcott Parsons (1957, 139), but ultimately the real problem for Poulantzas (1978, 118) on this point was not theoretical, but political.[20] Poulantzas was concerned that a zero sum concept of power suggests that power is a quantity (instead of a relation) that can be redistributed from one group to another and, therefore, this idea "is the basis of several contemporary forms of reformism." In other words, Mills' power structure analysis does not necessitate proletarian revolution, which as the touchstone of structuralist political correctness means that Mills' thinking, however empirically grounded, must be inherently incorrect.

Yet, Goran Therborn's (1976, 19) assessment of C. Wright Mills was even harsher when he writes that "C. Wright Mills was not primarily a theoretician." In fact, Goran Therborn gives *The Power Elite* only two minor (and dismissive) footnotes in *What Does the Ruling Class Do When it Rules?* (1978, 130 fn. 2, 131 fn. 3), a book published two years after the conclusion of the Poulantzas-Miliband debate. In the end, Therborn (1978, 131, fn. 3) dismisses Mills as merely "a radical liberal." Martin Carnoy's survey of *The State and Political Theory* (1984) makes only three insignificant references to C. Wright Mills in the context of discussing Miliband, while Bob Jessop's influential book on *The Capitalist State* (1982) does not contain a single mention of C. Wright Mills.

Moving Beyond C. Wright Mills?

There is really not much in the Poulantzas-Miliband debate that was not already present in Poulantzas' criticism of C. Wright Mills and therein lays the problem. The Poulantzas-Miliband debate merely replayed many of the same issues that had been addressed in earlier critiques of Mills, but the problem for Poulantzas is that Miliband had already moved beyond Mills empirically and conceptually. Miliband constructed a theory of the state anchored in classical Marxist theory, while Mills operationalized elite theory as he inherited it from Vilfredo Pareto and Gaetano Mosca. There are numerous differences that flow from this distinction starting with the fact that Miliband developed a far more nuanced analysis of the capitalist *class* and its relationship to the working *class*, while Mills saw only "elites" and "masses." Miliband marshalled empirical data to conceptualize the structure of class conflict in Western industrialized nations, while Mills saw a loose aggregation of venal elites who were rich, powerful, and famous, but he never went beyond descriptive sociology to an explanatory political economy. Thus, where Miliband saw working class struggle as an ever-present element of contemporary capitalism (as did Poulantzas), Mills could only see an acquiescent and inchoate mass being prodded by discontented intellectuals. In order words, Mills did not articulate a theory of the state, a theory of ideology, or a theory of capitalist development. There were actors and institutions in his description of American elites, but no structures and no theory.

Consequently, the early structuralist critique of Miliband was largely directed at a straw man if for no other reason than it failed to recognize the theoretical and empirical advances in Anglo-American Marxism occurred after 1956. Poulantzas seems to have read Miliband through a Millsian lens and, partly for that reason, failed to acknowledge that Miliband's analysis of the state included a significant structural dimension that was lacking in Mills. Furthermore, Miliband was able to draw on newer power structure research that had identified additional mechanisms of ruling class cohesion, while specifying the processes of ruling class domination. Moreover, Miliband's analysis did not assume the analytic separation of the economic and political, but it did share Mills' dictum that this relationship had to be specified in particular historical and geographic configurations. The standard Marxist criticisms of Mills are simply not applicable to Miliband, who had apparently learned from the earlier debate between Mills and the Marxists.

Yet, instead of carrying the debate to a higher level of empirical, historical, and theoretical sophistication, as has been done by Sweezy, Aptheker, Harrington, Domhoff, and Miliband, the state debate of the 1970s and 1980s degenerated into an artificial methodological stalemate, which Domhoff (1986–1987, 295) argues became little more than "a dispute among Marxists concerning who was the most Marxist and whose theories were the most politically useful." Interestingly, in that regard, Mills (1962, 98) observed in an almost prophetic statement that "politically, the plain marxists have generally been among the losers," because they generally stand outside positions of institutional authority. In fact, Frances Fox Piven (1994, 24) notes that an important historical outcome of the Poulantzas-Miliband debate is that Poulantzasian structuralism achieved hegemony among Marxists. This ideological hegemony gave it the power to (temporarily) write the history of Marxism and the ability to expunge C. Wright Mills from Marxist theory and even a great deal of left-wing analysis generally. Until recently, the name of C. Wright Mills had been largely erased from the memory and vocabulary of Marxism, except as an epithet and an example of what did not count as "real" Marxism. To the extent that Miliband was identified with Mills, his work mistakenly suffered the same fate (Wetherly et al., 2007). At the same time, it should be recognized that the type of work exemplified by C. Wright Mills performs the important function of ideology critique by standing as a critical bridge between the ideology of pluralism and a theoretical critique of the capitalist state.

FOUR

The Analytic (Mis)Construction of Instrumentalism

Ralph Miliband never used the term "instrumentalism" to describe his theory of the state, but rather it was Nicos Poulantzas (1969, 74) who first identified Miliband's book with "a long Marxist tradition" that allegedly considers the state to be "only a simple tool or instrument manipulated at will by the ruling class." As documented in Chapter 1, Miliband did anchor his work in a classical Marxist tradition, but Poulantzas' epithet was not an accurate description of either Miliband's book or the tradition of instrumentalist theory. However, Poulantzas' *ad hominin* is an oversimplification that quickly took hold in the state debate of the 1970s and 1980s and it is a misconstruction that persists to the present time. The significance of this misconstruction is that it has institutionalized an artificial conceptual antinomy between structuralism and instrumentalism, when the two types of analysis should be viewed as simultaneous forms of analysis that are both necessary to an explanation of specific state policies and to an understanding of the historical development of state forms.

The Defining Moment for an Ideal-Type

A defining moment in the extended reproduction of Poulantzas' theoretical caricature of instrumentalism was the seminal article in *Monthly Review* by David A. Gold, Clarence Lo, and Erik Olin Wright (1975a, 31) on "Recent Developments in Marxist Theories of the Capitalist State." This highly influential article followed Poulantzas' lead by defining instrumentalism as "a theory in which the ties between the ruling class and state are systematically examined, while the structural context within which those ties occur remains largely theoretically unorganized." Shortly thereafter, in an equally influential *Socialist Review* article, Fred Block (1977, 8) defined instrumentalism as "the orthodox Marxist view of the state because it views the state as a simple tool or instrument of ruling-class purposes."[1] These forays into state theory effectively began the process of institutionalizing Poulantzas' polemical jibe as a permanent part of the state debate even though G. William Domhoff (1976) correctly pointed out at the time that if one accepted this definition of instrumentalism then no one, especially Ralph Miliband, actually subscribed to an instrumentalist theory of the state. Indeed, it should have been highly instructive at the time that Block's (1977, 8–10) subsequent critique of instrumentalism does not cite a single published work or author to exemplify his specific claims about instrumentalism.

Ironically, even the most strident critics of instrumentalism recognized early on that very few theoretical works on the state could actually be considered "pure examples of an instrumentalist, structuralist, or Hegelian-Marxist perspective" (Gold, Lo, and Wright, 1975a, 31), because these concepts are themselves analytically constructed ideal-types. However, this did not prevent Gold, Lo, and Wright (1975a, 32) from proclaiming that "Ralph Miliband expresses this position clearly." Similarly, Bob Jessop's (1982, 15) influential work on *The Capitalist State* identified *The State in Capitalist Society* as "a classic work" of instrumentalist theory, while Gordon L. Clark and Michael Dear (1984, 6–27) labeled *The*

State in Capitalist Society as "probably the best example of the instrumentalist model."

Yet, even as Gold, Lo, and Wright (1975a, 33) were in the process of constructing the instrumentalist-structuralist dichotomy, they simultaneously acknowledged that "there are, of course, examples of instrumentalist work done at various levels of sophistication" and they conceded that Ralph Miliband "most notably" had "attempted to situate the analysis of personal connections in a more structural context." Jessop (1982, 15) also qualified his critique of Miliband with the observation that "it would be wrong to suggest that Miliband is committed to a simple instrumentalist position." Thus, one critic after another acknowledges the sophisticated, nuanced, and multilevel analysis developed in *The State in Capitalist Society*, but then still proceed to dismiss his work on the basis of criticisms that apply only to an artificially constructed ideal type, rather than to his actual published works.

It is not Miliband's actual theorizing that was ever at issue, but the so-called logic of a theoretical position artificially imputed to him by critics. Consequently, a long list of broadsides have been directed against Miliband's alleged instrumentalism and most of these criticisms revolve around four major "problems" that had been articulated earlier by Poulantzas: (1) the problem of the subject, (2) the problem of the ideological apparatuses, (3) the problem of state autonomy, and (4) the problem of economic and social reform. Once extracted from the epistemological and methodological issues that preoccupied Poulantzas, it is easier to recognize the extent to which these problems were falsely ascribed to Miliband by Poulantzas and his followers largely by ignoring significant elements of Miliband's political theory.

The Problem of the Subject

In his critique of Miliband's instrumentalism, Poulantzas (1969, 70–71) defines the problem of the subject as "a problematic of *social actors*, of individuals as the origin of *social action*." If individuals or groups of individuals are considered as social actors, then Poulantzas argues that theoretical research is diverted from "the study of the objective coordinates that determine the distribution of agents into social classes and the contradictions between these classes . . . to the search for *finalist* explanations founded on the *motivations of conduct* of the individual actors." Historically, this is one of the attributes that has always defined "historicism," "voluntarism," and even Vulgar Marxism. In this respect, Poulantzas (1969, 71) claims that Miliband's empirical and institutional analysis of states in capitalist societies "constantly gives the impression" that:

> social classes or "groups" are in some way reducible to *inter-personal relations,* that the State is reducible to inter-personal relations of the members of the diverse "groups" that constitute the State apparatus, and finally that the relation between social classes and the State is itself reducible to inter-personal relations of "individuals" composing social groups and "individuals" composing the State apparatus.

Consequently, Poulantzas chastises Miliband for offering explanations of the corporate elite, the state elite, and state managers that are "founded on the *motivations of conduct* of the individual actors" (i.e., ideology and conscious interests) and that Miliband fails to comprehend "social classes and the State as *objective structures,* and their relations as an *objective system of regular connections,* a structure and a system whose agents, 'men,' are in the words of Marx, 'bearers' of it." According to Poulantzas, the same problem of the subject resurfaces in Miliband's treatment of the state bureaucracy, the army, regulatory agencies, and other personnel of the state system. The problem appears to reside in the fact that Miliband places so much emphasis on the role of ideology in linking these agents to the capitalist class and the governing state elite, because this explanatory mechanism suggests that the criterion for membership in a particular class is the shared motivations and subjective orientations of a group of individuals. Hence, Poulantzas (1969, 73) concludes that Miliband "seems to reduce the role of the State to the conduct and 'behavior' of the members of the State apparatus."

In contrast, Poulantzas (1969, 73) claims that:

> . . . the *direct* participation of members of the capitalist class in the State apparatus and in the government, even where it exists, is not the important side of the matter. The relation between the bourgeois class and the State is an *objective relation*. This means that if the *function* of the state in a determinate social formation and the *interests* of the dominant class in this formation coincide, it is by reason of the system itself: the direct participation of members of the ruling class in the state apparatus is not the *cause* but the *effect*, and moreover a chance and contingent one, of this objective coincidence.[2]

According to Poulantzas, it is the general function of the state that gives cohesion and unity to the state apparatuses and personnel and that make it possible to refer both to *a* state and to *the* capitalist state. However, from Poulantzas' perspective, Miliband relies on factors exterior to the state itself and, therefore, he lacks a theoretical capacity to *conceptualize the necessary unity and cohesion of the state*. Poulantzas (1969, 77) insists that "the State in the classic Marxist sense of the term, possesses a very rigorous internal unity which directly governs the relation between the diverse branches of the apparatus."[3]

Poulantzas' critique was aimed mainly at Miliband's and others' efforts to empirically document the extent to which capitalist elites colonized the top command posts of the state apparatus. While my earlier reconstruction of Miliband's theory of the state in Chapter 2 demonstrates that this was only one component of his overall analysis, Gold, Lo, and Wright (1975a, 33) nevertheless sanctioned this misrepresentation of Miliband's position by claiming that "most of his analysis still centers on the patterns and consequences of personal and social ties between individuals occupying positions of power in different institutional spheres." Indeed, they (1975a,

34) insist that even in "sophisticated variants of instrumentalism," such as Miliband's, the functioning of the state is still "fundamentally understood in terms of the instrumental exercise of power by people in strategic positions, either directly through manipulation of state policies or indirectly through the exercise of pressure on the state."

In fact, Gold, Lo, and Wright (1975a, 35) contend that with "rare exceptions, there is no systematic analysis of how the strategies and actions of ruling-class groups are limited by impersonal, structural causes . . . the exercise of state power and the formation of state policy seem to be reduced to a kind of voluntarism on the part of powerful people." Bob Jessop (1977, 357) echoes this theme with the claim that Miliband "reproduces the liberal tendency to discuss politics in isolation from its complex articulation with economic forces. To the extent that he does relate them it is only through interpersonal connection" (Cf. Jessop, 1982, 22).[4] Simon Clarke (1991, 19) repeats this assertion by claiming that the main weakness in Miliband's theory of the state is its lack of "any theory of the *structural* relationship between civil society and the state."

Miliband on Structural Constraint

Miliband firmly rejected this indictment of his work by pointing out that Poulantzas and others had greatly underestimated the extent to which he did take account of the objective structural relations that constrain elite decision making and the role of the state, but he also argued that the nature of the state elite was not irrelevant to understanding the concrete differences between states and state policies in various capitalist societies.[5] In fact, in a chapter on "The Purpose and Role of Governments" that follows his analysis of the state elite, Miliband (1969, 79) specifically takes account of the structural constraints on state elites:

> The "bias of the system" may be given a greater or lesser degree of emphasis. But the ideological

> dispositions of governments have generally been of a kind to make more acceptable to them the structural constraints imposed upon them by the system; and these dispositions have also made it easier for them to submit to the pressures to which they have been subjected by dominant interests.

However, Miliband does not regard the "bias of the system" or its "structural constraints" as purely a limitation of state elites' and state managers' ideological outlook, or even as the exclusive result of campaign contributions, lobbying, and the other political processes of ruling class domination (Cf. Domhoff, 1978). Indeed, in a chapter entitled "Imperfect Competition," Miliband (1969, 146) argues that "business enjoys a massive superiority *outside* the state system as well, in terms of the immensely stronger pressures which, as compared with labour and any other interest, it is able to exercise in the pursuit of its purposes." In fact, the analysis of state power in this chapter spins off a passage that clearly articulates the mechanism of structural constraint later identified with the works of Amy Beth Bridges, Claus Offe, Fred Block, and Charles E. Lindblom (Barrow, 1993, 58–63). In defining capital's "massive superiority *outside* the state system," Miliband (1969, 147) observes that:

> One such form of pressure, which pluralist "group theorists" tend to ignore, is more important and effective than any other, and business is uniquely placed to exercise it, without the need of organisation, campaigns, and lobbying. This is the pervasive and permanent pressure upon governments and the state generated by the private control of concentrated industrial, commercial, and financial resources. The existence of this major area of independent economic power is a fact which no government, whatever its inclinations, can ignore in the determination of its policies, not only in regard to economic matters, but to most other matters as well.

Thus, as Domhoff (1990, 193) has pointed out previously, it should have been clear even at the time that when Miliband (1969, 23) states that "in the Marxist scheme, the 'ruling class' of capitalist society is that class which owns and controls the means of production and which is able, by virtue of the economic power thus conferred upon it, to use the state as its instrument for the domination of society" that he means exactly "what more recent theorists mean with their talk about structures and autonomy and privileged position." If there were any doubt about Miliband's meaning or intent, he (1969, 150) further clarified his position a few pages later in a discussion about whether government can use its political power and financial resources "as an instrument of long-term economic policy" by compelling individual firms or industries to radically change their methods of doing business. Miliband (1969, 150) concludes that there is not much evidence that "governments have been notably effective in the use of this power in their relations with private enterprise." The underlying structural reason for this failure, according to Miliband (1969, 150), is that:

> in the abstract, governments do indeed have vast resources and powers at their command to "wield the big stick" against business. In practice, governments which are minded to use these powers and resources—and most of them are not—soon find, given the economic and political context in which they operate, that the task is fraught with innumerable difficulties and perils.

So what is this economic and political context? What are the difficulties and perils that state elites confront in their relations with corporations and private businesses? Miliband (1969, 150) states that:

> These difficulties and perils are perhaps best epitomised in the dreaded phrase "loss of confidence." It is an implicit testimony to the power of business that all governments, not least reforming ones, have always

> been profoundly concerned to gain and retain its "confidence." Nor certainly is there any other interests whose "confidence" is deemed so precious, or whose "loss of confidence" is so feared.

What is remarkable about such a "discovery" in Miliband's work is that many of his critics were explicitly aware of this structural component in his theory, but chose for unarticulated reasons to downplay or ignore it. For example, Gold, Lo, and Wright (1975a, 33) concede that Miliband was well aware that "the policies of the state would still be severely constrained by the economic structure in which it operates" even if "personal ties were weak or absent—as sometimes happens when social democratic parties come to power." Furthermore, he avoids a voluntaristic version of instrumentalism by stressing the social processes which mold the ideological commitments of the "state elite." Jessop (1982, 22) also recognized that in later chapters of *The State in Capitalist Society* "Miliband emphasises the veto power of "business confidence" entailed in the institutional separation of the economic and political—a power that is independent of interpersonal connections—and also discusses the role of ideological practices rooted in civil society in shaping the political agenda. In this way Miliband moves well beyond the simple voluntarism and instrumentalism ascribed to him by most scholars.

In contrast, Stan Luger (2000) is one of the few scholars to have incorporated this observation into his thinking about Miliband's theory of the state with his suggestion that Miliband "offers a perspective that balances a focus on interest group activity with that of the privileged position of business." At the same time, Luger observes that "state dependence on business, while an important pressure, does not automatically mean that government officials know how to respond to each particular policy battle." The structural dependence of the state on capital confers an asymmetrical advantage to business in the political process, but it does not obviate the need for business to involve itself in the political and public policy-making processes. This is particularly true in capitalist democracies, where "officials cannot simply ignore citizens' demands if they wish to maintain legitimacy in the eyes of the electorate" (Luger, 2000, 28).[6] In other words, Miliband understood quite well that states in capitalist societies must simultaneously maintain the business confidence necessary to promote capital accumulation, while adopting policies that maintain the state's political legitimacy with a democratic electorate.

The Problem of Ideological Apparatuses

The problem of political legitimacy was cast primarily as a problem of the ideological apparatuses in the Poulantzas-Miliband debate. Given its prominence in Miliband's analysis, Poulantzas was not inclined to dismiss ideology altogether, but instead he proposes to reconceptualize its production and distribution within a Marxist theory of the state. Poulantzas (1969, 76–77) was quite correct to point out that "the classic Marxist tradition of the theory of the State is principally concerned to show *the repressive role of the State,* in the strong sense of organized physical repression." On the other hand, ideology had been dismissed as epiphenomenal (rather than constitutive) of social and political relations, mainly because ideology had been equated "with ideas, customs or morals without seeing that ideology can be embodied, in the strong sense, in *institutions*: institutions which then, by the very process of institutionalization, belong to the system of the State." Poulantzas proposes that the realm of ideology be brought inside the state by reconceptualizing the state as a dual matrix of apparatuses that either perform repressive functions or ideological functions.[7] Poulantzas follows Althusser's (1978) lead by defining the ideological state apparatuses to include churches, political parties, trade unions, schools and universities, the press, television, radio, and even the family.

Poulantzas' observations were again echoed by Gold, Lo, and Wright (1975a, 35), who argue that instrumentalism cannot account for ideology because there are "important realms of state-related activity which are clearly not manipulated by specific capitalists or coalitions, such as culture, ideology, and legitimacy" (Gold, Lo, and Wright, 1975a, 35). This cavalier assertion was anything but self-evident even in the context of the mid-1970s, when many highly respected works on the manipulation of culture, ideology, education, and legitimacy were readily available, including books by scholars such as Murray Edelman (1964), Joel H. Spring (1972), David N. Smith (1974), and Stewart Ewen (1976).[8] On the other hand, Block (1977, 8) asserts that instrumentalism simply "neglects the ideological role of the state."

These are both misdirected criticisms, because Miliband (1969, 178) concludes Chapter 6 of *The State in Capitalist Society* with the observation that:

> The subordinate classes in these regimes [i.e., capitalist democracies], and "intermediary" classes as well, have to be persuaded to accept the existing social order and to confine their demands and aspirations within its limits. For dominant classes there can be no enterprise of greater importance, and there is none which requires greater exertion on a continuous basis, since the battle, in the nature of a system of domination, is never finally won.

Miliband then proceeds to devote two entire chapters to analyzing the process of legitimation and thus adopts exactly the method of analysis proposed by Poulantzas and his followers. However, as noted in Chapter 2, Miliband does reject the structuralist view that all ideological institutions should be conceptualized as part of the state apparatus (Althusser, 1971; Poulantzas, 1980, 28–34; Therborn, 1980). Miliband insists that political theorists cannot ignore the fact that in bourgeois democracies most of the ideological apparatuses are not part of the state, but part of a wider political, ideological, or cultural system. Miliband (1970b, 59) agrees that ideological institutions *are* increasingly subject to a process of "statization," particularly schools and universities, and he concedes that their statization "is likely to be enhanced by the fact that the state must, in the conditions of permanent crisis of advanced capitalism, assume ever greater responsibility for political indoctrination and mystification." Thus, for Miliband, the question of whether the ideological institutions that generate and distribute ideology in capitalist societies are ideological *state apparatuses* is a theoretical question that can only be answered with historical and empirical analyses specific to time and place (i.e., what Poulantzas called particular theories of the state).

Miliband also insists that it is necessary to recognize that although state power may be the main and ultimate means of maintaining ruling class domination, it is not the only form of class power as Poulantzas' formulation implies. Miliband argues that state power is not the only form, nor the only site, of ruling-class domination, because the ruling class can directly exert power through other nonstate institutions (i.e., economic and ideological institutions). This is another reason why Miliband rejects the structuralists' suggestion that institutions such as churches, political parties, the press, radio, television, publishing, and the family, all be brought within the realm of state theory and regarded as components of an ideological state apparatus. Indeed, Miliband (1973, 88, fn. 16) scoffs at the suggestion as carrying "to caricatural forms the confusion between different forms of class domination and, to repeat, makes impossible a serious analysis of the relation of the state to society, and of state power to class power."

The Problem of State Autonomy

Another derivative aspect of the so-called problem of the subject is the assertion that Miliband, and instrumentalists generally, fail "to recognize that to act in the general interest of capital, the state must be able to take actions against the particular interests of capitalists" (Block, 1977, 9). For example, Fred Block argues that "in order to serve the general interests of capital, the state must have some autonomy from direct ruling-class control." Similarly, Jessop (1982, 12) suggests that even in instrumentalism's most developed form "the state is not an independent and sovereign political subject but is an instrument of coercion and administration which can be used for various purposes by whatever interests manage to appropriate it." Jessop (1990, 27–28) goes on to insist that the instrumentalist approach also encounters difficulties "where the state acquires a considerable measure of independence from the dominant class owing to a more or less temporary equilibrium in the class struggle."

However, even in his chapter on "The State System and the State Elite," which is the basis of so many of the criticisms directed at Miliband, he (1969, 55) observes:

> it is obviously true that the capitalist class, as a class, does not actually "govern." One must go back to isolated instances of the early history of capitalism, such as the commercial patriciates of cities like Venice and Lubeck, to discover direct and sovereign rule by businessmen. Apart from these cases, the capitalist class has generally confronted the state as a separate entity—even, in the days of its rise to power, as an alien and often hostile element, often under the control and influence of an established and land-owning class. . . . Nor has it come to be the case, even in the epoch of advanced capitalism, that businessmen have themselves assumed the major share of government. On the other hand, they have generally been well represented in the political executive and in other parts of the state system as well; and this has been particularly true in the recent history of advanced capitalism.

On this point, Miliband (1973, 85) agrees that it "is absolutely right" to reaffirm "that the political realm is not, in classical Marxism, the mere reflection of the economic realm, and that in relation to the state, the notion of the latter's 'relative autonomy' is central." Indeed, in a significant and lengthy footnote in one of his rejoinders to Poulantzas, Miliband (1973, 85, fn. 4) argues that the concept of relative autonomy is fully contained in:

> . . . the most familiar of all the Marxist formulations on the state, that which is to be found in the *Communist*

> *Manifesto,* where Marx and Engels assert that "the modern State is but a committee for managing the common affairs of the whole bourgeoisie" . . . what they are saying is that "the modern state is but a committee for managing the *common* affairs of the *whole* bourgeoisie": the notion of common affairs assumes the existence of particular ones; and the notion of the whole bourgeoisie implies the existence of separate elements which make up that whole. This being the case, there is an obvious need for an institution of the kind they refer to, namely the state; and the state *cannot* meet this need without enjoying a certain degree of autonomy. In other words, the notion of autonomy is embedded in the definition itself, is an intrinsic part of it.

The Problem of Economic and Social Reform

The false assertion that instrumentalism does not accord any relative autonomy to the state has led to two further, but mutually contradictory criticisms of Miliband's theory of the state. On the one hand, Gold, Lo, and Wright (1975a, 35) assert that instrumentalists "treat all reforms as the result of an instrumentalist use of the state by capitalists," which is to theoretically "deny the possibility of struggle over reform." On the other hand, Jessop (1990, 27) argues that a fundamental problem of instrumentalism is its "tendency to assume that the state as an instrument is neutral and can be used with equal facility and equal effectiveness by any class or social force." Thus, rather than negating the possibility of reform, Jessop (1982, 14) suggests that an instrumentalist theory of the state "underlies the reformism of social democratic movements," which "tend to see the state apparatus in liberal parliamentary regimes as an independent neutral instrument which can be used with equal facility and equal effectiveness by all political forces and they have therefore concentrated on the pursuit of electoral victory as the necessary (and sometimes even sufficient) condition of a peaceful, gradual, and majoritarian transition to socialism."

In fact, neither violent revolution nor parliamentary reform was ever advanced by Miliband, who instead emphasized the importance of mass politics and social movements as the basis for realigning the relationship between the state and civil society. From his early *Parliamentary Socialism* (1961) to *Socialism for a Skeptical Age* (1995), Miliband was always a critic of parliamentary socialism and he never viewed electoral politics alone as sufficient for a transition to socialism, precisely because state power is more than governmental power and class power is more than state power. In *The State and Capitalist Society*, Miliband (1969, 265) explicitly rejects the view that the state "can be and indeed mostly is the agent of a 'democratic' social order, with no inherent bias towards any class or group." Miliband (1969, 265–266) rejects the idea of state neutrality as "a fundamental misconception," because the state in capitalist societies "is primarily and inevitably the guardian and protector of the economic interests which are dominant in them."

At the same time, Miliband (1969, 266) acknowledges that class rule in the advanced capitalist societies "has remained compatible with a wide range of civil and political liberties" that provide the political basis for mass social and political movements. Miliband (1969, 266) contends that the historical exercise of these liberties "has undoubtedly helped to mitigate the form and content of class domination in many areas of civil society" and the state has been "the main agent of that mitigation." Miliband (1969, 77) is quite explicit in pointing out that state elites "have in fact been compelled over the years to act against *some* property rights, to erode *some* managerial prerogatives, to help redress *somewhat* the balance between capital and labour, between property and those who are subject to it." However, Miliband (1969, 266, 271) also concludes that "this mitigating function does not abolish class rule," because economic and social reforms have "to be confined within the structural limits created by the economic system in which it occurs." Thus, in Miliband's (1969, 271) theory of the state, reform is possible in exceptional circumstances, but only "when popular pressure is unusually strong" (Cf. Piven and Cloward, 1977). Thus, Simon Clarke (1991, 19) correctly observes that an important implication of "Miliband's analysis was that socialism could not be achieved by purely electoral means, but only by a mass political movement which could mobilise and articulate popular aspirations in order to conduct the democratic struggle on all fronts."

The Mirage of Instrumentalism

It is beyond doubt that critics of Miliband's theory of the state have not only distorted instrumentalism by representing it through an artificial and simplistic ideal-type, but these critics openly gloss over significant aspects of Miliband's thought—indeed entire chapters of *The State in Capitalist Society*—that contravene this ideal-type. For this reason, I (1993, 168) have previously suggested that many of Miliband's critics appear to "have never read more than the first half of Miliband's *The State in Capitalist Society*." Thus, a mere *reading* of Miliband should be sufficient to document that his work has not only been "defamed and distorted" by critics, as (Domhoff, 1990, 190) argues, but that starting with Poulantzas many have even misrepresented the book as "claiming the opposite of what it actually said."

For example, during the 1970s, Gold, Lo, and Wright (1975a, 33) were well aware of the fact that Miliband "attempted to situate the analysis of personal connections in a more structural context." They (1975a, 33) note that "Miliband stresses that even if these personal ties were weak or absent—as sometimes happens when social democratic parties come to power—the policies of the state would still be severely constrained by the economic structure in which it operates." These same authors (1975a, 33) even concede that Miliband "argues that the state must have a certain degree of autonomy from manipulation by the ruling class," which allows him to move away "from a voluntaristic version of instrumentalism." Similarly, Bob Jessop (1982, 22) explicitly recognized that in the later chapters of *The State in Capitalist Society* Miliband introduced the concept of business confidence as a structural constraint on decision-making in a way that "pointed beyond institutionalism and instrumentalism" as those concepts were defined by most scholars at the time. Yet, even after this long list of concessions, Gold, Lo, and Wright (1975a, 33) still concluded that "in spite of these elements in Miliband's work, the systematic aspect of his theory of the state remains firmly instrumentalist."

Thus, what are we to do with the concept of instrumentalism? In light of the foregoing analysis, one possibility is to jettison instrumentalism as nothing more than an artificially constructed straw man that does not accurately describe any actually existing work on the capitalist state. Scholars who employ a power structure methodology could simply follow G. William Domhoff's (1976) lead and declare that "I am not an instrumentalist" if it is the critics' version of instrumentalism that is to pass for instrumentalism among other scholars. An alternative strategy is to retain the concept of instrumentalism, because it is so well established in the state debate literature, while emphasizing that instrumentalism is both well-grounded in classical Marxism and a more sophisticated theory in practice than critics have acknowledged in the past.

FIVE

The Poulantzas-Althusser Debate

Frances Fox Piven (1994, 24) observes that once *Political Power and Social Classes* became more widely available to Anglo-American (and Spanish speaking) scholars it was the Poulantzasian structuralists who tended to prevail in the broader state debate and thereafter "to dominate the intellectual fashion contest" that emerged in the ensuing decade. Despite Poulantzas' and the structuralists' apparent triumph in the early state debate, renewed discussion among state theorists about Poulantzas' writings is leading a new generation of state theorists to recognize that there is room for considerable disagreement about how to understand Poulantzas' political theory and particularly its relation to Althusserian structuralism. Nicholas Abercrombie, Bryan Turner, and John Urry (1976) have praised Poulantzas' political theory as one of "the most sophisticated and developed products of the Althusserian revolution in the reading of Marx." On the other hand, following the translation of Poulantzas' *Political Power and Social Classes* (1973) into English, Ralph Miliband (1973, 83–84) criticized the book for being "obscurely written for any reader who has not become familiar through painful initiation with the particular linguistic code and mode of exposition of the Althusserian school to which Poulantzas relates."[1] Miliband initially criticized Poulantzas' theory of the state for its "structural super-determinism," because the latter seemed to claim that state elites and state institutions automatically respond to the functional imperatives of the capitalist system to such an extent that there is no place for personal ideological beliefs, party affiliations, political institutions, or even class struggle in a theoretical analysis of the capitalist state (King, 1986, 77).[2] Moreover, in a subsequent critique, Miliband condemned the "structuralist abstractionism" of Poulantzas' analytical method, which seemed to favor the elaboration of abstract concepts over empirical, historical, and institutional analyses of actually existing states.

There is no question that Poulantzas eschews what he calls "the demagogy of the 'palpitating fact', of 'common sense', and the 'illusions of the evident'." At one point in the Poulantzas-Miliband debate, he (1976, 65) even berates "the dominant 'Anglo-Saxon culture' as a whole" for succumbing to "the demagogy of common sense." However, in the debate's final exchanges, even Poulantzas conceded that he used "sometimes needlessly difficult language" and that in *Political Power and Social Classes* he had shared "an over-rigid epistemological position" with Althusser. Nevertheless, he (1976, 66–68) defended his position as one necessitated at the time by the requirements of a concentrated "attack against empiricism and neo-positivism, whose condensates, in the Marxist tradition, are economism and historicism."

While Poulantzas seemed to shift his position toward the end of the Poulantzas-Miliband debate, his work on the theory of the capitalist state has consistently been read by proponents, and similarly dismissed by critics, as being dependent on a rigid Althusserian structuralism. Sympathetic commentators have attempted to supersede the legacy of structuralist abstractionism either by exaggerating Poulantzas' shift of position or by dismissing Miliband's epithets as a mere caricature of his real position. Paul Thomas, for example, argues that shortly after the initial rounds of the Poulantzas-Miliband debate, Poulantzas "quickly, adroitly, and in principle moved beyond this hidebound *point d'appui*" toward a class struggle approach that first appears in *Fascism and Dictatorship* (1970), but is only fully developed in *State, Power, Socialism* (1978).

Thomas (2002, 74) attributes this transition to an "epiphany" (i.e., an epistemological break) that resulted from the events of May 1968.[3] Similarly, Stuart Hall (2002, viii) describes *Political Power and Social Classes* as Poulantzas' "most studiously 'Althusserian' text" and one that is situated "firmly within the Althusserian schema." This structuralist interpretation of Poulantzasian structuralism isolates *Political Power and Social Classes* as a short-lived theoretical episode and, thereby, dismisses the entire Poulantzas-Miliband debate as a distraction from Poulantzas' mature political theory.

A second approach to the problems of structural superdeterminism and structural abstractionism is offered by Stanley Aronowitz and Peter Bratsis. They argue that the Poulantzas-Miliband debate generated caricatures of both theorists' "true positions, offering no substantive insight into a theory of the state." Aronowitz and Bratsis (2002, xii) claim that "state theory was never the object of a rigorous and sustained critique" during the Poulantzas-Miliband debate. Instead, each theorist's caricature of the other was perpetuated by subsequent authors, who eventually dismissed Poulantzas, Miliband, and other state theorists with "a couple of paragraphs and footnotes."

The (re)reading of Poulantzas in this chapter documents that he was neither a "structural superdeterminist" nor a "structural abstractionist," but that attaching these labels to his early work during the Poulantzas-Miliband debate obscured the fact that structuralism was not a monolithic methodological or theoretical perspective even within the narrow confines of state theory. It is my contention that a close reading of the leading 1970s structuralists, such as Louis Althusser and Etienne Balibar, Goran Therborn, Samir Amin, Barry Hindess and Paul Q. Hirst, Eric Olin Wright, and Nicos Poulantzas would have revealed significant (if sometimes suppressed) theoretical differences between them, which divided this school of thought into structural determinist, technological determinist, and historical structuralist (or class struggle) approaches from the outset.[4] Balibar (1996, 109) later confirmed that "there was nothing like an Althusserian 'school', with a more or less unified doctrine, a research program, or an institutional frame."[5] In fact, Poulantzas never embraced the metaphysical structural determinism of Althusser and Balibar, nor the technological determinism of Therborn, but he did not articulate those differences explicitly (i.e., in a polemical form) until political events in the 1970s brought those theoretical differences into sharp relief.[6]

Thus, while correcting the caricature of Poulantzas inherited from the Poulantzas-Miliband debate requires a more sophisticated analysis of his position *within* structuralism, it is also not necessary to allude to epiphanies to rescue a "mature Poulantzas" from an "early Poulantzas."[7] Instead, I suggest that because the Poulantzas-Miliband debate was always about epistemology and methodology, rather than state theory, if we re-read Poulantzas outside this legacy and thereby shift the focus of analysis from the methodological to the conceptual level, one finds a remarkable continuity in Poulantzas' thinking about *the capitalist state*.[8] Moreover, the theory that emerges from a non-Althusserian understanding of Poulantzas' structuralism is much different and far more useful in the analysis of actually existing states than the legacy of structuralist abstractionism inherited from the Poulantzas-Miliband debate. In fact, Poulantzas (1976a, 76) states that the only reason he continued the debate in 1976 was because "certain authors, especially in the United States, have perceived the debate between Miliband and myself as a supposed debate between instrumentalism and structuralism, thus posing a false dilemma."

As noted in Chapter 2, Poulantzas (1976a, 63–64) dismissed these terms "as an utterly mistaken way of situating the discussion." Although Miliband and his followers generally rejected any description of their position as instrumentalism, it is not widely recognized that Poulantzas also rejected the structuralist label by 1976 if not earlier. Indeed, Poulantzas was apparently stung by Miliband's references to structural super-determinism and structuralist abstractionism and, as I demonstrate below, his consternation was justified due to his very real differences with Althusser. In fact, Poulantzas (1976a, 70) ended the Poulantzas-Miliband debate by declaring that: "I would like to state quite clearly that I have no intention of replying to this [charge of structuralism] . . . all those who have not yet understood, or who have yet to be convinced . . . are certainly not going to be convinced by the few lines I could possibly add here on this subject."

The unfortunate fact is that while Poulantzas was rejecting the Althusserian label applied to him by Miliband, "Poulantzasian structuralists" all over the world were embracing Miliband's caricature of Poulantzas and defending it with great polemical vigor! It was primarily these epigones who perpetuated an overly Althusserianized Poulantzas.[9] In fact, Poulantzas rejected Althusser's epistemological and methodological positions, at least implicitly, on many important points in *Political Power and Social Classes*.[10] However, his disagreements with Althusser and the other structuralists became more pronounced and more explicit during the 1970s in what might be termed the Poulantzas-Althusser debate, but so-called Poulantzasian structuralists were so busy reenacting the old debate on new stages that the new debate's implications for state theory were largely ignored in the wider state debate.

The Poulantzas-Althusser Debate

The epistemological and methodological differences between Poulantzas and the other structuralists manifest themselves more explicitly after 1968, mainly because Poulantzas shifts the focus of his epistemological critique from historicism and voluntarism (e.g., C. Wright Mills) to what he called formalism (e.g., Balibar) and economism (e.g., Therborn) (Benton, 1984, 13). In *Political Power and Social Classes*, Poulantzas' (1978, 11, 37–40) epistemological criticisms are directed mainly against the major variants of Marxist "historicism," that is, Lukacs, Korsch, Labriola, and Gramsci. After the publication of *The State in Capitalist Society* (1969), Poulantzas immediately identified Miliband as a contemporary exemplar of Marxist historicism, which (if inaccurately) put him directly in the crosshairs of Poulantzas' epistemological critique. Significantly, the critique of historicism is a philosophical project that Poulantzas shared with Althusser and the other structuralists until about 1970, when he published *Fascism and Dictatorship*.

Louis Althusser defined the original philosophical and political objectives of structural Marxism in a series of articles published in French Communist Party journals between 1960 and 1964. These articles were republished in French as *Pour Marx* in 1965. According to Althusser, Marx had "established a new *science*: the science of the history of 'social formations'," but this science was threatened by the emergence of historicist (e.g., Lukacs) and humanist (e.g., Sartre) strains of Marxism. In this intellectual context, the first purpose of Althusser's essays was "to 'draw a line of demarcation' between Marxist theory and the forms of philosophical (and political) subjectivism which have compromised it or threaten it: above all, *empiricism* and its variants, classical and modern—pragmatism, voluntarism, historicism, etc." Althusser's (1969, 12; Althusser and Balibar, 1977, 119–144) second objective was "to 'draw a line of demarcation' between the true theoretical bases of the Marxist science of history and Marxist philosophy on the one hand," and allegedly "pre-Marxist idealist . . . interpretations of Marxism as a 'philosophy of man' or a 'Humanism'."

However, the artificial *political* unity between Althusser and Poulantzas that had been maintained by shared opponents began to disintegrate after May 1968, when despite a series of major upheavals around the world, capital began to reestablish and reconstitute the basis of its political and economic power; first, in individual nations, and then on a global scale.[11] In response to the Greek and Latin American coups d'état, Poulantzas (1974, 11) turned his attention to the analysis of the "exceptional states" of Nazi Germany and fascist Italy, because as the "sharpness of class struggle" intensified inside the imperialist heartlands (i.e., the United States, Europe, and Japan), it was not only accelerating a worldwide crisis of imperialism, as manifested in the Vietnam debacle and other anti-colonial struggles, it was putting the question of fascism back on the political agenda as a possible response by the capitalist class. Moreover, the state's response to popular upheavals in the United States, Germany, Mexico, Japan, and elsewhere was growing increasingly violent, while many governments in the United States and Europe were also expanding the use of covert domestic surveillance and the subversion of foreign governments (U.S. Congress, 1976).

However, by 1974, Poulantzas (1978b, 47), was also warning that the political and ideological conditions for a new American imperialism were being put in place "by establishing relations of production characteristic of American monopoly capital and its domination actually inside the other metropolises."[12] While fascism had appeared as a realistic political strategy for capital (i.e., the state as repression), the major defeats for the working class and other popular movements were not generally being inflicted by direct political repression, but through economic reforms that were reconstituting the social relations of production inside national social formations.

Thus, in *Fascism and Dictatorship*, Poulantzas begins more explicitly to differentiate his position from Althusser's on two points that he would elaborate in subsequent works in much greater detail. First, Poulantzas (1974, 300–301 fn. 2) argues that Althusser's (1978) widely acclaimed essay on ideological state apparatuses "suffers to some extent from both abstractedness and formalism: it does not give the class struggle the place it deserves."[13] Second, Poulantzas (1974, 303 fn. 5) claims that Althusser badly underestimates "the economic role of the State apparatuses, to the extent of completely neglecting it theoretically" in his famous formula: The State = Repression + Ideology.

While both critiques are muted as mere footnotes deep inside *Fascism and Dictatorship*, it is notable that several years prior to being labeled a structural abstractionist by Miliband, Poulantzas was actually criticizing Althusser for his "abstractedness and formalism"! Moreover, while the challenge to Althusser's formula The State = Repression + Ideology was overlooked by many as a minor conceptual difference, the economic function of the state (i.e., its role in the extended reproduction of the social relations of production) is actually the *primary maintenance function* attributed to the state in *Political Power and Social Classes*. For Poulantzas, Althusser's failure to conceptualize this function was a major theoretical flaw in his one attempt to develop a regional theory of the superstructural instances. Furthermore, Poulantzas' concept of the economic functions as primary functions further differentiates him from the other structuralists, because it locates the state's presence *inside* the economic instance as an element necessary to *constituting and reproducing* the social relations of production. Moreover, as documented in Chapter 2, this concept of the state was not a new departure in *Fascism and Dictatorship,* but a central feature of his analysis in *Political Power and Social Classes.*

Yet, Poulantzas evidently believed these differences had been lost on his audience, because in *Classes in Contemporary Capitalism* (1978b) instead of ending his work with a muted critique of Althusser, as he had done in *Fascism and Dictatorship,* he explicitly begins this book by calling attention to the differences between his structuralism and that of the Althusser/Balibar school. While he notes that several of the *concepts and theoretical analyses* presented in his latest book assume a knowledge of both *Political Power and Social Classes* (1978a) and *Fascism and Dictatorship* (1974), he observes that "certain analyses and formulations that figure there, particularly in the first work, have been rectified and adjusted in the present text." Poulantzas does not call direct attention to any of these adjustments, but indicates that "the reader will find all the relevant developments of theory embodied in the following concrete analysis." Indeed, Poulantzas (1978b, 11) apologizes for the "critical and sometimes even polemical character" of this book, but he states that "instead of suppressing differences and thus inevitably choosing to brush fundamental problems under the carpet, I have preferred to dwell on them, in so far as criticism alone can advance Marxist theory."

In a passage that would seem to contravene Thomas' references to an epistemological break or an epiphany, Poulantzas insists that the arguments advanced in *Classes in Contemporary Capitalism* "are based on those of *Political Power and Social Classes,*" but they "are made somewhat more detailed and are in some respects rectified, a process already begun in *Fascism and Dictatorship.*" Nevertheless, Poulantzas (1978b, 13 fn.

1) emphasizes that "both the theoretical framework and the essence of the earlier arguments are maintained."[14] This might leave a reader wondering what has been rectified in *Classes,* except that Poulantzas launches an opening salvo on the first page of his introduction that should have commanded more attention at the time. Poulantzas (1978b, 13 fn. 1) not only calls attention to his differences with the Althusser/Balibar school of structuralism, but points out that such differences had always existed:

> I should mention here that although my own writings and those of a number of my colleagues have been received, and have even to a great extent functioned, as if they shared a common problematic, fundamental differences have always existed between some of these texts. In the domain of historical materialism, for instance, fundamental differences already existed between, on the one hand, my *Political Power and Social Classes* . . . and on the other hand Balibar's text in *Reading Capital,* "The Basic Concepts of Historical Materialism" (1966), which is marked by both economism and structuralism.

Imagine that following in the wake of the first two rounds of the Poulantzas-Miliband debate, it is Poulantzas criticizing Balibar for economism and *structuralism*! Yet, in *State, Power, Socialism,* Poulantzas (1980, 15) continues this critique with the observation that "today more than ever it is necessary to distance ourselves from the formalist-economist position," which he identified with the works of Althusser, Balibar, and Therborn, among others. While *State, Power, Socialism* is frustratingly devoid of footnotes, or other simple references to authors and titles, his earlier references can leave no doubt that his lengthy critique of the formalist-economist position in that book is meant to draw out and emphasize the "fundamental differences" that had always existed between himself and those he called "the structuralists." These differences were not a new departure, an epiphany, or an epistemological break in his thinking, but were differences simply lost on readers engulfed in the exaggerated polemics of the Poulantzas-Miliband debate.

Poulantzas (1980, 15) identifies the main limitation of the formalist-economist position with its assumption that "the economy is composed of elements that remain unchanged through the various modes of production—elements possessing an almost Aristotelian *nature* or *essence* and able to reproduce and regulate themselves by a kind of internal combinatory." It views the economic instance, as well as the state-political instance, as a fixed set of structural relations between essentially immutable forms. Poulantzas (1980, 15) correctly criticizes "the formalist position" for conceptualizing modes of production:

> . . . in the form of *instances* or *levels* that are by nature or by essence autonomous from one another. Once the economy is apprehended in terms of a series of elements occupying their own spaces and remaining unchanged through the diverse modes of production (slavery, feudalism, capitalism), the conception will be extended by analogy to the superstructural instances (the State, ideology). It will then be the *a posteriori* combination of these inherently autonomous instances that will produce the various modes of production, since the essence of these instances is prior to their mutual relation within a mode of production.

This is a distinction that Poulantzas had made in *Political Power and Social Classes,* but the *political* significance of the distinction had become more salient by 1978 (when the French edition of *SPS* was published), because of the limitations formalism imposed on a theory of the capitalist state. First, the metaphysical conception of the levels of a mode of production was questionable in its own right for any *historical* materialist, but the theoretical (as opposed to epistemological) problem with this type of formalism is that it led to the "old misunderstanding" of representing the relation between the economic and the political as one "of 'base' and 'superstructure';

namely, a conception of the State as a mere appendage or reflection of the economic sphere, devoid of its own space and reducible to the economy" (Poulantzas 1980, 15). What disturbs Poulantzas (1980, 16) about this formulation is that "the essential autonomy of the superstructural instances (the State, ideology) would then serve to legitimize the autonomy, self-sufficiency and self-reproduction of the economy." This is not to say that formalists did not recognize the existence of structural "interventions" by one instance into another, but that such interventions occurred from "relations of exteriority" as a *deux ex machina*. He insists that structuralist references to the State's "intervention" in the economy are theoretically incorrect, because they suggest that the State is something external to the economic that only periodically intrudes into its otherwise autonomous functioning and development.

A second major flaw with this theoretical position, as Poulantzas (1980, 15) notes, is that it "obscures the role of struggles lodged in the very heart of the relations of production and exploitation." In *State, Power, Socialism*, Poulantzas (1980, 16) reiterates a point he had made with equal vigor in *Political Power and Social Classes*:

> These conceptions also have an effect on the delimitation and construction of objects for theoretical investigation for they both admit the possibility and legitimacy of *a general theory of the economy* taken as an epistemologically distinct object—the theory, that is to say, of the transhistorical functioning of the economic space. In this perspective, the differences presented by the object (the economy) from one mode of production to another are to be explained purely in terms of a self-regulating and rigidly demarcated economic space, whose *internal* metamorphoses and transformations are unraveled by the general theory of the economy ("economic science").

Poulantzas is adamant about reiterating two additional points in *State, Power, Socialism*. First, he again rejects

Althusser's and Balibar's claim that it is possible to deduce an *a priori* science, or general theory, of the modes of production. This claim has two bases in what I call Poulantzas' *historical* structuralist epistemology. For Poulantzas, theoretical analysis begins with the concept of the mode of production itself, rather than its elements, because it is the totality of these economic, political, and ideological determinations that fixes the boundaries of these elemental spaces in each mode of production.[15] Consequently, these concepts will have different meanings, extensions, and boundaries in each mode of production and this makes it impossible to develop anything more than regional and particular theories.

Poulantzas had actually made the same point in *Political Power and Social Classes,* although he articulated it in such abstruse structuralist language that it was probably not recognized by most readers: "We are concerned with a combination (*combinsaison*) and not with a combinatory (*combinatoire*), because the relations of the elements determine *their very nature,* which is modified according to the combination." Indeed, in this earlier work, Poulantzas (1978a, 25, 25–26 fn. 9) was already criticizing "modern structuralism," and he cites Althusser's and Balibar's *Reading Capital* as its exemplar, for relying too heavily on Leibniz and thus reproducing "this ideology in its concept of a combinatory, a formal pattern of relations and (arbitrarily occupied) places which recur as homologous patterns with a different content throughout the social formation and its history."[16]

Furthermore, Poulantzas observes that at the superstructural levels, the formalist-economist position diverges into two distinct structuralisms that he considers equally flawed. The formalist variant—what is properly called structuralist abstractionism—argues that the general theory of the economy "has to be duplicated by analogy in a *general theory* of every superstructural field—in this case, the political field of the State." The economist variant—what is generally called technological determinism—conceptualizes the superstructural instances "as mechanical reflections of the economic base" (Poulantzas, 1980, 16).[17] Thus, in essentially two or three sentences, Poulantzas draws a firm distinction between his position and that of other leading structuralists. Poulantzas (1980, 19) reiterates this difference in his conclusion that:

> . . . just as there can be no general theory of the economy (no "economic science") having a theoretical object that remains unchanged through the various modes of production, so can there be no "general theory" of the state-political (in the sense of a political "science" or "sociology") having a similarly constant object. . . . What is perfectly legitimate, however, is a *theory of the capitalist State.*

Second, Poulantzas carries this critique a step further by emphasizing that he retains the distinction between *mode of production* as an abstract-formal object and concrete *social formations* as articulations of several modes of production at a given historical moment. While Poulantzas (1978a, 145–147) never clarifies the epistemological status of an abstract-formal object, he definitely rejects structuralist abstractionism (i.e., formalism), which seems to assign an objective (i.e., Platonist) reality to these concepts, but he is also equally vehement in rejecting Max Weber's heuristic notion of an ideal-type. Nevertheless, Poulantzas (1980, 25) clearly distinguishes himself from Althusser, Balibar, and Therborn by insisting that one cannot deduce the characteristics of a social formation "as merely heaped up concretizations of abstractly reproduced modes of production; nor, therefore, should a concrete State be considered as a simple realization of the-State-of-the-capitalist-mode-of-production." Quite the contrary, Poulantzas (1980, 25) emphasizes that:

> Social formations are the actual sites of the existence and reproduction of modes of production. They are thus also the sites of the various forms of State, none of which can simply be deduced from the capitalist type of State understood as denoting an abstract-formal object. . . . A theory of the capitalist State can be elaborated only if it is brought into relation with the history of political struggles under capitalism.

An additional theoretical basis for this conclusion is found in Poulantzas' understanding of the relative autonomy of the economic instance. In *State, Power, Socialism,* Poulantzas (1980, 17) restates nearly verbatim his earlier observation that the economy has never been "a hermetically sealed level, capable of self-reproduction and possessing its own 'laws' of internal functioning" in any mode of production. Instead, he repeats the argument from *Political Power and Social Classes* that "*the political field of the State* (as well as the sphere of ideology) *has always, in different forms, been present in the constitution and reproduction of the relations of production.*"[18] However, Poulantzas now acknowledges that "the position of the State vis-à-vis the economy has changed not only with the mode of production, but also with the stage and phase of capitalism itself." This point is actually the major argument in *State, Power, Socialism* and the reason why a critique of formalist-economism had moved from the background to the forefront of Poulantzas' critical agenda.[19]

In *State, Power, Socialism,* Poulantzas (1980, 167) argues that in the stage of competitive capitalism, and even in the early phases of monopoly capitalism, "the State's strictly economic functions were *subordinated,* though not reduced, especially to its repressive and ideological functions." The State was mainly involved in "organizing the socio-political space of capital accumulation" by establishing its political and material conditions within specific territories, that is, nations. However, while others were bemoaning an emerging crisis of the welfare states in the 1970s, Poulantzas was already theorizing this development as the beginning of a transition to a new form of capitalist state. According to Poulantzas, "the State's present role in the economy alters the political space as a whole, economic functions henceforth occupy the *dominant place* within the State. . . . *The totality of operations of the State are currently being reorganized in relation to its economic role.*"[20] The state was now actively responding to the sharpening of domestic class struggle, and to the crisis of imperialism, by managing these contradictions with new strategies and policies designed to reconstitute the relations of production, the division of labor, the reproduction of labor-power, and the extraction of surplus value.

While the state's social welfare responsibilities were being curtailed as part of the transition to a new state form, Poulantzas observed that its economic functions were simultaneously increasing to such an extent that one could now theoretically identify a specialized *state economic apparatus* in addition to the repressive and ideological state apparatuses (e.g., the strengthening of central banks, business friendly tax reform, finance and trade ministries, state labor exchanges, workforce retraining, economic development agencies). While Poulantzas had already called attention to the shortcomings of Althusser's conception of the state, the Althusserian view of autonomous instances and independently functioning apparatuses was now completely incapable of theorizing this restructuring of the state form. Thus, Poulantzas (1980, 170) insisted that "unless we break with the analogical image according to which the state apparatuses are divided into watertight fields, we cannot grasp the reorganization, extension, and consolidation of the state economic apparatus as the restructuring principle of state space."[21]

In a period of historical transition from one state form to another, Miliband's alleged historicism was now of less concern to Poulantzas than Althusser's formalism, which presumed a fixed set of formal theoretical categories, and economism, which would see post-Fordist globalization as an autonomous, inexorable economic development determined by new technological innovations that circumvented the state.[22] The capitalist state was actively reconstituting the relations of production on a new basis, while the abstract and immutable concepts employed by most structuralists were incapable of comprehending this (or any) process of *transition* to a new state form, that is, the problem of recombination. This theme was quickly picked up and carried forward by the regulationist school (Aglietta, 1979) and the post-Fordists (e.g., Bonefeld and Holloway, 1991; Jessop, 1993, 1994). While Aglietta used an essentially Poulantzasian formulation to conceptualize and analyze the structures of the Fordist mode of regulation, (i.e., a specific phase of capitalism), the post-Fordists were more concerned with identifying the key structures of the emerging "post-Fordist" phase of capitalism.

From Structuralist Abstractionism to Historical Structuralism

The stated objective of *Political Power and Social Classes* (1978a, 16) was to produce a concept of the capitalist state and to produce "more concrete concepts dealing with politics in capitalist social formations." For Poulantzas, this constellation of concepts, including the general function of the state, constitutes a *regional* theory of the capitalist State. However, the purpose of a regional theory is to organize and facilitate the development of particular theories of actually existing states in capitalist social formations. State theory is thus an activity and not a fixed body of concepts, because the production of concepts does not end in a theory, but rather theorizing is an activity that employs these concepts.

Poulantzas (1980, 24–25) was remarkably consistent in his use and deployment of the basic concepts of historical materialism, but he was also cognizant of the fact that a theory of the capitalist state must "grasp the reproduction and historical mutations of its object at the very place where they occur—that is to say, in the various social formations that are the sites of the class struggle" and this means that "*the theory of the capitalist State cannot be isolated from the history of its constitution and reproduction.*" This type of analysis can be done only at the level of particular theories, which is why the transition from a Fordist to a post-Fordist state form required Poulantzas to sharpen the distinction between his type of historical structuralism and the structuralist abstractionism (i.e., formalist-economism) of Althusser, Balibar, and Therborn.

However, understanding the distinction between Poulantzas' and Althusser's structuralism does not necessarily mean that the Poulantzas-Miliband debate was a grand diversion that is now irrelevant to state theory. Although the Poulantzas-Miliband debate is frequently dismissed as "sterile and misleading," it continues to capture our attention, because this early dispute remains symptomatic of unresolved epistemological issues within Marxism that have far reaching methodological repercussions even beyond state theory (Holloway and Picciotto, 1978, 1–31; Jessop, 1982, xiv). This is equally true of the Poulantzas-Althusser debate, which was either ignored, or not understood, by Poulantzas' followers. However, those enthusiasts who continued the debate clearly misunderstood it when they either dismissed the importance of particular theories as articulated by Miliband or accepted the assertion that Poulantzas' regional theory of the capitalist state actually depended on Althusser's structuralist metaphysics.

Others who were more attentive to the differences between Poulantzas and Althusser, successfully elaborated mechanisms of functional constraint (e.g., investment strikes and public debt) that added detail to Poulantzas' concept of the general function of the State, but did not rely on any form of abstractionism or functionalist metaphysics (Block, 1977; Bridges, 1973; Mandel, 1971; Offe, 1975).[23] Thus, in its appropriate form, Poulantzas' work on the theory of the capitalist state provides a compelling conceptual apparatus for analyzing and explaining capitalist states, particularly when its conceptual apparatus is not confused with Althusserian metaphysics. In the end, however, Poulantzas' categories of analysis are most functional when they are deployed in the analysis of actually existing capitalist states, as he exemplified in *Fascism and Dictatorship* (1974) and *Crisis of the Dictatorships* (1976b), because real class struggles only take place in historical social formations.[24] Indeed, for this reason, Aglietta (1979, 29) has argued that even a structuralist theory of the capitalist state must be "open to internal analyses of the political field such as those of Ralph Miliband, which study in detail the organization of the state apparatuses, their penetration by forces that represent social groups, and the relationships that form within them" (similarly, see Konings, 2010).

Further advances in state theory require that we no longer start our discussions by posing a false dichotomy between Poulantzasian abstractionism and Milibandian empiricism, even though both caricatures emerged from the Poulantzas-Miliband debate. State theory must move beyond this false dichotomy precisely because Poulantzas left us with an unfinished research agenda starting with the need to describe, conceptualize, and theorize the emergence of a state economic apparatus. Moreover, he presciently diagnosed the expansion of this apparatus, as the newly dominant state apparatus, as the basis for creating the political and ideological conditions for a new American imperialism *within* the territories of nation-states. There is ongoing work that reconceptualizes this new capitalist state form at a regional level (e.g., post-Fordism, regulation theory, globalization theory), but there is even more work to be done at the level of particular theories that describe and analyze this process theoretically within individual nation-states or geographic areas. Finally, Poulantzas (1969, 68) offers a timely reminder that the revolutionary objective of socialism is not "only a shift in *State power*, but it must equally *'break'*, that is to say radically change, the State apparatus." The objective is not to capture the capitalist State, or to merely change its personnel, but to alter its structural configuration as an apparatus and its class relation to the mode of production.

SIX

The Return of the State

The interest in state theory that swept academic circles following the Poulantzas-Miliband debate waned considerably by the late-1980s and much of the last two decades was notable for the impoverishment of state theory (Barrow, 2002b; Panitch, 2002). There were few significant theoretical advances and many radical scholars simply drifted away from state theory. First, by the mid-1980s state theory had generated a complex of intractable antinomies and stalemates that led the proponents of various theories to simply retreat to their own corners where they pursued "theoretically informed fact gathering" around narrowly specialized questions of policy analysis and political development within the confines of their chosen theory (Barrow, 1993, 157).

Second, the abandonment of grand theory took place in the context of a more widespread intellectual disillusionment with grand scale meta-narratives, such as state theory, and their attendant transformational political projects (Barrow, 1993, 157). The shift from Marxist to post-Marxist to post-structuralist and postmodernist theory shifted analysis from macroscopic to microscopic forms of power and, therefore, to the multiple "technologies of power" such as language, family, interpersonal relationships, culture, leisure and entertainment, and the configurations of repressed desire (Deleuze and

Guattari, 1987; Foucault, 1972).[1] In this effort to identify the "polymorphous techniques of power" the concept of the state became merely the effect of a discursive practice (political theory) that concealed power more than it revealed it (Foucault, 1980, 11; Mitchell, 1991).[2]

Finally, the 1990s was the decade when "globalization" became a common buzzword among scholars in numerous fields. The new interest in globalization sparked a renewal of political economy (the dreaded "economism" of postmodernism), but in its initial stages globalization theory continued to push state theory into the background. Indeed, there was a never-ending litany of books and articles on the crisis of the nation-state (Poggi, 1990), the eclipse of the state (Evans, 1997), the retreat of the state (Strange, 1996), and even the end of the nation-state (Ohmae, 1990).[3] The central theme in these eulogies was that nation-states had lost control of their national economies, currencies, territorial boundaries, and even their cultures and languages and that macroscopic forms of power were shifting from the nation-state to the global market, transnational corporations, and globalized channels of communication (Castells, 1997, 243). Why study an institution in retreat or one in the twilight of its sovereignty? (Wriston, 1992).

This chapter reexamines the relationship between globalization theory and state theory to argue that nation-states are still the principal agents of globalization as well as the guarantors of the political and material conditions necessary for global capital accumulation. Nation-states have proliferated in the wake of decolonization, the fall of the Soviet Union, and other national secessionist movements with membership in the United Nations (2014) increasing from the 51 original members in 1945 to 193 members in 2013. As Ellen Wood (2003, 141; 1999, 11) observes: "the world today is more than ever a world of nation states," but more importantly for our purposes, she suggests that "global capitalism is nationally organized and irreducibly dependent on national states." In contrast to those who see a nebulous logic of empire, a network state, or even a global state as the repositories of a new sovereignty,[4] I suggest that globalization, in its current form, is actually a new form of American imperialism.

As Poulantzas was among the first to see, this "new imperialism" is characterized by the direct penetration of U.S. capital into foreign social formations, which induces the restructuring of economic, political, and ideological relationships with those nation-states and their subordinate articulation with a new American superstate (Sakellaropoulos, 2007).[5] However, within the new global political economy, state elites must still manage the contradictory pressures of (global) capital accumulation and (national) political legitimation. This enduring contradiction is being managed by a restructuring of the capitalist state form and a realignment of internal power relations within national state apparatuses. It is this transition to a new form of capitalist state that many scholars have incorrectly identified as a decline of the nation-state (Sakellaropoulos, 2009; Sakellaropoulos and Sotiris, 2015).

Globalization: The Form and Function of the Nation-State

In *A Theory of Capitalist Regulation* (1979), Michel Aglietta identifies "the wage-relation" as the cornerstone of the capitalist mode of production, since it is the basis of exploitation and therefore capital accumulation.[6] Aglietta anticipated globalization as a territorial expansion of the wage-relation, but in extending the territorial reach of the capitalist wage-relation, he observes that capitalist enterprises come into conflict with the reciprocal obligations of traditional societies. Thus, in substituting the capitalist wage-relation for the relationships of traditional societies, the introduction of capitalist social relations tears apart the social ethos and other forms of social regulation that constitute the older civil societies. The result is that new social norms must be instituted by the state and this process requires the state to intervene in civil society and to restructure it in ways that are compatible with the emerging wage-relation. Following Poulantzas, Aglietta (1979, 32) suggests that historical and empirical investigations of this process would demonstrate that *"the state forms part of the very existence of the wage relation."*[7]

Thus, for Aglietta, the existence and reproduction of capitalism on a global scale (or any other scale) is theoretically inconceivable without the state, which must penetrate civil society and restructure its norms through laws, coercion, and inducements to provide the general political and material conditions for capital accumulation (Cf. Altvater 1973a, 1973b). Moreover, this process requires a comparatively strong state, because "the policies, mentalities and institutions which interfere with the determinant factors of capital accumulation do not develop at the same rate as techniques, working methods and markets" and, consequently, states must manage a great deal of conflict within and between the territorial boundaries of capitalism (Aglietta, 1979, 414). Despite such tantalizing insights as early as 1979, Aglietta (1979, 29) notes that his analysis of the state was "incomplete," because his analysis was restricted to the structure and dynamics of the wage-relation in United States Fordism.[8]

Similarly, even as the concept of imperialism was being jettisoned for theories of postcolonialism and postimperialism, Aglietta was still referring to imperialism as "a terrible reality" of the emerging global economy, but it is an ambiguous notion not studied in his work, precisely because he rejects the idea that a theory of imperialism can be constructed on the basis of *economic* concepts alone. Aglietta (1979, 32) defines imperialism as a system of hegemony through which "one state manages to influence a series of other states to adopt a set of rules that are favorable to the stability of a vast space of multilateral commodity relations guaranteeing the circulation of capital."[9] Consequently, it is not multinational or transnational firms that organize imperial economic and political relationships, but rather the existence of transnational firms would not be possible without a system of states maintaining stable relations of unequal influence across the globe. Thus, Aglietta (1979, 29–30) argues that to the extent that imperialism is a constitutive element of the current form of globalization, "it can only be grasped on the basis of a fully developed theory of the state, capable of studying the significance of inter-state relations" in the process of globalization. While

Aglietta (1979, 32–33) does not construct such a theory, he does assert that:

> From the formulation of the "Open Door" doctrine at the turn of the century, through Bretton Woods and the Marshall Plan to Nixon's monetary maneuvers of 1971, the strategic concern of the US financial community and those industrial interests with an overseas orientation has always been to deploy political influence to ensure the prevalence of those types of social organization in other nations and procedures for settling international conflicts that would safeguard the expansion of American capital.[10]

Robert W. Cox extended these observations in *Production, Power, and World Order* (1997) by challenging the idea that the state was in retreat and proposing instead a concept of the *internationalization of the state*. Cox argues that state policies such as health, education, welfare, and tax reform, as well as institutional restructuring of the state apparatus through decentralization, deregulation, and the privatization of public assets, did not signal a retreat of the nation-state, but an internationalization of the nation-state.[11] Cox (1987, 254) identifies the internationalization of the state with three processes:

> *First,* there is a process of interstate consensus formation regarding the needs or requirements of the world economy that takes place within a common ideological framework (i.e., common criteria of interpretation of economic events and common goals anchored in the idea of an open world economy). *Second,* participation in this consensus formation is hierarchically structured. *Third,* the internal structures of states are adjusted so that each can best transform the global consensus into national policy and practice, taking account of the specific kinds of obstacles likely to arise in countries occupying the different hierarchically arranged positions in the world economy.[12]

Cox suggests that the common element in the process of internationalization is the conversion of "the state into an agency for adjusting national economic practices and policies to the perceived exigencies of the global economy. The state becomes a transmission belt from the global to the national economy, where heretofore it had acted as the bulwark defending domestic welfare from external disturbances" (Cox, 1992, 30–31). While many globalization theorists have interpreted these policies as a retreat of the state in the face of global market pressures, the domestic implementation of neoliberal policies has actually generated a great deal of social and political conflict over the last two decades and it has generally required "strong states" to implement these policies against domestic opposition. Indeed, even Hardt and Negri (2000, 248–249) paradoxically note that "when the proponents of the globalization of capital cry out against big government, they are being not only hypocritical but also ungrateful . . . where would imperial capital be if big government were not big enough to wield the power of life and death over the entire global multitude?"

In fact, what some have interpreted as the retreat of the state is an internal realignment of power within the state apparatus to privilege the institutions, offices, and agencies in closest contact with the centers of the global economy, while subordinating or disempowering those offices and agencies that draw support primarily from domestic constituencies.[13] The offices of presidents and prime ministers, treasuries, and central banks now assume the leading role in state policy, while ministries of commerce, labor, health, welfare, and education, among others, are being subordinated ideologically to the tenets of international competitiveness and further disempowered through budget and staffing reductions. Cox (1992, 31) does not follow up on this observation except to say that the internal realignment of state apparatuses "needs much more study."[14] In fact, Aglietta (1979, 29) suggests in a similar vein that the internal realignment of state power, the internal restructuring of the state apparatuses, and their systematic articulation with the institutions of global capitalism now requires us to conduct new "internal analyses of the political field such as those of Ralph Miliband, which study in detail the organization of the state apparatuses, their penetration by the forces that represent social groups, and the relationships that form within them."

In this formulation, the internationalization of the nation-state entails an internal restructuring of the state apparatus and a realignment of its attachments to various class forces, but its policies continue to be generated by the systemic requirement that it manage the contradiction between (now) global accumulation and domestic legitimation (O'Connor 2002, xiii–xviii). The function of the nation-state has not been diminished as a result of globalization, although the form of state intervention in the economy and society has changed considerably. As Leo Panitch (1994, 69) puts it: "The state now takes the form of a *mediator* between the externally established policy priorities and the internal social forces to which it also still remains accountable."

In this regard, Panitch (1994, 63) argues that there has been a tendency among globalization theorists "to ignore the extent to which today's globalisation both is authored by states and is primarily about reorganising, rather than by-passing, states." Panitch (1994, 63) contends that "far from witnessing a by-passing of the state by a global capitalism, what we see are very active states and highly politicised sets of capitalist classes."[15] Indeed, Panitch (1994, 64) identifies nation-states as the authors of a new global regime, which now:

> defines and guarantees, through international treaties with constitutional effect, the global and domestic rights of capital. This process may be understood in a manner quite analogous to the emergence of the so-called laissez-faire state during the rise of industrial capitalism, which involved a very active state to see through the separation of polity from economy and guarantee legally and politically the rights of contract and property.[16]

Ian Robinson articulates the same concept in his analysis of the North American Free Trade Agreement (NAFTA) by noting that many international trade agreements, including the WTO, go far beyond the effort to merely liberalize trade between nations, or construct an international division of labor, as previously characterized the world capitalist system (Schirm, 2002, Chaps. 3–5; Cf. Wallerstein, 1980). These new treaties between nation-states prohibit discrimination between national and foreign owned corporations (so-called national treatment) and even create new corporate property rights such as guarantees of intellectual property rights, the repatriation of profits, and extended patent protection, among others. In this respect, the more recent trade agreements do not merely liberalize trade between countries, but "function as an economic constitution, setting the basic rules governing the private property rights that all governments must respect and the types of economic policies that all governments must eschew" (Robinson 1993, 2).[17] These new private property rights typically go well beyond those previously established in most countries, although they frequently mirror U.S. property and contract law and, thus, effectively extend the U.S. Constitution's 5th and 14th Amendment protections to virtually the entire globe (Hartmann, 2011).

The Internationalization of the State: A Case Study

Mexico provides an excellent illustration of how nation-states act as the agents of globalization and how trade agreements like NAFTA give constitutional effect to the new global and domestic rights of "foreign" capital. Historically, Mexico relied heavily on import-substitution and managed trade policies that emphasized industrialization, infrastructure development, and domestic economic diversification. Mexico's emerging industries were protected from import competition through high tariffs, quotas, and licensing, while the costs of protection were borne by established economic activities, particularly the agricultural and oil sectors (Babb, 2001, Chaps. 4–5; MacLeod, 2004, Chap. 2; Organization for Economic Cooperation and Development [OECD], 1995; OECD, 1996, 9). These policies were sustained by the state-owned monopoly in oil and petrochemical products, which allowed the government to use super-profits from high worldwide oil prices in the 1970s to modernize infrastructure, subsidize other sectors of the economy, and to subsidize low food prices. While this policy established an industrial base and allowed Mexico to modernize much of its economy, the policy reached its limits in the small size of the country's domestic market, the growing inefficiency of many state enterprises, a large trade management bureaucracy, and the lack of international competitiveness in protected sectors of the economy. The government's ability to subsidize inefficient and noncompetitive sectors of the economy, as well as low food prices for citizens, collapsed with the decline in oil prices during the 1980s. These pressures were magnified by the Latin American debt crisis, which allowed the United States and the International Monetary Fund to exert considerable pressure on the Mexican government for structural adjustment.

In response, the Mexican government began "unilaterally" liberalizing its trade and investment regimes in the early 1980s under the Presidency of Miguel de la Madrid in a bid to attract new foreign direct investment. President Miguel de la Madrid (1981–1988) initiated the liberalization of Mexico's trade and FDI regimes as part of the government's solution to the 1982 debt crisis (Gestrin and Rugman, 1996, 65–70). The debt crisis emergency softened political resistance to policy change and Madrid used this window of opportunity to initiate a sustained and far-reaching program of economic reform. Madrid's short-term strategy for dealing with the debt crisis included a large devaluation of the peso, a reduction of real wages in the public sector, and a privatization program that reduced the number of state-owned enterprises from 1,214 to 468 during his presidency (MacLeod, 2004, 70–78). These policies were designed to restore investor and business confidence by increasing exports and reducing the federal budget deficit.

De la Madrid's reforms explicitly broke with Mexico's history of import substitution and rejected managed trade as a theoretical basis for a viable model of long-term economic development. However, it was not until 1984 that the de la

Madrid Administration reached a consensus that trade restrictions were an additional obstacle to further economic recovery (Babb, 2001, Chap. 7; Ramirez de la O, 1993, 60–86). In 1979, 60% of the total value of imports to Mexico was subject to licensing requirements and by December of 1982 this coverage had been extended to 100%. However, this policy was softened in December of 1984 when licensing requirements were eliminated for 17% of the total value of all imports to Mexico. After several months of negotiations, Mexico joined the General Agreement on Tariffs and Trade (GATT) in June of 1986 and, as part of its accession commitments, Mexico eliminated import licensing requirements on all but 27.8% of the value of its imports. In addition, the trade weighted average tariff on imports was reduced from 16.4% to 13.1% and tariff dispersion was reduced.

President de la Madrid also challenged Mexico's highly nationalist view of foreign direct investment (FDI), which is partly ensconced in the Mexican Constitution (petroleum and land) and partly in federal legislation. In particular, President de la Madrid's abandonment of the import substitution regime was accompanied by modifications to the 1973 Law to Promote Mexican Investment and Regulate Foreign Investment. The 1973 Foreign Investment Law limited foreign equity in Mexican firms to a maximum of 49%, subject to exceptional case-by-case rulings by the National Foreign Investment Commission (NFIC). In 1984, President de la Madrid issued new "Guidelines for Foreign Investment and Objectives for Its Promotion," which stipulated that foreign ownership shares up to 49% in private firms would no longer need federal authorization, but simply had to be registered with the government (excluding numerous sectoral exemptions). The new guidelines also included a list of sectors where foreign investors could hold shares in excess of 49% subject to approval by the NFIC. The new guidelines did not guarantee automatic approval, but the change was designed to encourage the expectation that approval would be expedited in the preapproved areas. Importantly, the new Guidelines did not change the 1973 law, but only altered its administration and implementation (Ramirez de la O, 1993, 67).[18]

The liberalization of trade and foreign direct investment accelerated under President Carlos Salinas de Gortari (1988–1995) (Grayson, 1993, 7–15). In 1989, the trade weighted average tariff on goods imported into Mexico was reduced from 13.1% to 9.7% and tariff dispersion was again reduced. Import licensing was again reduced from 27.8% to 20.0% of the value of imports. By 1993, less than 2% of Mexico's tariff lines were subject to licensing requirements (OECD, 1996, 86). President Salinas also changed the 1973 Foreign Investment Law in 1989 to grant automatic approval to foreign ownership shares in excess of 49% if six criteria were met. These criteria included an investment ceiling of $100 million, full compensation of imports by exports, location outside the main urban areas, and technology suitable for Mexico. In lieu of meeting these criteria, the 1984 Guidelines requiring approval by the NFIC still applied to foreign majority ownership. In December of 1993, however, even the watered-down version of the Foreign Investment Law was replaced with a completely new and far more liberal legal framework.

A major result of trade liberalization is that imports into Mexico rose from 9.5% of GDP in 1985 to 12.5% in 1989, 15.3% in 1993, and 30.2% in 1998 (Banco de Mexico, 1999; Ramirez de la O, 1993, 63). Mexico has recorded a balance of trade deficit for most years since liberalizing its trade policies, but Mexican officials anticipated this situation at the time. They were convinced that the trade deficit would eventually turn to a surplus, because the rate of growth in Mexico's exports accelerated from an 11.9% average annual rate of increase from 1987 to 1994 to 18% between 1994 and 1998 (Banco de Mexico, 1999, 258). In fact, with the exception of 1995 and 1996, Mexico began recording trade deficits every year after 1991, compared to a consistent record of trade surpluses in the 1980s (see Banco de Mexico, 2005).

The main source of export growth during the first decade of liberalization (1984–1993) was the maquiladora industry, which recorded export growth rates well in excess of the national average. However, both within and outside the maquiladora industry, export growth was supported mainly by U.S. investment in the automobile, auto parts, and electronics manufacturing sectors. In 1982, the leading manufactured exports from Mexico to the United States were in primary resources such as food, drink, and tobacco, petroleum derivatives, and chemicals. By 1993, transportation equipment (automobiles) and electronic equipment had become Mexico's leading exports to the United States. By 1994, fully 78% of Mexico's total exports were machinery and transportation equipment, that is, mainly automobiles, panel trucks, and auto parts as Mexico shifted from an agricultural and resource-based economy to a manufacturing economy that provided low-cost inputs (machinery, auto parts) and consumer products (electronics, apparel) to the United States (OECD, 1996, 25). The investment liberalization reforms also had the expected effect of increasing foreign direct investment in Mexico. The flow of FDI into Mexico increased from 8.3% of gross fixed capital formation in 1986–1991 to 14.25% in 1996. As a result of increased foreign investment, Mexico's total stock of FDI nearly tripled from $24.1 billion in 1989 to $65.8 billion in 1993 with about two-thirds of the developed countries' FDI in Mexico coming from the United States (United Nations Conference on Trade and Development [UNCTAD], 1998, 391).

Hence, when *Mexico initiated* the discussions for a free trade agreement with the United States in 1991, it was a logical extension of the nation's previous trade and investment liberalization policies, which were designed to restore the confidence on foreign and international lenders and foreign (particularly U.S.) investors. NAFTA institutionalized—or gave constitutional effect—to the liberalizing reforms of previous presidential administrations, who believed that Mexico's future economic growth and political stability depended on access to foreign export markets and foreign direct investment (Rubio, 1999). In short, the North American Free Trade Agreement mandated the elimination of tariffs and nontariff barriers (NTBs) on substantially all trade between the three signatories over a 10-year period that concluded on December 31, 2003 (Hufbauer and Schott, 1993). The cornerstone of NAFTA's investment provisions is Article 1102.1, which requires that each party to the agreement accord the investors and investments of other NAFTA parties "treatment no less favorable than it accords, in like circumstances, to its own investors." NAFTA's national treatment clause for foreign direct investment (FDI) goes beyond the WTO's most favored nation provisions by establishing *common norms* for the treatment of international investments between the three countries.[19] NAFTA further modified Mexico's Foreign Investment Law by removing the requirement that foreign majority ownership by a NAFTA-based parent company receive government approval. The agreement also strengthened the Mexican government's 1987 reforms on intellectual property rights by subjecting intellectual property disputes to the agreement's dispute settlement process. In addition, NAFTA's provisions on intellectual property rights go beyond those adopted in the Uruguay Round of GATT, mainly by extending better protections to products that are still under development, which was a provision deemed particularly important to U.S. high-technology industries where up-front research and development costs are high, lead times to market are long, and product life cycles are short (Gestrin and Rugman, 1996, 69–70). A 1996 OECD (p. 9) report on the country's economic reforms leading up to NAFTA concludes that "Mexico has undergone an economic transition in the last decade and a half that is extraordinary by any standards. In its pace, breadth and depth, Mexico's reform process has surpassed those of most other developing countries that have undergone similar economic adjustments in recent years."

Yet, the Mexican officials who initiated the NAFTA negotiations were not seeking to introduce new trade and investment liberalization policies, but sought to preempt domestic opposition to their policies and prevent the potential rollback of these economic reforms by locking them in through a trade agreement that effectively constitutionalized statutory legislation and executive decrees.[20] Nathan Jensen's (2006, 1) more far-reaching analysis of the political economy of foreign direct investment reminds us that "foreign direct investment entails a substantial and lasting ownership stake in a venture in a host country." Consequently, Jensen (2006, 1) finds that "political factors have marked influence on these decisions:

governments that can commit to future economic policies conducive to multinationals' interests will achieve higher levels of FDI inflows . . . political institutions that provide commitments to these 'market-friendly' policies for multinationals will systematically attract higher levels of foreign direct investment inflows."

The New Imperialism

In this regard, Panitch (1994b, 75) is correct to point out that trade treaties such as NAFTA and the WTO are not being imposed on national states throughout the world by American capital or the American state, but instead operationalize these states' role *in representing the interests of their bourgeoisies and bureaucracies as these are already penetrated by American capital and administration.* The NAFTA case again provides an excellent and perhaps not extreme example of what Panitch means when he refers to the penetration of foreign social formations by American capital. A central feature of Canada's economy is the relatively high level of foreign ownership of productive assets, despite decades of trade and domestic economic policies designed to insulate Canadian industries and protect its national autonomy. By the late 1980s, approximately 45% of Canada's manufacturing assets were held by foreign owners, particularly by parent firms based in the United States. In 1989, when the Canadian-U.S. Free Trade Agreement (CUFTA) was adopted, U.S. parent companies controlled 71% of the assets in Canada's transportation equipment industry (mostly trucks and automobiles), 59% of the assets in the rubber products industry (tires), 51% of the assets in chemicals and chemical products, and 33% of the assets in petroleum and coal. U.S. ownership accounted for 12% to 25% of the assets in several other industries such as wood, paper, primary metals, food and beverages, and mining. Thus, the Canadian economy was already highly dependent on foreign direct investment, particularly U.S. investment, which means that many of the strategic business decisions affecting key sectors of the Canadian economy were increasingly tied to the global competitiveness strategies of transnational companies based in the United States. Thus, it is little wonder that following CUFTA, Canada's corporate and government leaders turned to Professor Michael E. Porter (1991), one of the architects of U.S. competitiveness policy, for recommendations about that country's strategic competitiveness policy (Porter, 1991, 15).

Similarly, in Mexico, 66% of the developed countries' FDI already came from the United States by 1990, which is a ratio that remained relatively constant over the next decade, although total FDI in Mexico quadrupled from $3.1 billion in 1986–1991 to $12.1 billion in 1997 after NAFTA's ratification (Gestrin and Rugman, 1996, 66; United Nations Conference on Trade and Development [UNCTAD], 1998, 363). Similarly, a great deal of economic integration between Mexico and the United States had already occurred in the decade prior to NAFTA as transnational enterprises (TNEs) began rationalizing production across the United States-Mexico border. The increasing depth of the cross-border economic integration in North America (and the world) is similarly illustrated by the growing *intra-firm* cross-border trade between U.S. majority-owned foreign affiliates (MOFAs) in Mexico and their parent companies in the United States. Intra-firm trade between MOFAs in Mexico and their U.S. parents accounted for 24% of total U.S.-Mexican trade in 1989. By 1992, intra-firm trade between MOFAs in Mexico and their U.S. parents had increased to 30% of total U.S.-Mexican trade. Just prior to the ratification of NAFTA, more than half of Mexico's manufactured exports to the United States were *intra-firm transactions* and the same was true of Canada's manufactured exports to the United States. Chrysler, General Motors, Ford, and Pepsi are now among the largest manufacturers in Mexico, while Walmex, the Mexican branch of Walmart, is now Mexico's largest retailer (UNCTAD, 1998, 249–258; Weintraub, 1993).

The penetration of the entire North American social formation by U.S. capital is highly advanced, but this trend has been occurring to varying degrees throughout the world for some time. In 1997 alone, there were 151 changes in FDI regulatory regimes made by 76 countries and 89% of these changes created a more favorable or liberalized environment for FDI. The value of international production attributable to some 53,000 transnational enterprises (TNEs) and their 450,000 foreign affiliates was $3.5 trillion in 1997, while the estimated global sales of these foreign affiliates was $9.5 trillion. Total FDI stocks are now equal to 21% of global GDP, while foreign affiliate exports account for one-third of world exports. The sales of foreign affiliates are currently growing faster than total world exports of goods and services. The ratio of total world FDI stocks to world GDP has also grown twice as fast as the ratio of world imports and exports to world GDP. These developments suggest that the expansion of transnational production, a process led by U.S. capital is deepening the global *penetration* of national social formations far beyond anything that could be achieved by international trade alone (UNCTAD, 1998, xvii–xix).

Consequently, Panitch (2000, 16) provocatively suggests that all of the international treaty-making in the last 25 years has induced nation-states to rapidly transform their domestic financial, legal, and educational systems "into facsimiles of the American." The new domestic arrangements induced or even required by these treaties establish the political and material conditions for the reproduction of American capital within foreign social formations, while creating a dense institutional network binding other states to the American empire through a hub-and-spoke network of financial, economic, military, and cultural linkages. Thus, Panitch (2000, 17) identifies a new form of imperial rule that is:

> characterized by the penetration of borders, not their dissolution. It was not through formal empire, but rather through the reconstitution of states as integral elements of an informal American empire, that the international capitalist order was now organized and regulated. Nation states remained the primary vehicles through which (a) the social relations and institutions of class, property, currency, contract and markets were established and reproduced; and (b) the international accumulation of capital was carried out. The

> vast expansion of direct foreign investment, whatever the shifting regional shares of the total, meant that far from capital escaping the state, it expanded its dependence on *many* states.

Therefore, it is important to recognize that while globalization is a multilateral process, it is one that unfolds in a context where states are not only unequal in their political and military power, but are representing "nations" already deeply penetrated by American capital and, to a lesser degree, by European and Japanese capital. In this context, Stephen Gill and David Law (1988, 84) emphasize that the continuing separation of the world into nation-states "creates a central condition for the power of internationally mobile forms of capital." It is the political fragmentation of the globalized economy that makes the threat of capital flight and disinvestment operative and real. The structural power of transnational capital can be effective only in a political world where capital has the ability to move from one state to another in search of competitive advantages (Picciotto, 1997). Transnational capital—American or otherwise— would have no long-term interest in constructing a global state or a transnational state, because such an arrangement would jeopardize, or at least mitigate, the political basis of its structural power. For Ellen Wood (2003, 6) this means that "the political form of globalization is not a global state but a global system of multiple states, and the new imperialism takes its specific shape from the complex and contradictory relationship between capital's expansive economic power and the more limited reach of the extra-economic force that sustains it."

Thus, against those who see the International Monetary Fund, World Bank, WTO, and NATO as the foundations of a transnational state, or a new multilateral world order, these institutions are more appropriately conceptualized as "the international mediators of US hegemony" (Gilbert and Vines, 2000; Panitch, 2000, 13–14).[21] More specifically, and following Panitch, globalization and its new institutions are a process that is further institutionalizing the hegemony and reproduction of American capital on an ever extending scale. Panitch points to Nicos Poulantzas' (1978b, 37–38) prescient essay, "The Internationalization of Capitalist Relations and the Nation State" as a basis for incorporating these new developments into the established framework of Marxian state theory. Panitch (2000, 8–9) suggests that Poulantzas' main contribution in this essay was to explain:

> (i) that when multinational capital penetrates a host social formation, it arrives not merely as abstract "direct foreign investment", but as a transformative social force within the country; (ii) that the interaction of foreign capital with domestic capital leads to the dissolution of the national bourgeoisie as a coherent concentration of class interests; (iii) but far from losing importance, the host state actually becomes responsible for taking charge of the complex relations of international capital to the domestic bourgeoisie, in the context of class struggles and political and ideological forms which remain distinctively national even as they express themselves within a world conjuncture.

These elements provide "the conceptual building blocks" for a theory of globalization capable of explaining "a new type of non-territorial imperialism, implanted and maintained not through direct rule by the metropolis, nor even through political subordination of a neocolonial type, but rather through the 'induced reproduction of the form of the dominant imperialist power within each national formation and its state'" (Panitch, 2000, 9; Sakellaropoulos and Sotiris, 2015). A crucial component of this new imperialism is that the same process also structures the relationship between the United States and other metropolitan centers so that in contrast to the imperialist rivalries described by Lenin:

> . . . relations between the imperialist metropolises themselves are now also being organized in terms of a structure of domination and dependence within the imperialist chain. . . . it [the new imperialism] has been

> achieved by establishing relations of production characteristic of American monopoly capital and its domination actually inside the other metropolises, and by the reproduction within these of this new relation of dependence. (Panitch and Gindin, 2003, 2004; Poulantzas, 1978b, 47)

While the growing interpenetration of American, European, and Japanese capital, as well as their attachment to international institutions, has been identified as the basis of an autonomous transnational capitalist class (Robinson and Harris, 2000; Sklair, 2001), such views fail to acknowledge that none of these institutions have the police powers that are the constitutive essence of stateness. Institutionalist, realist, and even structuralist concepts of the state apparatus conceptualize it as an organization that attempts "to extend coercive control and political authority over particular territories and the people residing within them," which is a definition that makes military and bureaucratic capacities synonymous with state power (Skocpol and Amenta, 1986, 131).[22] The enforcement of compliance with international regimes still depends on nation-states and within the system of nation-states the American superstate remains preeminent.

For example Panitch notes that despite numerous international financial crises (e.g., Mexico, East Asia, Russia, Argentina), a global financial crisis (2007), and various political challenges to its continuing hegemony (e.g., China), the U.S. state and capital have been amazingly successful (from the standpoint of its own hegemony) at restructuring global capitalism in forms that reproduce their imperial dominance. Moreover, the interpenetration of American capital by European and other capitals has actually Americanized the latter's political interests by attaching their fortunes to the American superstate's successful enforcement of the new global trade and investment regime (Beck, Klobes, and Scherrer, 2005).

For example, German capitalists roundly chastised former Chancellor Gerhard Schroeder for his populist anti-Americanism prior to the first Iraq invasion with Thomas Middelhoff, the CEO of Bertelsmann, having already stated publicly that he considered himself an "American who by sheer coincidence has a German passport" (quoted in Ewing, 2000). Indeed, a *Businessweek* review of German acquisitions in the United States concludes that:

> . . . Germany's business elites come across more like a bunch of American wannabes, showing off their English, being envious of the unfettered capitalism enjoyed by U.S. companies, and embracing U.S. business articles of faith such as shareholder value. . . . Germany's push abroad seems more an attempt to embrace America than conquer it. Its companies often eschew their German-ness and install foreign managers. (Ibid.)

Despite two decades of earlier hand wringing about America's "decline" by U.S. public officials, journalists, and scholars, it would appear that the "coming economic battle" between the United States, Japan, and Europe has been postponed for the foreseeable future (Thurow, 1992). In retrospect, it is now clear that many claims about the decline of U.S. economic hegemony projected domestic economic trends from 1971 to 1991 (e.g., productivity) into the indefinite future, while they also presumed that other centers of regional capitalist hegemony were emerging to challenge U.S. dominance, such as a Pacific Rim anchored by the Japanese economy, a resurgent East Asia, and a new Europe powered by the German economy (Arrighi, Mamashita, and Selden, 2003; Meyer-Larsen, 2000). These claims also assumed that the United States would not (or could not) take effective measures to counter long-term challenges to its world economic and political hegemony. Yet, G. William Domhoff points out "for all the outcry and worry [in America] over the rise of Japan and Germany, the United States is without doubt the largest, most populous, and richest industrial democracy in the world" (Berberoglu, 2003; Domhoff, 1998, 298–299; Cf. Wallerstein, 2003).

Indeed, by 1997, the Japanese and German economies combined were only 56% as large as the U.S. economy, while the Japanese, German, British, and French economies combined were 87% as large as the U.S. economy. Moreover, during the 1990s, a 10-year cycle of uninterrupted productivity and GDP growth actually widened the economic gap between the United States, Europe, and the rest of the world as the rate of U.S. economic growth exceeded both the European and the world average.[23] From 1990 to 1998, the United States reversed a four-decades long trend of its economy shrinking as a share of world gross domestic product so that during this time the U.S. economy not only grew in absolute terms—to $11 trillion gross domestic product—it increased proportionately from 22% to 25% of world gross domestic product (World Bank, 1999).

Christoph Scherrer (2003, 52) has analyzed the resurgence of American capitalism to conclude that "the liberal world-market order of the post-war era may be interpreted as a project of internationally-oriented capital fractions in the United States (notably New York banks and law practices as well as transnational corporations from the various sectors). These fractions succeeded in hegemonically integrating into their project important groups in the United States on the one hand, and—through the resources of the US government—the other capitalist industrial nations on the other" (also, Gill, 1990; Starrs, 2013). Similarly, Leo Panitch and Sam Gindin (2003, 72) call attention to "the overwhelming power—and above all the penetrative capacity—of the American state and capital vis a vis even the other leading capitalist states in the world today." Consequently they each emphasize the need to theorize other "capitalisms"—whether Japanese, European, or North American—in relation to American capital and the American state.

Thus, theoretically Panitch and Gindin (2003, 75) are led to the proposition that "globalization is a development not external to states, but internal to them," particularly because nation-states and nation-based fractions of capital (however internationalized) have played an active role in creating the newly liberalized and globalized international financial and trade regimes ensconced in the post-Bretton Woods monetary arrangement, the World Trade Organization, and the implementation of United Nations and NATO mandates. It is these nation-states, especially the United States, that still carry the responsibility for the implementation, enforcement, and success of international arrangements within their borders.[24] Thus, an understanding of "global" governance first requires "an examination of the role played by foreign capital as a social force within each nation state, as well as the increasing transnational orientation to accumulation on the part of domestic capital" (Panitch and Gindin, 2003, 75).

Toward a New State Form?

A central theoretical challenge to this neo-imperialist thesis revolves around the concepts of "nation" and "state," which though linked historically since the early 1300s are by no means analytically identical, nor necessarily permanent features of the historical terrain. In fact, as Martin Van Creveld (1999, 415) observes, historically speaking the state is merely one of the forms that the organization of government, or political authority, has assumed at different times and places and therefore it should "not be considered eternal and self-evident any more than were previous ones."[25] In responding to this theoretical challenge, Bob Jessop (2002a, 205) also deploys a "Poulantzasian" analysis and concurs with Panitch's position that the inability of national states to control world markets has "far less to do with any alleged inherent 'ungovernability' of footloose global capital than with real class contradictions within national power blocs as these are increasingly shaped by the process of internationalization itself." Jessop also suggests that an understanding of the emerging forms of political authority "will surely be found in the internal contradictions of capital itself rather than the simple incapacity of states to control financial capital" Thus, Jessop (2002, 196) also rejects the "alleged decline in power of nation-states in the face of globalization or the world market" (Cf. Strange, 1998).

While Jessop (2002a, 206) concurs with critics of neo-imperialism that global and domestic forms of governance are in transition, he too does not see a decomposition of "the political," but rather a rearticulation of the economic and the political in a new state form that continues to be structured internationally "by the continuing hegemony of the United States within the interstate system." While Jessop (2002a, 207) acknowledges many of the structural and institutional tendencies advanced by critics of neo-imperialist theory, he concludes that the new world order must still be theorized within the current "resurgence of a reinvigorated and relatively unchallenged American 'super state' with revitalized capacities to project its power on a global scale."

A focus on the arcane provisions of the WTO, IMF structural adjustment policies, and World Bank lending policies can often evade the issue of how much of these institutions' influence is derived from other states' dependence on American capital, the global market, and international lending as opposed to how much of that power is derived from the American state's internal political, diplomatic, and military strength. Domhoff (1998, 298) echoes Jessop's claim by noting that "the end of the Soviet Union has left the United States as far and away the most powerful country in the world, with no serious rivals in the economic, political, or military realms."[26] At the turn of the century, the U.S. economy was supporting military expenditures nearly double those of Japan, Germany, France, and the United Kingdom combined and nearly equal to the military expenditures of the entire world combined. This rate of military spending was achieved by committing only 4% of U.S. GDP to these expenditures (which is less than the 6% to 7% committed during the Cold War) (Domhoff, 1998, 298–299; Shaw, 2000, 204–205). These expenditure figures do not even begin to capture the immense technological gap between the United States and any potential military competitors. Domhoff (1998, 299) surmises that "the most likely result of this unrivaled power is that the American foreign policy establishment will intervene militarily anywhere in the world that it chooses" to protect "American" interests.

The disputes between Europe and the United States over diplomatic (e.g., Iraq) and trade issues (e.g., steel tariffs) are intra-class conflicts about the American state's deployment on behalf of the particular interests of American capital, or even particular fractions of capital, in betrayal of the superstate's function to promote the global interests of capital under an internationalized regime of accumulation. From this perspective, the American state has been captured (in Milibandian terms) by a mere fraction of American capital that is pursuing a myopic definition of American "national interest," rather than the larger neo-imperial interests of globalizing capital (Panitch and Gindin, 2003, 95; Shaw, 2000, 246). When embarked on this trajectory, the only foreseeable limit to U.S. economic and military power will be the internal contradictions of the American social formation and the tendency of a messianic state elite to over-reach strategically until it is disciplined by some disastrous military adventure (Barrow, 2004). Martin Shaw (2000, 249–250) is convinced that intra-class contradictions will successfully restrain this chauvinism in the long run, because "the majority of large transnational corporations are American–based" and this gives American capital "a profound interest in the internationalization of law, especially commercial law." The latter scenario has been predicted (incorrectly thus far) in every U.S. military expedition from Haiti to Kosovo to the second Gulf (U.S.-Iraq) War.[27]

Thus, at the international level, Jessop (2002a, 205) also sees a crisis *in* imperialism, rather than a crisis *of* imperialism and he theorizes this crisis, drawing on regulation theory, as a crisis of Atlantic Fordism that is having significant repercussions on the capitalist state form. Jessop argues that the state form in the current phase of imperialism is the effect of a central contradiction faced by all contemporary nation-states in the globalizing economy; namely, the increasing difficulty of reconciling the "pressure to take measures directly and visibly beneficial to capital with the need to maintain political legitimacy and the overall cohesion of a class-divided social formation" (Cf. O'Connor, 1978; Offe, 1984). In Jessop's (2002, 200) analysis, this transition is a *response* to the "challenges to the continued dominance of the national state both as a *national* state and as a national *state* in managing" the global process of capital accumulation (see also, Jessop, 1994; Lipetz, 1987).

Jessop observes three major structural shifts in the state form that are still ongoing in response to the continuing development of a new regime of global accumulation. A first response involves the internationalization of domestic policy regimes that incorporate the personnel and interests of those fractions of capital involved in global accumulation directly into the national policy regime. The international context of capital accumulation increasingly provides the basis of policy formation, decision making, and state actions through its incorporation *into* domestic policy-making processes and political discourse. The internationalization of domestic policy regimes certainly requires the incorporation of extraterritorial or transnational agreements and processes into state policy making and action (e.g., IMF, WTO, NAFTA, EU), but "the key players in policy regimes have also expanded to include foreign agents and institutions as sources of policy ideas, policy design, and implementation" (Jessop, 2002a, 208).

However, in many ways, the internationalization of policy regimes may well intensify the central contradiction between the requirements of accumulation and legitimation. Thus, Jessop (2002a, 205) identifies a second response to this contradiction as "the displacement of crisis through the reallocation of functions to different levels of economic and political organization." Jessop refers to this process of political development as "a general trend toward the *denationalization of the state*" (see also, Jessop, 2002b, Chaps. 5–7). Jessop (2002a, 206) argues that the national state apparatuses are being hollowed out in a process where both old and new state capacities are "being reorganized territorially and functionally on sub-national, national, supranational, and trans-local levels" (see also, Pierson, 1996, 204). This process is most visible in the European Union, but it is also occurring to a lesser degree in the NAFTA region and in other formal intergovernmental blocs (Zurn, 2005).

This *development* of the state form is not occurring because the national state is unable to control capital flows, but is occurring precisely because national states continue to facilitate the conditions necessary to capital accumulation under the new regime (Weiss, 1998). In the new regime of flexible (global) accumulation (Harvey, 1982, 1990, 2003), Jessop (2002a, 203) argues that the scope of governance continues expanding into new areas of social life and penetrates ever deeper into the fabric of national social formations, precisely because global "competitiveness is now widely believed to depend far more on formally extra-economic institutional forms, relations, resources, and values than in the past, and this belief is leading in turn to increased pressure to subsume these factors under the logic of capital" (i.e., as social capital, human capital, intellectual capital). This process is visible in the subsumption of family policy, neighborhood development, public education, university research, patents and copyrights, and many other facets of social life once considered "private," "cultural," "social," or "intellectual" into the structure of economic and workforce development policy.[28]

The expansion and deepening of the scope of governance required to facilitate capital accumulation necessitates a structural denationalization of the state. Jessop (2002a, 206) observes that this process has "major implications for the role of local and regional governments and governance mechanisms insofar as supply-side policies are supposedly more effectively handled at these levels and through public-private partnerships than at the national level through traditional legislative, bureaucratic, and administrative techniques." However, the rising significance of local and regional forms of subnational governance cannot be confined merely to traditional forms of "the local state" (Gottdeiner, 1987), precisely because economic regions, supply chains, and industrial clusters have emerged as the new centers of global competitiveness (Porter, 1990, Chap. 6–7). These regional clusters not only exceed the geographic reach of existing forms of the local state, but they are frequently international regions defined by cross-border economic linkages (Perkmann and Sum, 2002).

The denationalization of the state is also required at another level by the continuing internationalization of capital accumulation through regional economic blocs (e.g., NAFTA and EU). The deepening of these supra-national regions of capital accumulation requires an increasing role for supranational institutions, which Jessop (2002a, 204) considers vehicles for organizing "countervailing imperialist strategies in Europe and Asia." Jessop does "not deny the continued domination of U.S. capital and the American state in an allegedly 'triadic' world," but he suggest that the United States will be increasingly checked by a shifting balance of power within the global triad, particularly since the European situation is now complicated by increasing linkages between European and East Asian capitals. However, Jessop (2002a, 199) insists that the process of supra-national state development should not be equated with the emergence of a "global state" or a "world state," since there is still no "supranational state with equivalent powers to those of the national state."[29]

Finally, a third major trend that Jessop (2002a, 207) identifies in contemporary state formation is the destatization of the political system, which is indicated by "a shift from govern*ment* to gover*nance* on various territorial scales and across various functional domains." This trend is empirically visible in the creation of partnerships at all levels of governance between government, para-governmental, and non-governmental organizations in which the state apparatus is often only first among equals. In these arrangements, state elites and state managers are involved primarily in steering and guiding "multiple agencies, institutions, and systems that are both operationally autonomous from one another and structurally coupled through various forms of reciprocal interdependence."

Claus Offe (1984, 249; 1996, 22–27) describes the same process as "a dissolution of the institutional separateness, or relative autonomy of the state, the withering away of the capitalist state as a coherent and strictly circumscribed apparatus of power." The process of destatization is one in which "policy-making powers are 'contracted out' to consortia of group representatives who engage in a semi-private type of bargaining, the results of which are then ratified as state policies or state planning." A key feature of destatization in Offe's view is the parallel trend toward strengthening intermediate organizations in national and international civil societies that are legally "private," but which are capturing sovereign functions from the state or receiving them as delegated powers of the state. As the state becomes overloaded with demands on its national and local administrative capacities, it continues to delegate and disperse regulatory and distributive powers to quasi-public corporations, trade associations, professional organizations, social service corporations, labor unions, chambers of commerce, scientific associations, and many other private nonprofit organizations. These collective actors are being delegated quasi-sovereign functions and thereby relieve the national state of a number of responsibilities (Drucker, 1993, 1–46; Flinders, 2006; Hall and Biersteker, 2002; Schmitter, 1985).

Conclusion

The restructuring of the nation-state entails its simultaneous internationalization, denationalization, and destatization, as described by Jessop, Offe, and others, but this process should not be equated with a decline, retreat, or end of the state. Nation-states should also not be seen as passively acquiescing to the irreversible logic of a global market or to the superior power of transnational corporations. First, the nation-state has been a profoundly contested terrain for nearly four decades as highly politicized capitalist classes have launched new business offensives in one country after another under the ideological rubric of neo-liberalism, competitiveness, economic modernization, and globalism. The fact that capitalist classes have vigorously and successfully deployed a range of economic, financial, political, and ideological power to recapture these states and to restructure their hegemony should actually be taken as an indicator of the state's continuing importance to economic globalization.

Second, these same states have acted as the principal agents of globalization by exercising enormous power to realign the state apparatuses with transnational capital, to reconstitute property and contract law, and to otherwise implement and enforce the provisions of international trade and investment agreements even against domestic opposition. The internal realignment of the state apparatuses that accompanies the internationalization of policy regimes has certainly resulted in the ideological subordination or disempowerment of those agencies with links to labor and other noncapitalist groupings. However, the fact that implementing such policies has entailed significant social struggles in one country after another should signal the enduring power of the state for it is labor and other social groups that are in retreat—not the state. In opening domestic economies to global competition and in facilitating the restructuring of those same economies, the nation-states of both developed (e.g., United States, Canada) and developing (e.g., Mexico) countries have demonstrated remarkable strength in relation to those groups seeking to promote social welfare, labor rights, and environmental protections. Meanwhile, nation-states have intervened directly in reconstituting private and corporate property rights, contract law, and labor markets to create the political and material conditions necessary for global capital accumulation. The only states that are visibly in retreat are those that once purported to be "socialist" (e.g., Russia, China) or that sought to promote some limited variant of that ideal (e.g., India, Mexico) and in these cases it is noncapitalist state forms that are being displaced by a new form of the capitalist state and simultaneously integrated into the global system of a new imperialism.

SEVEN

The Return to State Theory

The Poulantzas-Miliband debate left Marxist state theorists with the discomfort of what appeared to be an unresolved divergence at the core of Marxian political theory and for most state theorists it brought an end to the illusion that there is something called *the* Marxist theory of the state. It is now widely recognized, in part due to the Poulantzas-Miliband debate that one cannot find a complete theory of the state in the writings of Marx and Engels in the sense that they never developed "a theoretical analysis of the capitalist state to match the scope and rigour of *Das Kapital*" (Editorial Collective, 1973, 2; Jessop, 1977, 354). Consequently, although Marxist political theorists still frequently turn to Marx's and Engels' so-called political writings for guidance in constructing this never-finished theory of the state, as Bob Jessop (1977, 354) points out, political theorists are relying at best on "a fragmented and unsystematic series of philosophical reflections, contemporary history, journalism and incidental remarks." Indeed, most Marxists have passed the point of believing that anyone can construct a fully developed Marxist theory of the state simply by reading Marx (Cf. Draper, 1977; Duncan, 1982). Indeed, after the Poulantzas-Miliband debate concluded in 1976, new conceptual modifications to state theory continued to emerge as exemplified by the works of critical systems analysis (e.g., Habermas and Offe), the German derivationists (e.g., Alvater), and the new institutionalists (e.g., Theda Skocpol) and each of these new approaches offered a still new reading of the Marxian classics (Barrow, 2000).

However, beyond the debate about what constitutes Marx's "political writings," the Poulantzas-Miliband debate had little to do with "Marxism," but focused on epistemological and methodological disputes that were in no way peculiar to Marxism. The Poulantzas-Miliband debate did not focus on conceptual or empirical disputes about how to define the state, the "function" of the capitalist state, or the internal structure of the state apparatus and its relations to different classes in specific social formations. Instead, the Poulantzas-Miliband debate digressed almost immediately into an epistemological dispute over whether there is any such thing as a specifically Marxist methodology, but even this question was incorrectly posed as the false dichotomy between structure and agency. Nevertheless, the debate once again brought into sharp relief a long-standing methodological impasse that has persisted since Eduard Bernstein (1961, Chap. 1) first argued that there is no such thing as a Marxist methodology and George Lukacs (1971, 1) replied that Marxist theory refers exclusively to a method.

In reconstructing the Poulantzas-Miliband debate, and in assessing its aftermath, I do not claim to answer the original epistemological question posed by Bernstein and Lukacs as to whether there is a Marxist methodology in some abstract sense of the term. However, as a particular historical observation, I do argue throughout this book that even though both theorists cite Marx extensively in staking their claims, their research is firmly anchored in the same *methods* employed by mainstream social scientists. The conclusion to my argument is that the distinctively "Marxist" element in Marxist theories of the state is the constellation of analytical concepts (as opposed to methodological assumptions) that can be derived from Marx's writings.[1] Thus, when we engage Poulantzas and Miliband at the practical level of doing empirical, historical, and institutional research on actually existing states, the false methodological antinomies of state theory tend to dissolve in practice. The alternative is to endlessly replicate the Bernstein-Lukacs impasse as the Poulantzas-Miliband debate, although I argue beyond mere pragmatism that Poulantzas and Miliband both create theoretical openings that allow us to potentially combine their work in theoretically informed analyses of actually existing states without becoming mired in a hopeless epistemological and methodological stalemate.[2]

If we jettison the instrumentalist label imposed on Ralph Miliband by his polemical critics and actually read *The State in Capitalist Society* then it should be clear that his theory of the state focuses on three sets of factors that define "the Western system of power." The first set of factors is Miliband's (Chaps. 2–5) empirical and historical analysis of class structure in contemporary capitalist societies, the internal institutional organization of the state apparatus, and the institutional linkages between the state apparatus and various classes and class fractions. As this analysis constitutes about one-half of Miliband's book, it received the most attention, particularly from his critics and, in fact, his theory of state has become synonymous with these chapters (although in a grossly distorted form). However, the second set of factors analyzed by Miliband are considered under the chapter heading of "Imperfect Competition" and, as I have documented in Chapter 5 of this book, Miliband explicitly introduces the principle of business confidence and structural constraint—he even uses those terms—as factors facilitating a natural alliance between state and capital, regardless of who *governs*, because the state is dependent on capital investment for economic growth and tax revenue. The latter are necessary to the state's political legitimacy, which depends on its ability to deliver needed public services and, especially, to ensure gainful employment for the working class.

Miliband did not use terms such as the *privileged position of business* (Lindblom), the *dependency principle* (Offe), or *major structural mechanism* (Block), which were introduced later in the state debate, but he is certainly talking about the same thing with his references to business confidence, structural constraint, and imperfect competition. He also understood that it is this structural constraint that is fundamentally important to ensuring that the state in capitalist society "functions" as a capitalist state. These observations by Miliband unquestionably dispel the assertion that he was a methodological "voluntarist" or a mere descriptive "empiricist."

Finally, Miliband devotes the last three chapters of *The State in Capitalist Society* (Chaps. 7–9) to "the process of legitimation" and to the problem of "reform and repression." As I have documented in Chapter 2 and Chapter 5, the assertion that Miliband did not deal with questions of ideology and legitimacy is preposterous. Miliband recognized that a key element in maintaining legitimacy in nominally democratic states was the role (function) of the ideological system. When states are unable to deliver the requisite services and employment demanded by the working class, it must be able to draw on a reservoir of public loyalty and this requires that citizens be submerged in ideological messages to contravene the obvious and chronic policy deficits of capitalist states. And when those messages fail, states in capitalist societies face the problem of reform or repression (or maybe revolution).

How at a conceptual level does any of Miliband's analysis differ substantially from the one proposed by Nicos Poulantzas beyond the obvious differences of terminology? The three sets of factors analyzed by Ralph Miliband in *The State in Capitalist Society* parallel the political, the economic, and the ideological instances (or levels) elaborated in structuralist theory (and by Marx). When Miliband examines the internal institutional organization of the state apparatus and its linkages to various classes and class fractions what is he doing other than demonstrating empirically that the state is an arena (or condensate) of class struggle? When Miliband describes the power of business confidence on state decision makers what is he doing other than elaborating a major mechanism of structural constraint that explains *why* the state in capitalist society functions as a capitalist state? When Miliband describes the process of legitimation as an essentially ideological process necessary to build consensus and maintain the stability of the existing order what is he doing other than elaborating yet another structural mechanism that "functions" to maintain the unity or cohesion of the social formation in which the capitalist class is dominant? And, finally, when Miliband refers to Marx's statement in *The Communist Manifesto* that "the modern State is but a committee for managing the common affairs of the whole bourgeoisie" exactly how is this different from Poulantzas' claim in *Political Power and Social Classes* (1978a, 127) that "with regard to the dominant classes, and particularly the bourgeoisie, the State's principal role is one of *organization.* It represents and organizes the dominant class or classes"?

It may well be that certain aspects of Miliband's analysis were undertheorized compared to those who wrote after him and he definitely did not adopt a jargon laden or specialized terminology to convey his ideas. However, the more salient difference between Miliband and Poulantzas in this regard is their intended audience as a political theorist and their conception of what it means to do radical political theory. In Chapter 2 of this book, I demonstrated that Miliband was consciously developing an immanent critique of pluralist-democratic theory, which Poulantzas acknowledges was the dominant form of bourgeois social science in the United States. Thus, Miliband starts his analysis by elaborating the basic assumptions and claims of bourgeois social science and then systematically sets out to use the same methods and types of evidence employed by those social scientists and to expose that social science as ideology by revealing its internal contradictions, empirical falsehoods, and mystifications. It is this type of immanent critique, broadly pursued and written in accessible language, that opens the conceptual space and creates the necessity for elaborating an alternative theory that can account for the new facts deployed by an immanent critique.

As I document in my reconstruction of the Poulantzas-Miliband debate, Poulantzas explicitly recognizes the value of Miliband's immanent critique, but then chooses to invoke the specter of "ideological contamination" as one potential outcome of Miliband's approach to political theory. The irony of this allegation, as I also demonstrated in Chapter 2, is that Poulantzas was also engaged in his own immanent critique of bourgeois social science by challenging the Anglo-American school of systems-functional analysis. Poulantzas proposes an immanent critique of systems-functionalism by concretizing the concept of the social system as a capitalist system and thus introduces the inherent dysfunction of class struggle as a permanent tendency toward system disequilibrium. Poulantzas took a comparatively marginal concept within systems analysis and structural-functionalism, and by moving it to the center of his own analysis, he developed a radical critique of the mainstream concept of the system maintenance function. Thus, one can feel justified in dismissing Poulantzas' epithet, because it should be clear that immanent critique and alternative theorizing go hand in hand and complement each other in the larger task of challenging bourgeois social science.[3]

Other disputes between Poulantzas and Miliband were actually empirical disagreements and this pertains especially to their argument about the ideological state apparatuses. Initially, Poulantzas followed Althusser's famous essay on the same topic, which absorbed virtually all of civil society into the concept of an ideological state apparatus—political parties, the media, churches, and even the family—which are all legally private nonstate institutions in capitalist societies. In this conceptualization, the only ideological counter-apparatuses were the radical trade unions and the French Communist Party (Therborn, 1980). Miliband agreed that there was a process of "statization" underway with respect to many of these institutions, but he argued that empirically most ideological institutions are still not part of the state apparatus and, therefore, should be conceptualized as part of a more diffuse ideological system that gradually dissipates into culture. While this disagreement was a conceptual "boundary dispute" about where to differentiate the various subsystems of the capitalist system, the resolution of this dispute is ultimately an empirical question that may well vary from time to time and place to place. At any rate, Poulantzas eventually distanced himself from Althusser's essay on the ideological state apparatuses.

Similarly, Poulantzas criticizes Miliband for not being able to adequately account for state cohesion and to explain why something as diffuse as "the state" is able to function *as if* it was a conscious subject. The basis of this dispute is also empirical, although it has significant theoretical implications, because it is exactly Miliband's point to suggest that the state is not always cohesive, but asymmetrical and uneven in its development and policies. While business confidence and other processes of ruling class domination may infuse the state with a certain degree of class coherence, Miliband recognizes that fissures within the state are one of the dysfunctions that provide openings for nondominant classes to establish strongholds within the state apparatus. In one of his last works (see below), Poulantzas also came to the conclusion that the state was becoming more diffuse even as it was becoming more authoritarian.

Finally, Poulantzas and Miliband had a significant disagreement over the concept of power, but as I discuss in Chapter 3, it is C. Wright Mills who actually provides a solution to this problem. Poulantzas (1978a, 115, fn. 24) defines an institution as "a system of norms or rules which is socially sanctioned. . . . On the other hand, the concept of structure covers the *organizing matrix* of institutions." In other words, whereas Miliband conceptualized power as the ability to authoritatively mobilize the key resources organized through institutions (i.e., decision making), Poulantzas conceptualized power as a structured relationship between classes, rather than merely an attribute of institutions or organizations. This problem is resolved by recognizing that the relationship among classes and the state, as organized by institutions, is asymmetrical as in the case of investment strikes. The structural power of capital is its ability to make decisions about capital investment and disinvestment and they would not have that power if they did not occupy the command posts of financial and industrial corporations and if bourgeois legality did not maintain a separation of the political and the economic. Structural mechanisms such as disinvestment and capital strikes are not automatic and impersonal market forces, but decisions made by economic elites occupying the top command posts of financial and nonfinancial corporations. When "the market" responds to an unfavorable business climate, it is signaling a series of decisions made by those in positions of economic power. This is the "organizing matrix" of capitalism.

Why Return to the State Theory?

However, with state theory in decline for the last twenty years, why now return to state theory? The answer is simple. We have recently lived through a financial crisis that originated in the United States. It began with a rise in mortgage delinquencies in early 2007 and was followed by the collapse of major financial institutions in 2008, the collapse of major industrial corporations in 2009, and these events precipitated a global financial crisis and the Great Recession—the worst recession in U.S. history since the Great Depression of the 1930s (Kotz, 2009). Despite the platitudes of an anti-statist free-market neo-liberal ideology, nation-states were deeply involved in managing this crisis.

The world's central banks began coordinated injections of liquidity into national financial systems by the summer of 2007 in response to growing mortgage delinquencies and the emerging crisis in mortgage backed obligations. Despite these injections, Bear Stearns, a leading global investment bank based in New York City imploded, but being "too big to fail," the U.S. Federal Reserve orchestrated its forced acquisition by JP Morgan Chase. This maneuver was soon followed in the summer of 2008 by the U.S. Federal Deposit Insurance Corporation's (FDIC) takeover of Indymac Bank, which was a major underwriter and holder of subprime mortgages. As the financial crisis accelerated, the U.S. Government took control of Fannie Mae and Freddie Mac in the early fall of 2008, forced the sale of Merrill Lynch to Bank of America, watched the failure of Lehman Brothers, and then rescued the American International Group (AIG) by nationalizing it. The U.S. Government effectively nationalized General Motors and Chrysler the following year (2009) with an $80 billion bailout (Crotty, 2008).

By April 30, 2011, the U.S. Treasury, the Federal Reserve, and other federal agencies had made commitments of $12.2 trillion to assist the struggling financial and industrial system. These commitments included the expenditure of $1.6 trillion in direct investments in financial institutions, as well as the purchase of high-grade corporate debt and the purchase of mortgage-backed securities issued by Fannie Mae, Freddie Mac, and Ginnie Mae. The U.S. Government had spent $330 billion to insure debt issued by financial institutions and to guarantee poorly performing assets owned by private banks and by Fannie Mae and Freddie Mac. The U.S. Government became the lender of last resort for private banks and other financial institutions in the amount of $528 billion. As a consequence of the Troubled Asset Relief Program (TARP), the U.S. Treasury acquired stock in hundreds of banks, including two of the largest banks in the United States—Bank of America and Citibank—as well as in General Motors, Chrysler, and AIG. Fannie Mae and Freddie Mac were put into conservatorship by the U.S. Treasury ("Adding Up the Government's Total Bailout Tab," 2011). Moreover, similar scenarios were played out across Europe and many other countries around the world. At the same time, approximately 5 million homes in the United States had been lost to foreclosure by mid-2013 and millions of additional foreclosures were to follow (Global Research, 2013).

It is no longer possible to pretend that the state is in retreat as the global financial and economic crisis resulted in massive state interventions and, once again, despite the myth of neoliberalism, the state visibly reemerged as the main structural and institutional mechanism for restabilizing and reproducing the capitalist mode of production on a global scale, and primarily through the actions of nations-states, albeit led by and coordinated with the United States. Thus, as Martijn Konings (2010, 174) observes, "the period since the onset of the global financial crisis in 2007 has seen unprecedented public interventions into economic life. As a result, the role and presence of states has taken on a new degree of visibility. . . . If the state's presence and active role were impossible to miss, so was the fact that the benefits of its interventions were distributed in a highly unequal manner."

If the state is significant, then so must (or should) be state theory. Konings (2010, 174) reminds us that "the deployment of public authority in ways that systematically benefit some interests more than others suggests the need for a more profound appreciation of the ways in which socio-economic sources of power make themselves felt in the political arena. The insights of Marxist state theory therefore remain indispensable." For example, Spyros Sakellaropoulos and Panagiotis Sotiris (2015, 99) have analyzed the Greek debt crisis as another reminder that "the formation of the current international financial architecture was not a spontaneous process, and the same goes for the lowering of barriers to the free flow of products and capital and for the political decision to expose capitalist social formations to the competitive pressure of world markets and capitalist movements." Sakellaropoulos and Sotiris (2015, 98) reveal how the Greek debt crisis exemplifies the new "non-territorial imperialism" and demonstrate how "the tendency of capital to transcend national borders is not an unmediated, purely economic process," because "political power and bourgeois hegemony are necessary conditions for the reproduction of capitalist social relations" and "the same goes for the internationalization of capital: some form of political intervention (and ideological legitimization) is necessary for it." However, as David A. Kotz (2009, 307) has also recently observed: "when a particular form of capitalism enters its crisis phase, this eventually gives rise either to a new form of capitalism or to a transition beyond capitalism. This suggests we can expect to see more changes ahead than just a bailout of the financial system and a big government stimulus program. If a restructuring of capitalism rather than its replacement lies ahead, history suggests that we will see the emergence of a more state-regulated form of capitalism in the United States" and elsewhere.

State Theory Beyond the Poulantzas-Miliband Debate

However, even if we must return to state theory to understand the post-2007 world, what is to be gained by a return to Miliband and Poulantzas, particularly when they both published their major works on state theory well before globalization became a major topic in the social sciences. Miliband (1989, 167) did not specifically articulate a concept of globalization, even in his later works, but by the end of his life, he did increasingly recognize that "the international dimension of class struggle has assumed extraordinary, unprecedented importance."[4] Miliband (1989, 171) suggested that international class relations in the post–World War II era had been shaped by a consensus among national power elites that they collectively had "to ensure by all possible means that the radicalism produced or enhanced by the war should be strictly contained, and prevented from bringing about revolutionary change anywhere in the world." In the post–World War II era before globalization, this meant that the Soviet Union and China had to be contained within their existing boundaries and that "third world" revolutions had to be prevented or suppressed through inducements (e.g., development aid and government loans) and coercion (e.g., support for authoritarian governments or direct military intervention). Moreover, this class-political strategy required the acceptance of American leadership by the power elites of other major capitalist nations, despite occasional disputes among them, because only the United States' immense military and economic power could underwrite and guarantee the dominance of capitalist classes throughout most of the world.[5] This claim remains a basic thesis of the new "non-territorial" concept of imperialism being advanced in state theory today.

Poulantzas also did not use the term *globalization,* but he was acutely aware of the "internationalization of capital" and he viewed this change in the geography of capitalism as one requiring a new state form. Poulantzas argued that nation-states were not "retreating," but restructuring their state apparatuses and realigning those apparatuses with the newly dominant fractions of internationalized capital. However, as Michel Aglietta observed at the time, it is necessary to undertake new "Milibandian analyses" to understand this process of state reconstruction in the various nation-states and to identify the contours of the new state form. Indeed, much of the best work being undertaken at the present time on the new state form is explicitly and directly indebted to the works of Miliband (e.g., Panitch and Gindin, 2012) and Poulantzas (e.g., Jessop, 2002a).

Moreover, Poulantzas did offer some prescient and significant observations in his later work that provide a foundation for the further empirical and theoretical development of state theory. As I document in Chapters 5 and 6, Poulantzas argues that one of the major shifts within the state apparatus is the growing dominance of a new state economic apparatus. This apparatus certainly includes central banks, treasuries, and trade offices, which coordinate their activities and are generally linked to supra-national entities, including the WTO, EU, NAFTA, IMF, but also directly to transnational capitalists (e.g., transnational corporations and global investment banks). However, the state economic apparatus is not merely confined to these obvious organs of power, but it has also entailed a realignment of the ideological state apparatus to economic needs by incorporating "education" into workforce development, job training, and technology transfer and thereby jettisoning what Claus Offe calls "decommodification policies." Similarly, social welfare and health-care expenditures have been increasingly linked to "workfare" and used as prods to shunt the surplus population into low-wage sectors. Social welfare entitlements have been replaced by more and more direct corporate subsidies in the form of workforce training funds, local tax abatements, investment tax credits, infrastructure and building subsidies, and ready-to-go industrial parks, which actually make capital more mobile by freeing it of any special physical constraints or the anchors of sunk capital. In a word, as the economic crisis of capitalism is displaced into a fiscal crisis of the state, there has been a shift from social expenditures to social investment as education, social welfare, and health care become *economic* policies valued only for their return on social investment (O'Connor, 1978). Thus, what were once counter-hegemonic arenas of decommodification are subsumed into support mechanisms for the "free" market.

What Next?

One of the last works published by Nicos Poulantzas (2008, 403–411) was a short essay entitled "Research Note on the State and Society," where he sought to "point out the essential problems and outline the themes" that "should guide research on the state and society in the world today." Poulantzas (2008, 405) called for a return to the state (or to continue with the state), but with the understanding that capitalist states were in a process of transition to a new state form. Consequently, Poulantzas (2008, 405) suggested that it was necessary "to clear the theoretical terrain" by identifying "a series of *common theoretical issues* with which all disciplines and schools of thought are faced in analyzing the state, even if they differ as to the solutions they propose."

The first common theoretical issue was to define and designate the subject and scope of the state (Poulantzas, 405). The mere definition of the state was again a problem because the state was not actually in retreat as many globalization theorists would claim, but instead the state apparatus and state power were actually being extended beyond "the state composed of government machinery under formal state control" to include institutions, which in terms of their form are legally private. The boundaries of the state were shifting and this required a reassessment of the basic concept as proposed in Chapter 6 of this book (i.e., denationalization, internationalization, and destatization).

In conducting this reassessment of the concept of the state, Poulantzas (2008, 409) succinctly reiterates the argument made in *Classes in Contemporary Capitalism* that "the nation-state is the core, and the kingpin of domination" (409) even though it is undergoing changes in its structural form as a result of the internationalization of capital. However, Poulantzas already recognized that in many parts of the world, the internationalization of capital is rupturing "the 'national unity' imposed by various states and a resurgence of a variety of national entities hitherto kept down by the dominant nation-states" is resulting in "the revival of national minority struggles the world over" and this is leading to a further proliferation of nations, states, and nation-states.

Second, Poulantzas (2008, 405) argues that "the connection between the economico-social sphere and the political-state sphere" is being rearticulated in terms of the form and extent of state intervention in the economy and civil society. Poulantzas (2008, 409) observes that capitalist societies are "undergoing such profound changes as to make it possible to speak of a new state form different qualitatively from any they have had in the past" and he calls this state form *authoritarian statism*. Authoritarian statism is defined by increasing state interventions in the economy, but Poulantzas predicts that the burgeoning "economic planning machinery of the state" will become a machinery for deeper and more pronounced state controls over social life.

In particular, Poulantzas (2008, 410) predicts that a crisis of the ideological hegemony of the ruling classes is being managed by shifting the process of consensus-building "away from ideological apparatuses such as schools and universities [which are now being reconstructed as part of the economic apparatus] towards the media" and, in this respect, Poulantzas moves closer to Miliband on the question of the ideological apparatuses and the legitimation process. The significance of this shift in the form of the ideological and legitimation processes is that 1,200 channels of cable television, religion, and talk radio all penetrate much deeper into "private space" than the public sphere of formal schooling. Thus, Poulantzas (2008, 410) concludes that new forms of social control are defined by "a decisive 'de-institutionalization' of the ideologico-repressive machinery" toward institutions and ideological processes "intended to isolate those who are thought to be 'abnormal', deviant, or dangerous' and extending this policy to the entire society." In a nod to Foucault, Poulantzas argues that the ideological processes of domination are being accelerated by "the technology of surveillance," and by "computerization and electronics," which invite the hegemonic classes into our last sanctuaries.

Third, Poulantzas (2008, 405) suggests that it is again necessary to reassess the "the state and forms or organization of hegemony" by reexamining the relations between the ruling classes and the institutional framework of the state. Poulantzas was clearly moving toward the conclusion that the state was becoming "an isolated impregnable fortress" accessible only to the highest levels of internationalized capital and, consequently, it was less and less a "field of manoeuvre within which power relations between classes are condensed" or an arena where the struggles of the people permeate the state. In this respect, Poulantzas (2008, 410) observes "a marked shift in the organizing role of the state away from political parties towards state bureaucracy and administration, and the overall decline of the representative role of political parties," but Poulantzas insists that "this is a subject which goes much further than the relatively old phenomenon of dwindling parliamentary prerogatives and a more powerful executive" elaborated earlier by Miliband. Instead, the new state form also involves a "significant massive shift in hegemony towards powerful monopolistic capital and the restructuring of the repressive machinery of state" (410). While Poulantzas (2008, 410–411) recognizes that the repressive apparatuses (i.e., military, police, administration, courts) are being strengthened as "formal overt networks" of repression, an equally important political development is that these apparatuses are becoming "tightly sealed nuclei controlled closely by the highest executive authorities," while there is a "constant transfer of real power from the former to the latter, entailing the spread of the principle of secrecy." Yet, even as the official repressive apparatuses tend toward secrecy, state elites increasingly deploy "a whole system of unofficial state networks operating concurrently with the official ones (para-state machinery) with no possible check by the representatives of the people" (e.g., special forces, intelligence agencies, private security contractors). On the other hand, Poulantzas (2008, 411) suggests that new sites of political struggle will emerge as the old forms of representative democracy recede in the wake of authoritarian statism. As the state becomes an "isolated fortress" the focus on representation, political parties, and juridical civil liberties is giving way to "new claims for self-management or direct democracy in the world today" (Poulantzas, 2008, 411; Ranciere, 2011).

While Poulantzas' observations provide valuable insights for articulating the emerging formal structure of the state in global capitalism, a state form is not a theory of the state, but what Poulantzas calls an *abstract-formal object*. A theory of the state identifies and describes the crisis that precipitated the necessity of a transition from one state form to another and explains how the new state form functions to extend the reproduction of capitalist relations of production. It explains the historical origins and development of a state form (i.e., type of state), but "form analysis" as such does not provide such a theory (Barrow, 1993, 63–66). Theories of the state in global capitalism must be articulated at the level of particular theories, especially in the era of global capitalism, where there are a multitude of states. A particular state form will not necessarily emerge simultaneously in capitalist social formations at exactly the same time or in the same way (although there may be some synchronicity), nor will they develop at the same rate of time or perform the same functions through exactly the same institutions. The dependency principle and the golden chain of public debt may function similarly, but these structural mechanisms will also function differently in different social formations (i.e., public debt is not the same in the United States as in Greece). These details can only be elaborated at the level of individual social formations—a Milibandian analysis—which may consist of individual nations, subnational regions, or international regions (e.g., ASEAN, NAFTA, EU) and it is at this level of pragmatic operationalization that the methodological and epistemological issues debated by Poulantzas and Miliband recede into the background.

However, in 1980, when Poulantzas (2008, 409) published his "Research Note on the State and Society," he was already aware of the fact that scholarly interest in state theory was declining despite the "growing economic functions of the state, which are plainly to be seen in the vastly increased state intervention in all spheres of social life." In a passage strongly reminiscent of Ralph Miliband's critique of bourgeois ideology, Poulantzas (2008, 409–410) observes that despite the increased economic role of states in establishing the political and material conditions for the internationalization of capital, the "dominant Anglo-Saxon tradition in the social sciences . . . from functionalism to systemism" was reestablishing its hegemony in the United States and even extending its reach to scholars in European, Asian, and Latin American universities. Of course, as Miliband had pointed out in 1969, one of the most obvious shortcomings of this social science "has been a neglect of the peculiar role and specific character of the 'state' which has been absorbed into a very broad concept of the 'political system' and into one of dividing up power into a multitude of 'power pluralisms' and micro-powers." Western social science was again plunging into the abyss of an intellectual crisis, because it continued to neglect the state—the most prominent feature of the contemporary global political and economic landscape. Thus, what is at stake intellectually in the state debate is the future of the illusion called the American science of politics (Crick, 1959).

NOTES

Preface

1. A collection of papers from the conference was published by Aronowitz and Bratsis (2002). Of the eleven papers published from this conference eight are clearly inspired by a Poulantzasian perspective.
2. The "How Class Works Conference" was held at the State University of New York at Stony Brook (June 10–12, 2004). The Annual Conference of the Political Studies Association was held at Leeds, U.K., April 5–7, 2005. The 3rd Annual Historical Materialism Conference on "New Directions in Marxist Theory" was held at the School of Oriental & African Studies, University of London, London, England, December 8–10, 2006.
3. More recently, Jessop (2008b, 32) has argued (correctly in this author's view) that "Poulantzas seriously misrepresented his own position in round one" of the debate, which was already moving toward (what Jessop calls) a relational analysis of the state.
4. Likewise, Martin (2008, 15), concurs that "the weakening of an overt structuralist presence in Poulantzas' work, his effort to capture the variations in the forms of state by reference to changing relations of production and class

struggle, and the conceptualization of the state as a relation whose form was inseparable from the political and ideological dimensions of struggle, these were all hallmarks of the 'mature' theory."

5. See, www.poulantzas-lesen.de/ and http://poulantzas-lesen.de/wp/?page_id=37
6. The best practical effort in this direction is the outstanding opus by Panitch and Gindin (2012).

Chapter 1. Marxism and the Critique of Bourgeois Social Science

1. Gerstenberger (1992, 151) concurs that "state analysis has not loomed large in the traditions of Marxist theory. There seemed to be no need for it, as long as the political experience of socialists could be summed up in the description of the state as an instrument of oppression in the hands of the ruling class(es)."
2. In Roettger's (1978) study, Miliband's name appears among an aggregated group of influential "left radicals," which includes Ira Katznelson, Herbert Marcuse, C. Wright Mills, James O'Connor, and Bertell Ollman. However, members of this group were mentioned by only 5% of the political scientists surveyed for the study. Thus, Roettger (1978, 8) concludes that "their inclusion, paradoxically, testifies to the general disaffection with the Left which characterizes American political science. Despite their prominence in the larger society, the individual members of the Left Radicals have made only a minor impression on the vast majority of the members of the APSA." Cf. Kadushin (1972), where "Left Radicals" enjoy much greater prominence in the larger "intellectual community."
3. For historical background, see, Singer (1970) and Touraine (1971).
4. Similarly, Martin (2008, 1) describes Poulantzas as "one of the leading Marxist theorists of the late twentieth century."

5. For example, Alford and Friedland (1985, 278) conclude that Poulantzas criticized Miliband "quite appropriately" for employing an "un-Marxist epistemology." Similarly, Wright (1978, 12–13) argues that "one of the central epistemological premises of Marxist theory is the distinction between the 'level of appearances' and the underlying social reality which produces those appearances. . . . Marxists, then, have generally stressed the importance of elaborating a theory of the underlying structures of social relations, of the contradictions embedded in those structures, of the ways in which those underlying structures generate the appearances which people encounter in everyday life."
6. Biographical information on Ralph Miliband is from Blackburn (1994); Piven (1994); Panitch (1994); Kovel (1994).
7. Harold Laski had taught government at Harvard University until 1920, where he was accused by local officials of being a "Red" for supporting the Boston police strike in 1919. In fact, Laski was critical of both American democracy and Soviet Communism, although like many Anglo-American "new liberals" of the time, his intellectual development traversed a long path from pluralism to socialism. By the 1930s, Laski had embraced an unorthodox (i.e., non-Soviet) version of Western Marxism. He was a highly influential member of the British Labour Party's National Executive Committee from 1937 to 1949 and was elected chairman of the party in 1945–1946.
8. Morris Hillquit (1869–1933) was a founder and political leader of the Socialist Party of America. During his own lifetime, Hillquit was often called "the American Kautsky," because he was one of the Socialist Party's most prominent and influential "American" political theorists (see, Hillquit 1909, 1910).
9. For example, see Poulantzas (2008), Chaps. 1–3.
10. Miliband's footnotes and other references draw on a fascinating and diverse array of radical scholars for theoretical insight, including C. Wright Mills, Murray Edelman,

Andrew Schonfield, P.K. Crosser, Barrington Moore, Gabriel Kolko, Paul Baran, Harry Magdoff, and Ernest Mandel.

11. Parsons (1951, 75, 126–127) states that political science "is concerned with the power relations within the institutional system and with a broader aspect of settlement of terms. . . . Neither power in the political sense nor the operation of government as a sub-system of the social system can be treated in terms of a specifically specialized conceptual scheme . . . precisely for the reason that the political problem of the social system is a focus for the integration of all of its analytically distinguishable components, not of a specifically differentiated class of these components. Political science thus tends to be a synthetic science, not one built about an analytical theory as is the case with economics."
12. Italics added by this author.
13. The National Advisory Commission on Civil Disorders was generally known as the "Kerner Commission" after its Chairman, Illinois Governor Otto Kerner.
14. Abercrombie, Turner, and Urry (1976, 512, 517) were among the first to explicitly recognize that Poulantzas' "similarities with conventional functionalist arguments as found in sociology and political science" meant one could read *Political Power and Social Classes* as "a sort of Marxist equivalent of Talcott Parsons' *The Social System*."
15. For example, Merton (1957, 25–36, 51) postulates "the functional unity of society," although he acknowledges that dysfunctional and nonfunctional elements may appear in a social system until it adapts to or eliminates those disturbances. Interestingly, Merton (1957, 39) specifically addresses the question of "functionalism as ideology" and concludes that because "functional analysis can be seen by some as inherently conservative and by others as inherently radical suggests that it may be *inherently* neither one nor the other."
16. Hay (2006, 78) argues insightfully that "the dualism of structure and agency (of which the structuralism-

instrumentalism battle is merely a reflection) is not only a problem within Marxism but has characterized social and political science since its inception." See, also Giddens (1984).

17. Piven (1994, 25) recounts that "a mutual friend told me not long ago that Ralph had been deeply moved as a young man by the *Communist Manifesto*." Similarly, Blackburn (1994, 22) observes that Miliband was deeply moved by the fact that "the young socialist militant who first lent him a copy of the *Communist Manifesto*" perished in a Nazi extermination camp.
18. Miliband (1977, 2) argues "none of the greatest figures of classical Marxism, with the partial exception of Gramsci, ever attempted or for that matter felt the need to attempt the writing of a 'political treatise'." Elsewhere, Miliband (1970a, 309), argues that "*The State and Revolution* is rightly regarded as one of Lenin's most important works. . . . In short, here, for intrinsic and circumstantial reasons, is indeed one of the 'sacred texts' of Marxist thought."
19. The best examples are Balibar in Althusser and Balibar (1977, 199–308); Hindess and Hirst (1977); Amin (1976, 13–26); Hindess and Hirst (1975, 1–12).
20. Strauss (1959, 56–77) draws a sharp distinction between the disciplines of "history" and "political philosophy," but the idea that political philosophy is concerned with reasoning about concepts in a timeless present is clearly not limited by the requirement that one accept a particular set of texts as the basis of one's interpretive canon. Also see, Strauss and Cropsey (1963).
21. Rancière contributed a chapter to *Reading Capital,* although his contribution was left out of the English translation by New Left Books (1970) that became the standard source on Althusser for Anglo-American scholars (see, Arditi, 2006, 183). Ranciere (1970, 2011) distanced himself from Althusser shortly after the May 1968 rebellion because, in Ranciere's view, Althusser's political theory did not allow for spontaneous uprisings of the sort that swept the world in 1968.

Chapter 2. The Poulantzas-Miliband Debate

1. Louis Althusser and Etienne Balibar, *Reading Capital* was published in English in 1970. Louis Althusser, *Lenin and Philosophy,* which includes Althusser's famous essay on ideological state apparatuses was published in English in 1971, while Nicos Poulantzas' *Social Classes and Political Power* was released in English in 1973. It is probably significant to Anglo-American interpretations of Poulantzas' work at the time that scholars had access to Althusser's work *before* most of them could read Poulantzas directly.
2. Note the similarity between Miliband's formulation and Sweezy (1942, 243), who asserts the state is "an instrument in the hands of the ruling class for enforcing and guaranteeing the stability of the class structure itself."
3. Likewise, see the excellent summary of this literature by Useem (1984, 29–33).
4. More recently, the Occupy Wall Street movement's effort to focus public attention on "the 1%" is a practical effort to make the public aware of this simple but unrecognized fact.
5. In contrast, Dahl (1958, 465) argues that "neither logically nor empirically does it follow that a group with a high degree of influence over one scope will necessarily have a high degree of influence over another scope within the same system."
6. Italics added by this author.
7. In the same passage, Miliband (1969, 59) notes that capitalists "have never constituted, and do not constitute now, more than a relatively small minority of the state elite as a whole."
8. The passage cited is Kautsky (1910, 29). Miliband cites this passage nearly a decade prior to the widely acclaimed article by Block (1977), which claimed "The Ruling Class Does Not Rule."
9. For other evidence, see Zweigenhaft (1975); Freitag (1975); Riddlesperger Jr. and King (1989). For historical data on the U.S. spanning nearly a century, see, Mintz (1975).
10. Importantly, Miliband (1969, 47) notes: "This does not

mean that they [capitalists] have always known how best to safeguard their interests—classes, like individuals, make mistakes—though their record from this point of view, at least in advanced capitalist countries, is not, demonstrably, particularly bad."

11. It is here that the work of the "new institutionalists," particularly Skowronek (1982) provides useful insights on how states administrative capacities are built into cohesive institutional networks with concentrated and centralized state power. See also, Barrow (1993, 130–136).
12. Miliband (1983, 12) elsewhere points to this distinction by noting that the concept of the state "refers to certain people who are in charge of the executive power of the state—presidents, prime ministers, their cabinets, and their top civilian and military advisers."
13. Miliband (1969, 78) observes that state elites "have often been forced, mainly as a result of popular pressure, to take action against *certain* property rights and capitalist prerogatives."
14. Poulantzas (1969, 67). Miliband (1970b, 55) observed early in the debate that a translation of Poulantzas' book "into English is urgently needed."
15. Balibar in Althusser and Balibar (1977, 201) claim that "the concept of the 'mode of production' and the concepts immediately related to it thus appear as the first abstract concepts whose validity is not as such limited to a given period or type of society, but on which, on the contrary, the concrete knowledge of this period and type depends." See also, also, Clarke (1977).
16. See, Balibar in Althusser and Balibar (1977, 199–308).
17. See also, respectively, Wright (1978) and Amin (1976).
18. Likewise, Poulantzas (1978a, 68, fn. 16): "Classes always denote class *practices, and these practices are not structures.*"
19. Marx (1906, 15) observes that "individuals are dealt with only insofar as they are the personifications of economic categories, embodiments of particular class relations and class interests." It is also difficult in retrospect to understand how Poulantzas thinks this differs fundamentally from Miliband's position.

20. The point here is that Poulantzas was already struggling with the adequacy of structuralist terminology, as well as the limitations of Althusserian epistemology and its consequent reading of the Marxist classics. As a result, Poulantzas is constantly qualifying this reading and softening its impact on his analysis, while struggling to distance himself from Miliband by mislabeling the latter's work as historicist and voluntarist.
21. Poulantzas (1978a, 48) insists that "a good deal of guidance on these questions is found in the Marxist classics," but in practice he cites David Easton, Karl Deutsch, David Apter, Gabriel Almond and James S. Coleman.
22. Also, Poulantzas (1978a, 51) reiterates that "there is a global function of cohesion which is ascribed to it [the state] by its place" in the mode of production. Also see Bridges (1973).
23. Poulantzas (1978a, 53): "We must remember here the relation between the state (through the agency of the dominant class) and the general direction of the labour process, with particular reference to the productivity of labour."
24. Poulantzas, (1980, 28), insists that "the state's major contribution to reproducing the economic relations of a capitalist social formation is the effect of its policies on the reproduction of labor power and the means of labor."
25. Poulantzas, *Political Power and Social Classes,* pp. 50, 53.
26. For an example, see Mamut in Jessop (1990, 95–105) and Hirst (1979).
27. Poulantzas (1978a 115, fn. 24) defines an institution as "a system of norms or rules which is socially sanctioned. . . . On the other hand, the concept of structure covers the *organizing matrix* of institutions." However, on this point, Poulantzas also notes "that structure *is not the simple principle of organization which is exterior to* the institution: the structure is present in an allusive and inverted form in the institution itself."
28. Italics added by author. Cf. Wright (1978, 1 fn.) who notes that "the point of the distinction is to emphasize that there are structural mechanisms which generate immediately encountered reality, and that a Marxist social theory

should be grounded in a revelation of the dynamics of those structures, not simply in a generalization about the appearances themselves."

29. This assumes that the important conditions of capitalist accumulation are the productivity of labor, the security of private property, and an efficient system of exchange and contract as claimed by Poulantzas.
30. See also, Therborn (1978, 35, 151). Clark and Dear (1984, 45) agree that "generally speaking, the term 'state apparatus' refers to the set of institutions and organizations through which state power is exercised."
31. Jessop (1982, 221) echoes this view with his observation that "the state is a set of institutions that cannot, *qua* institutional ensemble, exercise power." Indeed, Jessop (1982, 224) argues that a key methodological guideline in formulating a Marxist theory of the state is a "firm rejection of all attempts to distinguish between 'state power' and 'class power' (whether as descriptive concepts or principles of explanation)."
32. Similarly, Therborn (1978, 132) contends that "the state as such has no power; it is an institution where social power is concentrated and exercised."
33. Poulantzas (1969, 69): ". . . the procedure chosen by Miliband—a *direct* reply to bourgeois ideologies by the immediate examination of concrete fact—is also to my mind the source of the faults of his book."
34. Indeed, Miliband would have considered the elaboration of an alternative theory of the state to be the *conclusion* of an empirical critique of bourgeois social science and not the starting point of an epistemological critique. Similarly, Wright (1978, 9), who was closely identified with the structuralist school in the United States found that: ". . . to the extent that the debate [between bourgeois and Marxist social science] raged simply at the level of theory, non-Marxists found it relatively easy to dismiss our challenges."
35. Poulantzas (1973, 47) again suggests that "the state is composed of *several apparatuses*: broadly, the *repressive* apparatus and the *ideological apparatus*, the principal role of the

former being repression, that of the latter being the elaboration and incubation of ideology. The ideological apparatuses include the churches, the educational system, the bourgeois and petty bourgeois political parties, the press, radio, television, publishing, etc. These apparatuses belong to the state system because of their objective function of elaborating and inculcating ideology."

36. For example, see, Hamm in Hamm and Smandych (2005, 18–30).
37. Similarly, Miliband (1965).
38. Miliband (1970b, 55) was willing to "readily grant that *The State in Capitalist Society* may be insufficiently 'theoretical' in the sense in which Poulantzas means it; but I also tend to think that his own approach, as suggested in his review and in his otherwise important book, *Pouvoir Politique et Classes Sociale* . . . errs in the opposite direction."
39. Similarly, Abercrombie, Turner, and Urry (1976, 513) refer to Poulantzas' methodological approach "as a form of omnipotent structuralism."
40. Miliband (1977) later returned to this theme by offering a close reading of Marx's writings in *Marxism and Politics.*
41. Ibid., p. 76.
42. More specifically, Poulantzas was rejecting an effort by Ernesto Laclau (1975) to mediate the debate.

Chapter 3. Plain Marxists and Sophisticated Marxists

1. Mills (1956, 343) asserts that the American public's "general acceptance" of the power elite's higher immorality "is an essential feature of the mass society."
2. Mills (1956, 9) observes that ". . . institutions are the necessary bases of power, of wealth, and of prestige, and at the same time, the chief means of exercising power, of acquiring and retaining wealth, and of cashing in the higher claims for prestige. By the powerful we mean, of course, those who are able to realize their will, even if others resist it." It is remarkable that Dahl's and Lukes' definitions of power were heralded as such important advances

in the concept of power when they offer nothing that is not already in the definition offered by Mills in *The Power Elite*. Even Bachrach's and Baratz's (1962, 1963) concept of "nondecisions" is already advanced in *The Power Elite*, where Mills (1956, 4) observes "Whether they [the power elite] do or do not make such decisions is less important than the fact that they do occupy such pivotal positions; their failure to act, their failure to make decisions, is itself an act that is often of greater consequence than the decisions they do make." Bachrach and Baratz do not even cite Mills' work.

3. I (2002a, 16–17) have pointed out elsewhere that Beard's 1945 edition of *The Economic Basis of Politics* "anticipates C. Wright Mills' *The Power Elite* (1956)," although Mills (1951, xx) dismissed Beard as "irrelevant."
4. In *The Power Elite*, Mills cites the work of only three economists: Thorstein Veblen, A.A. Berle, and John Kenneth Galbraith. Mills (1958, 8) was deeply influenced by Veblen, which he learned at the University of Texas from the institutional economist, Clarence E. Ayres, who was a Veblen disciple (Judis, 2001). However, in *The Power Elite*, Mills (1956, 58) rejects Veblen's work as "no longer an adequate account of the American system of prestige." He (1956, 125) later argues that "neither the search for a new equilibrium of countervailing power conducted by the economist John K. Galbraith, nor the search for a restraining corporate conscience, conducted by the legal theorist, A.A. Berle Jr., is convincing." Mills (1956, 272–273) also argues that the New Deal (Keynesianism) did not reverse the supremacy of corporate economic power, because in due course the corporate rich "did come to control and to use for their own purposes the New Deal institutions whose creation they had so bitterly denounced."
5. Mills (1948, 3): "Inside this country today, the labor leaders are the strategic actors: they lead the only organizations capable of stopping the main drifts towards war and slump." By the mid-1950s, Mills (1958, 37) was arguing that organized labor had been integrated into the middle-level of the American power structure: "labor remains

without political direction. Instead of economic and political struggles it has become deeply entangled in administrative routines with both corporation and state."

6. The same criticism was leveled by Rossi (1956). More recently, Alford and Friedland (1985, 199) correctly note that Mills' "theoretical ambiguity is linked to the lack of any theory of the societal contradictions of capitalism, despite his radical rhetoric and politics. Systemic power does not exist for Mills. Power is manifest in organizational form with elites commanding resources."
7. In fact, every major class movement develops a theory of exploitation to justify or criticize the existing social structure. For example, the American Physiocrats (i.e., early Jeffersonians) offered the theory that "agricultural interests" were exploited by "mercantile and manufacturing interests," who plundered value through the exchange process and protective tariffs (see Taylor, 1977, esp., 318–324). A modified version of this theory resurfaced during the farmers' revolt of the 1880s and 1890s. Southern slaveholders turned Marx on his head by constructing a theory of exploitation to simultaneously *justify* slavery and denounce Northern manufacturing interests, see Fitzhugh (1960, 21–51). The Social Darwinists also developed a theory of economic exploitation to justify inequality and free markets during the Gilded Age, see Sumner (1986). The institutional economists, who influenced New Deal labor policy offered an explanation of exploitation based on competition between rights in different degrees and types of "property"—land, capital, and labor, see Commons (1965).
8. Bottomore (1966, 34–35) states further that Mills "emphasized the unity of the elite, as well as the homogeneity of its social origins–all of which points to the consolidation of a ruling class. . . . he insists that the three principal elites—economic, political, and military—are, in fact, a cohesive group, and he supports his view by establishing the similarity of their social origins, the close personal and family relationships between those in the different elites, and the frequency of interchange of personnel between

the three spheres. But because he resists the conclusion that the group is a ruling class he is unable to provide a convincing explanation, as distinct from description, of the solidarity of the power elite."

9. For instance, Aptheker (1960, 33) argues that "despite Mills' three-point elite, his own work, in its descriptive passages, shows not only that the economic and political and military are inter-dependent but also that the economic is ultimately decisive and fundamentally controlling." Similarly, Alford and Friedland (1985, 199) identify this problem as "a crucial theoretical ambiguity in Mills, because, on the one hand, he defines the power elite as separate hierarchies . . . and, on the other hand, he shows the close relations among the three hierarchies: the interchange of personnel, borrowings of status, social contacts, intermarriages, and commons sources of recruitment." Also, see, Highsaw (1957, 145); Parsons (1957, 126); Reissman (1956, 513); Rogow (1956, 614); Rossi (1956).
10. Mills (1956, 7) states merely that "the economy . . . has become dominated by two or three hundred giant corporations, administratively and politically interrelated, which together hold the keys to economic decisions." However, Aptheker's criticism ignores the fact that Mills does draw an important structural and ideological distinction between "sophisticated conservatives" (i.e., corporate liberals) and "practical conservatives" (i.e., ultraconservatives).
11. Paul Sweezy's contribution to this report is entitled, "Interest Groups in the American Economy." It is included as Appendix 13 to Part I of Means (1939) and provides the empirical foundation for much of the report's analysis of the U.S. economy. This appendix was republished in Sweezy (1953, Chap. 12).
12. The TNEC was established as a joint Congressional-Executive branch committee, composed of members of both houses of Congress and representatives of several executive departments and commissions, by joint resolution of Congress, on June 16, 1938. Its purpose was to study monopolies and the concentration of economic power

and to make recommendations for remedial legislation. Sweezy also conducted research for the TNEC (see Foster, 2004).

13. Mills (1951, 37, 103, 127) was at least aware of the TNEC report, because he makes three brief and unimportant references to it in *White Collar* (1951). However, it is never mentioned in *The Power Elite* and does not appear to have influenced him theoretically except to recognize that the "big corporation" had replaced "the little man" as a foundation of the American economy.
14. Mills (1962, 96) defines Vulgar Marxists as those "who seize upon certain ideological features of Marx's political philosophy and identify these parts as the whole." For the most part, Marxists have identified Vulgar Marxism with "economic reductionism," that is, the explanation of all social phenomena in terms of economic *motives*, see Seligman (1924, 25).
15. The 1960s and 1970s structuralists, as represented by Louis Althusser, Etienne Balibar, Nicos Poulantzas, Goran Therborn, and others would seem to exemplify what Mills called Sophisticated Marxism.
16. This distinction seems quite similar to Poulantzas' (1978a, 16–22) differentiation between a regional theory of the capitalist state and particular theories of states in capitalist societies.
17. Mills (1962, 97) observes that "sophisticated marxists generally are committed to current marxist practice on political as well as intellectual grounds." Another defining characteristic is that "even when Marx's terminology is obviously ambiguous and plainly inadequate they are often reluctant to abandon it" (ibid., 98).
18. Schneider (1968, 13) states that "Mills explicitly labeled himself a 'plain Marxist'." Zeitlin (1977, 238 fn. 3) also claims that Mills listed himself among the plain marxists. Mills (1962, 98) does not quite make such an explicit statement, but instead says "it [plain marxism] is . . . the point of view taken in the present essay" (i.e., in *The Marxists*). Miliband (1964, 77) is more circumspect in suggesting that "one feature of Mills' political commitment, which

immediately invites attention is that it is very difficult to give it an obviously appropriate name. . . . He obviously belongs on the left, but his particular place there is not easily determined."

19. Poulantzas (1978a, 329) later reiterates this same claim in slightly different language: ". . . this [power elite] school attempts to discover *parallel* sources of political power, considering the economic itself as one source of power and the state as another. The elites, including the bureaucracy, though they are reduced to their relations to these various sources, are nonetheless unified, according to Wright Mills, by the fact that the 'heads of economic corporations', the 'political leaders' (including the heights of the bureaucracy) and the 'military leaders', that is to say all the elites belong to what he calls the 'corporate rich'. In this case, this conception, which wanted to supersede so-called Marxist economic determinism and examine the autonomous functioning of the bureaucracy, appears to reduce the problem to an economic over-determinism. The political functioning of the state apparatus is absorbed into the fact that its members, along with other elites, belong to the unifying centre of the high income group."
20. Elsewhere, I have documented the influence of Talcott Parsons and other structural-functionalists on Poulantzas theory of the state (Barrow, 2002b).

Chapter 4. The Analytic (Mis)Construction of Instrumentalism

1. Block (1977, p. 6, 28 fn. 1) cites Gold, Lo, and Wright (1975a, 1975b) in the first sentence of his article and specifically thanks Clarence Y.H. Lo for his "help on this article."
2. King (1986, 77) observes that in Poulantzas' formulation "state bureaucrats are constrained to act on behalf of capital because of the logic of the capitalist system, irrespective of their personal beliefs or affiliations."
3. Likewise, Poulantzas (1969, 75) insists that: ". . . the State apparatus forms an objective system of special 'branches'

whose relation presents a specific internal unity and obeys, to a large extent, its own logic."

4. See also, Jessop (1982, 22), where he states for Miliband "it is the activities of the people who occupy the leading positions in these institutions and thus constitute the 'state elite' that are said to determine the class nature of state power."
5. This line of argument is taken directly from Domhoff (1990, 190–194).
6. Luger does not undertake an extensive conceptual analysis of Miliband's work, but his book calls attention to the fact that some scholars were starting to recognize that Miliband was a far more sophisticated thinker than he was given credit for in the 1970s and 1980s.
7. Poulantzas (1973, 47) elsewhere claims that "the state is composed of several apparatuses: broadly, the repressive apparatus and the ideological apparatus, the principal role of the former being repression, that of the latter being the elaboration and incubation of ideology. The ideological apparatuses include the churches, the educational system, the bourgeois and petty bourgeois political parties, the press, radio, television, publishing, etc. These apparatuses belong to the state system because of their objective function of elaborating and inculcating ideology."
8. More recently, see Schiller (1989).

Chapter 5. The Poulantzas-Althusser Debate

1. Similarly, Hall (2000, vii) identifies Poulantzas as part of "the core of the 'Althusser' group along with Etienne Balibar and others."
2. This claim is based on Poulantzas' (1969, 73) polemical assertion that ". . . the *direct* participation of members of the capitalist class in the State apparatus and in the government, even where it exists, is not the important side of the matter. The relation between the bourgeois class and the State is an *objective relation*. This means that if the *function* of the state in a determinate social formation and the

interests of the dominant class in this formation coincide, it is by reason of the system itself: the direct participation of members of the ruling class in the state apparatus is not the *cause* but the *effect*, and moreover a chance and contingent one, of this objective coincidence."

3. See also, Thomas (1994).
4. Balibar in Balibar and Althusser (1977, 199–308); Therborn (1976); Amin (1976, 13–26); Hindess and Hirst (1975, 1–12); Hindess and Hirst (1977); Wright (1978). The proposed close reading of the structuralists will be left for another time, because the present chapter focuses on the development of Poulantzas' explicit understanding of his differences with the other structuralists, which in substance correspond to these three categories.
5. In this vein, Poulantzas warrants only one minor bibliographical entry, and no entry in the index, in Lewis' (2005) recent book on *Louis Althusser and the Traditions of French Marxism*. Poulantzas also does not figure prominently in Elliott's (2009, 191) book on *Althusser*, except for the passing comment that the young Poulantzas "exchanged Sartrean for Althusserian loyalties."
6. Significantly, even Hall (2000, viii), who describes the Poulantzas of *Political Power and Social Classes* as an "Althusserian," simultaneously recognizes that the class struggle component of this work "was already a sort of correction for the hyper-structuralism of *Reading Capital* and the integral functionalism of some aspects of 'Ideological State Apparatuses.'"
7. Jessop (2008b, 120) has also recently argued that in *State, Power, Socialism*, Poulantzas was concerned with "changes in contemporary capitalism and the rise of a new form of capitalist state." Jessop (2008b, 120) recognizes that although this book presents "some basic theoretical guidelines and arguments," for the first time it is still the case that "many are found in his earlier work."
8. In Barrow (1993, 9–12 and Chap. 6), I argue that political theories have an analytic and a methodological dimension. The analytic dimension of a political theory consists of the key concepts that select, name, and logically interrelate a

specified range of phenomena; in this instance, a range of phenomena identified as "the state." The central problem at the analytic level of state theory is to define what range of phenomena are encompassed by a concept of the state. However, in selecting and interrelating phenomena, political theories simultaneously put forward specific claims about how various events and phenomena are related to one another. Hence, political theories must also advance a methodological position that enables scholars to specify what kinds of research and evidence are necessary to test those hypothetical claims and to provide rules about what counts as an adequate explanation of the state. Competing theoretical approaches to the state emerge from the various ways in which these two dimensions—analytic and methodological—are linked together by different theorists. The point of this argument is that Poulantzas did *not* anchor the basic concepts of state theory in *Althusserian* structuralism, but in a type of historical structuralism that is fundamentally compatible with Miliband's empirical analysis.

9. For example, in Oxford's recent *Dictionary of Critical Theory* (Buchanan, 2010, 381), Poulantzas warrants a short entry, primarily for his debate with Miliband, but Miliband does not receive a comparable entry.
10. Benton's (1984, 141) analysis of structural Marxism draws a weak relationship between Poulantzas and Althusser with his observation that Poulantzas "employed broadly Althusserian ideas" in his theory of the state (i.e., the basic concepts of historical materialism), but he does not extend this relationship to the epistemological or methodological level. Poulantzas does even warrant a single mention in the index to Montag's *Althusser and His Contemporaries* (2013), which focuses exclusively on structuralist epistemology and method.
11. Balibar (2014, 146) has recently affirmed that "deep cleavages opened up between us [Althusser/Balibar and Poulantzas] during this period ['the 1960s and 1970s' (p. 145)]. They concerned both the critique of the Marxist and Leninist concept of the state and the analysis of

institutions or political forms in the framework of a new relation of forces just as the hegemonic state, that of the capitalist bourgeoisie, was shaken by the internationalization of capital (what we did not yet call globalization) and reacted to its declining economic efficacy by an authoritarian turn more or less accentuated and disguised by a liberal discourse." Cf. Jacques Ranciere, "On the Theory of Ideology," *Radical Philosophy* 7 (1974): 2–15, who challenges Althusser's theory of ideology for similar reasons.

12. The internalization of American capitalism within a "foreign" national social formation was symbolized in France amid media fanfare and cultural shock over the opening of the first McDonald's on the Champs-Élysées in 1972. There are now more than 1,200 McDonald's in France, including locations at the Louvre and Sorbonne, two on the Champs-Élysées, and several more across the French Riviera. France has the most McDonald's locations per capita in Europe and the fourth-highest rate per capita in the world (Wile, 2014). Similarly, Crothers (2010).
13. Althusser's essay on ideological state apparatuses was originally published in *La Pensee* in 1970.
14. Only later does Poulantzas (1980, 53), *State, Power, Socialism* inform us that it was the "peculiarities of the workers movement" in May of 1968 that taught Poulantzas "the lessons concerning the importance of the social division of labor in the constitution of classes." Since "changes in the State themselves refer above all to the struggles of social classes," the failure to thoroughly analyze the contemporary social division of labor was a "limitation" of his earlier book, even though he was "already following this line of research in *Political Power and Social Classes.*"
15. See, Balibar, "On the Basic Concepts of Historical Materialism," in Althusser and Balibar, (1977, 201–216, 225–253) for his discussion of "The Elements of the Structure and Their History." Balibar argues that the basic concepts of historical materialism are "the 'mode of production' and the concepts immediately related to it." The elements in this "system of forms" are the means of production, the laborer, the nonlaborer, the property relation, and the

relation of real appropriation. For Althusser and Balibar, the basic concepts of historical materialism are not historical generalizations or empirical inductions, but "abstract concepts whose validity is not as such limited to a given period or type of society."

16. Poulantzas (1980, 51–53) draws on these same arguments to dismiss the *Ableitung* or German derivationist approach to state theory. For background, see, Barrow (1993, Chap. 3); Altvater (1973a, 1973b); Holloway and Picciotto (1978).
17. See also, Therborn (1976, 353–385).
18. Balibar (2014, 147ff) observes that "I have long since conceded this point to Poulantzas, first of all for a reason he himself mentioned while implicitly giving the basis for his difference with Althusser: only such a conception allows us to put an end to the myth of the exteriority of revolutionary forces (parties or movements) in relation to the functioning of the state in advanced capitalism."
19. Likewise, Poulantzas (1980, 15) observes that "the basis of the material framework of power and the State has to be sought in the relations of production and social division of labour. . . . I do not refer to an economic structure from which classes, the class struggle and forms of power are absent." Hence, he (1980, 17) argues "the position of the State vis-à-vis the economy is never anything but the modality of the State's presence in the constitution and reproduction of the relations of production."
20. Poulantzas (1980, 167) further argues one concrete result of this strategy was that "a number of previously 'marginal' fields (training of labour-power, town-planning, transport, health, the environment, etc.) are directly integrated, in an expanded and modified form, into the very space-process of the reproduction and valorization of capital." Cf. Harvey (1982).
21. Poulantzas (2008, 409) makes the same point in a 1980 essay entitled "Research Note on the State and Society," where he comments on the "growing economic functions of the state, which are plainly to be seen in the vastly increased state intervention in all spheres of social life."

22. For example, Strange (1996); Ohmae (1990); Castells (1997), Vol. 2, 243, claims that "State control over space and time is increasingly bypassed by global flows of capital, goods, services, technology, communication, and information."
23. See, Barrow (1993, 58–63) for a summary.
24. Gerstenberger (1978) made a similar point in the context of the German state derivation debate. She later reiterated the same critique in response to other post-Poulantzasian forms of structuralism for example, regulation and social structure of accumulation theories (see, Gerstenberger, 1992).

Chapter 6. The Return of the State

1. For example, Henri-Levi (1977, 68) called for "a provisional politics, a small-scale program, which some of us think can only be precarious, uncertain, and circumstantial—in a word, a matter of feeling."
2. Mitchell (1991, 95) applies Foucault's approach to state theory to conclude that "focusing on the state as essentially a phenomenon of decision making or policy is inadequate," because the state is "an effect of detailed processes of spatial organization, temporal arrangement, functional specification, and supervision and surveillance, which create the appearance of a world fundamentally divided into state and society" and, consequently, "the state should not be taken as a free-standing entity, whether an agent, instrument, organization or structure, located apart from and opposed to another entity called society."
3. In the conclusion to my 1993 analysis of critical state theory, I (1993, 145) proposed that "we could well be witnessing the disintegration of the state as a form of institutionalized political authority, at least as it has heretofore been understood in the modern era."
4. Hardt and Negri (2000, xi) suggest that "along with the global market and global circuits of production has emerged a global order, a new logic and structure of

rule—in short, a new form of sovereignty. Empire is the political subject that effectively regulates these global exchanges, the sovereign power that governs the world." Castells (2004), Shaw (2000), Robinson and Harris (2000) argue for the existence of a new transnational state apparatus linked to a transnational capitalist class.

5. This stands in direct contrast to Hardt and Negri (2000, xiii–xiv) who argue that "*the United States does not, and indeed no nation-state can today, form the center of an imperialist project*. Imperialism is over." Likewise, Shaw (2000, 240) asserts that "the idea of American hegemony is too simple to characterize relations within the Western [transnational] state."
6. Aglietta's analysis of the Fordist mode of regulation starts from an explicitly Poulantzasian assumption. Cf. Poulantzas (1980, 17), who argues that "*the political field of the State* (as well as the sphere of ideology) *has always, in different forms, been present in the constitution and reproduction of the relations of production*," that is, that "the function of the state primarily concerns the economic level, and particularly the labour process, the productivity of labour" (Poulantzas 1978a, 52).
7. Likewise, Gill and Law (1988, 84), contend that "states are essential for economies, in that they provide the legal conditions for the establishment and maintenance of property rights, which are defined in private terms within capitalism. . . . In the modern world, these systems of property rights are further defined in the context of the widespread acceptance of national sovereignty and territorial jurisdiction." For example, see Marx (1977, Chap. 10) on "The Working Day," which revolves around state interventions in the wage-relation through Acts of Parliament. Similarly, see Cleaver (1979).
8. Destanne De Bernis (1990, 36) cautions that "our approach is not a complete theoretical system . . . we are extremely aware that a number of very important issues concerning the theory of regulation have not been yet sufficiently analyzed and studied. Among these issues is the building of a multi-stage theory of the role of the state."

9. For background see Brewer (1990); Arrighi (1978).
10. For a historical analysis, see Domhoff (1990, Chaps. 5–6, 8).
11. Wood (2003, 140) observes that "globalization has certainly been marked by a withdrawal of the state from its social welfare and ameliorative functions; and, for many observers, this has perhaps more than anything else created an impression of the state's decline." It has also led some scholars, such as Evans (1997) to arrive at the questionable conclusion that the Nordic states are "strong states" in the global economy, while the United States and Great Britain are "weak states" in the new order. Waddell (2001, 3–4) poignantly challenges the new institutionalists' and many globalization theorists' focus on domestic welfare policies, because it "leads to inadequate and misleading assessments of 'feeble' U.S. national capabilities compared with the welfare states of western Europe. U.S. national governance, after all, is not only defined by its welfare state but also by a powerful and encompassing national security 'warfare' state that rivals European welfare states in its commitment of societal resources."
12. On the globalist consensus, see Steger (2002). Paradoxically, the "pyramid of global constitution" described by Hardt and Negri (2000, 309–314) bears a striking resemblance to Cox's description on the one occasion where the former authors substitute empirical analysis for postmodernist jargon.
13. John Holloway, "Global Capital and the National State," *Capital and Class,* 23–49.
14. Panitch (1994, 72) argues that an important aspect of this realignment of the state apparatuses is that "ministries of labour, health, and welfare are perhaps not so much being subordinated as themselves being restructured" through a general process "determined more from within the state itself" than by direct linkages to international capital. Panitch speculates that even state agencies without direct international links "but which nevertheless directly facilitate capital accumulation and articulate a competitiveness ideology, are the ones that gain status, while those which fostered social welfare and articulated a class harmony

orientation lose status. Whether the loss of status is considerable, or even permanent, however, partly depends on the transformations which these latter agencies are today going through in terms of being made, or making themselves, more attuned to the exigencies of global competitiveness and fiscal restraint." For example, an interesting study would be to examine the shift *inside* the U.S. Department of Health and Human Services from an emphasis on entitlement welfare provision to workfare or the U.S. Department of Education's decreasing concern with equal opportunity and its increasing emphasis on "workforce training" and transferable (flexible) "competencies" and "workplace skills."

15. For example, Useem (1984); Edsall (1984); Piven and Cloward (1982); Peschek (1987).
16. For more detailed analysis, see Gearey (2005, Chap. 3) and Dezalay and Garth (2005). For an analysis of the form and functions of the early "accumulative state" see Wolfe (1977, Chap. 1).
17. Similarly, Gill (1992).
18. Other important reforms include the Automotive Decree of 1983, which was a first step toward the more important 1989 Automotive Decree that radically liberalized the automobile industry in Mexico, and the Pharmaceutical Decree of 1984. In 1987, Mexico strengthened intellectual property rights by revising the 1976 Invention and Trademark Law to increase patent protection from 10 to 14 years and increase penalties for patent infringements.
19. The MFN investment provisions are also included in NAFTA. According to Gestrin and Rugman (1996, 68): "One of the main reasons for having both MFN and national treatment coverage is to ensure that when one of the signatories holds a reservation against the national treatment provisions (in other words, the signatory in question reserves the right to discriminate in favour of domestic over foreign investors), investors from the other signatory parties are at least still guaranteed that they will receive the best possible treatment with the group of other foreign investors."

20. The archetypal illustration for constitutionalizing treaties is the supremacy clause (Article VI, paragraph 2) of the U.S. Constitution, which effectively incorporates such agreements into the U.S. Constitution such that they override federal, state, and local statutes: "This Constitution, and the Laws of the United States which shall be made in Pursuance thereof,; and all Treaties made, or which shall be made, under the Authority of the United States, shall be the supreme law of the land; and the judges in every State shall be bound thereby, any Thing in the Constitution or Laws of any State to the Contrary notwithstanding."
21. For historical analysis, see Domhoff (1990, 153–186).
22. Similar definitions are found in Miliband (1969, 54); Hall and Ikenberry (1989, 1–2; Poggi (1990, 19–33). Therefore, Block (2001) argues that a genuinely global state "would need to have an effective monopoly on the legitimate use of violence" to be considered a state of any kind.
23. See, Panitch and Gindin (2003, 81–91) for a review of indicators documenting the resurgence of U.S. economic strength and comparative advantage in the 1990s.
24. Gilpin (2001, 363) argues persuasively that "the nation-state continues to be the major actor in both domestic and international affairs . . . even though its role may have diminished somewhat, the nation-state remains preeminent in both domestic and international economic affairs." See also, Boyer and Drache (1996).
25. See, Larson (2009) on the origins and history of the nation-state and its transformation in the era of globalization.
26. Many critics of U.S. military power have pointed to China as a possible new counterweight to that power. However, Beckley (2011, 73–74) documents that despite an estimated 800% increase in Chinese military spending since 1989, its military spending has actually declined relative to U.S. military spending since 2001.
27. Rice (2000, 51) acknowledges that in the 1990s the United States' "already thinly stretched armed forces came close to a breaking point." Similarly, Lt. General James R. Helmly, who commanded the U.S. Army Reserve, complained to the U.S. Army Chief of Staff that his branch of

200,000 soldiers "is rapidly degenerating into a 'broken' force'" due to simultaneous commitments in Afghanistan and Iraq, see, Gorham (2005, A–1).

28. On the capitalist subsumption of social capital, see, Negri (1991, 105–125; 1989, 177–191).
29. A possible shortcoming in Jessop's (2002, 199) analysis of the triad is that it relies on the claim that "European and East Asian capitals have continued to catch up with American capital," which is a claim that is no longer factually correct, particularly with respect to Europe and Japan.

Chapter 7. The Return to State Theory

1. For example, Balibar (1977, 199–308); Therborn (1976); Amin (1976, 13–26); Hindess and Hirst (1975, 1–12); Hindess and Hirst (1977); Wright (1978).
2. The false dichotomy between agency and structure was actually surmounted rather quickly by Lukes (1974, 2005) with his "three dimensions of power" formulation.
3. This question surfaced during the Greek debt crisis as Yanis Varoufakis (2015), the former Greek Finance Minister observes: "A radical social theorist can challenge the economic mainstream in two ways. . . . One way is by means of immanent criticism. To accept the mainstream's axioms and then expose its internal contradictions. To say: 'I shall not contest your assumptions but here is why your own conclusions do not logically flow on from them'. This was, indeed, Marx's method of undermining British political economics. . . . The second avenue that a radical theorist can pursue is, of course, the construction of alternative theories to those of the establishment, hoping that they will be taken seriously. My view on this dilemma has always been that the powers that be are never perturbed by theories that embark from assumptions different to their own. The only thing that can destablise and genuinely challenge mainstream, neoclassical economists is the demonstration of the internal inconsistency of their own models."

4. Miliband (1989, 184) did note that "external economic and financial pressure—particularly on reforming governments—constitutes a permanent part of class struggle; and given the ever-greater integration of the world into a global economy, such pressure must be expected to be even greater in the future than in the past."
5. It may (or may not) be viewed as a limitation of Miliband's (1989, 182) class analysis that he considered the international dimension of class struggle as "for the most part *supplementary to internal class struggles.* It is usually in order to help indigenous conservative forces to repel challenge from below that intervention has occurred. Such intervention, in other words, must be seen as part of the class struggle from above which is waged by local dominant classes." In other words, he continued to see the nation-state, and particularly American hegemony, as central to understanding the international class struggle.

BIBLIOGRAPHY

Abercrombie, Nicholas, Bryan Turner, and John Urry. (1976). "Class, State and Fascism: The Work of Nicos Poulantzas." *Political Studies*, Vol. 24, No. 4 (December): 510–519.

"Adding Up the Government's Total Bailout Tab." (2011). *New York Times*, July 24. www.nytimes.com/interactive/2009/02/04/business/20090205-bailout-totals-graphic.html?_r=0

Aglietta, Michel. (1979). *A Theory of Capitalist Regulation: The US Experience*. London: Verso.

Alford, Robert R. and Roger Friedland. (1985). *Powers of Theory: Capitalism, the State, and Democracy*. Cambridge: Cambridge University Press.

Allender, Paul. (1996). "A 'New' Socialist Party?" *Capital and Class* 59 (Summer): 144–149.

Almond, Gabriel. (1988). "The Return to the State." *American Political Science Review* 82:853–874.

Almond, Gabriel, and James S. Coleman. (1960). *The Politics of Developing Areas*. Princeton: Princeton University Press.

Althusser, Louis. (1969). *For Marx*. New York: Pantheon Books.

Althusser, Louis. (1971). "Ideology and Ideological State Apparatuses: Notes Towards an Investigation." Pp. 127–186 in *Lenin and Philosophy and Other Essays*. New York: Monthly Review Press.

Althusser, Louis. (1993). *The Future Lasts Forever: A Memoir.* New York: New Press.

Althusser, Louis, and Etienne Balibar. (1977). *Reading Capital.* London: New Left Books.

Altvater, Elmer. (1973a). "Notes on Some Problems of State Interventionism (I)." *Kapitalistate* (1): 97–108.

Altvater, Elmer. (1973b). "Notes on Some Problems of State Interventionism (II)." *Kapitalistate* (2): 76–83.

Amin, Samir. (1976). *Unequal Development.* New York: Monthly Review Press.

Apter, David. (1958). "A Comparative Method for the Study of Politics." *American Journal of Sociology* 64 (November): 221–237.

Aptheker, Herbert. (1960). *The World of C. Wright Mills.* New York: Marzani and Munsell.

Arditi, Benjamin. (2006). "Louis Althusser." Pp. 182–195 in Terrell Carver and James Martin, eds., *Palgrave Advances in Continental Political Thought.* London: Palgrave Macmillan.

Aronowitz, Stanley. (2003). "A Mills Revival?" *Logos* (Summer): 67–93.

Aronowitz, Stanley, ed. (2004). *C. Wright Mills,* 3 vols. Thousand Oaks, CA: Sage.

Aronowitz, Stanley. (2012). *Taking It Big: C. Wright Mills and the Making of Political Intellectuals.* New York: Columbia University Press.

Aronowitz, Stanley, and Peter Bratsis, eds. (2002). *Paradigm Lost: Revising State Theory.* Minneapolis: University of Minnesota Press.

Aronowitz, Stanley, and Peter Bratsis, eds. (2002). "State Power, Global Power," Pp. xi–xxvii in Stanley Aronowitz and Peter Bratsis, eds., *Paradigm Lost: State Theory Reconsidered.* Minneapolis: University of Minnesota Press.

Arrighi, Giovanni. (1978). *The Geometry of Imperialism: The Limits of Hobson's Paradigm,* translated by Patrick Camiller. London: New Left Books.

Arrighi, Giovanni, Takeshi Mamashita, and Mark Selden, eds. (2003). *The Resurgence of East Asia.* London: Routledge.

Ashcraft, Richard. (1980). "Political Theory and the Problem of Ideology." *Journal of Politics* (August): 687–705.

Babb, Sarah. (2001). *Managing Mexico: Economists from Nationalism to Neoliberalism*. Princeton: Princeton University Press.

Bachrach, Peter, and Morton S. Baratz. (1962). "Two Faces of Power." *American Political Science Review*, Vol. 56, No. 4 (December): 947–952.

Bachrach, Peter, and Morton S. Baratz. (1963). "Decisions and Non-Decisions: An Analytical Framework." *American Political Science Review*, Vol. 57, No. 3 (September): 632–642.

Balbus, Isaac. (1971). "Modern Capitalism and the State: Ruling Elite Theory vs. Marxist Class Analysis." *Monthly Review*, Vol. 23, No. 1 (May): 36–46.

Balibar, Etienne. (1977). "The Basic Concepts of Historical Materialism." Pp. 199–308 in Louis Althusser and Etienne Balibar, *Reading Capital*. London: New Left Books.

Balibar, Etienne. (1994). "Althusser's Object." *Social Text* 39 (Summer): 157–188.

Balibar, Etienne. (1996). "Structural Causality, Overdetermination, and Antagonism." Pp. 109–119 in Antonio Callari and David F. Ruccio, eds., *Postmodern Materialism and the Future of Marxist Theory: Essays in the Althusserian Tradition*. Hanover, NH: University Press of New England.

Balibar, Etienne. (2014). *Equaliberty: Political Essays*, translated by James Ingram. Durham, NC: Duke University Press.

Banco de Mexico. (1999). *The Mexican Economy, 1999*. Mexico City: Direccion de Organismos y Acuerdos Internacionales.

Banco de Mexico. (2005). "Balance of Payments: Foreign Trade (Monthly Indexes): 1980–2005." www.banxico.org.mx/site BanxicoINGLES/eInfoFinanciera/FSinfoFinanciera.html

Baran, Paul A., and Paul M. Sweezy. (1966). *Monopoly Capital: An Essay on the American Economic and Social Order*. New York: Monthly Review Press.

Barrow, Clyde W. (1990). *Universities and the Capitalist State: Corporate Liberalism and the Reconstruction of American Higher Education, 1894-1928*. Madison: University of Wisconsin Press.

Barrow, Clyde W. (1993). *Critical Theories of the State: Marxist, Neo-Marxist, Post-Marxist*. Madison: University of Wisconsin Press.

Barrow, Clyde W. (1997). "The Diversionary Thesis and the Dialectic of Imperialism: Charles A. Beard's Theory of Foreign Policy Revisited." *Studies in American Political Development* 11 (Fall): 248–291.

Barrow, Clyde W. (2000). "The Marx Problem in Marxian State Theory." *Science & Society*, Vol. 64, No. 1 (Spring): 87–118.

Barrow, Clyde W. (2002a). "Political Theory and the Economic Basis of Politics." Pp. 1–22 in Charles A. Beard, *The Economic Basis of Politics*, edited, indexed, and annotated with a new introduction by Clyde W. Barrow. New Brunswick: Transaction Publishers.

Barrow, Clyde W. (2002b). "The Poulantzas-Miliband Debate: An Intellectual History." Pp. 3–52 in Stanley Aronowitz and Peter Bratsis, eds., *Paradigm Lost: Revising State Theory*. Minneapolis: University of Minnesota Press.

Barrow, Clyde W. (2004). "God, Money, and the State: The Spirits of American Empire." *Forschungsgruppe Europaische Gemeinschaften Arbeitspapier* (22): 1–48.

Barrow, Clyde W. (2005). "Die Ruckkehr des Staates: Globalisierung, Staatstheorie, und der neue Imperialismus." *Sozialismus*, 32 Jahrgang Heft Nr. 7–8 (July / August 2005): 40–54.

Barrow, Clyde W. (2007). "Ralph Miliband and the Instrumentalist Theory of the State: The (Mis)Construction of An Analytic Concept." Pp. 84–108 in Paul Wetherly, Clyde W. Barrow, and Peter Burnham, eds., *Class, Power, and the State in Capitalist Society: Essays on Ralph Miliband*. London: Palgrave Macmillan.

Barrow, Clyde W. (2014). "The Intellectual Origins of New Political Science." Pp. 7–36 in Nancy S. Love and Mark Mattern, eds., *Studying Politics Today: Critical Approaches to Political Science*. New York: Routledge.

Beard, Charles A. (1913). *An Economic Interpretation of the Constitution of the United States*. New York: Free Press.

Beck, Stefan, Frank Klobes, and Christoph Scherrer, eds. (2005). *Surviving Globalization?: Perspectives for the German Economic Model*. Dordrecht, The Netherlands: Springer.

Beckley, Michael. (2011). "China's Century? Why America's Edge Will Endure." *International Security*, 36 (3): 41–78.

Bell, Daniel. (1960). *The End of Ideology: On the Exhaustion of Political Ideas in the Fifties*. Glencoe, IL: Free Press.

Benton, Ted. (1984). *The Rise and Fall of Structural Marxism: Althusser and His Influence*. New York: St. Martin's Press.

Berberoglu, Berch. (2003). *Globalization of Capital and the Nation-State: Imperialism, Class Strugge, and the State in the Age of Global Capitalism*. Lanham, MD: Rowman & Littlefield.

Bernstein, Eduard. (1961). *Evolutionary Socialism*. New York: Schocken Books.

Blackburn, Robin. (1994). "Ralph Miliband, 1924–1994." *New Left Review*, No. 206 (July / August): 15–25.

Block, Fred. (1977). "The Ruling Class Does Not Rule: Notes on the Marxist Theory of the State." *Socialist Revolution* (7): 6–28.

Block, Fred. (2001). "Using Social Theory to Leap Over Historical Contingencies: A Comment on Robinson." *Theory and Society*, 30 (2): 215–221.

Bonefeld, W., and J. Holloway, eds. (1991). *Post-Fordism and Social Form: A Marxist Debate on the Post-Fordist State*. London: Macmillan.

Bottomore, Tom B. (1966). *Elites and Society*. London: Penguin Books.

Bottomore, Tom, and Robert J. Brym, eds. (1989). *The Capitalist Class: An International Study*. New York: New York University Press.

Boyer, Robert, and Daniel Drache, eds. (1996). *States Against Markets: The Limits of Globalization*. London: Routledge.

Bretthauer, Lars, Alexander Gallas, John Kannankulam, und Ingo Stutzle (Hrsg.). (2006). *Poulantzas Lesen: Zur Aktualitat Marxistischer Staatstheorie*. Hamburg, Germany: Verlag-Springer.

Bretthauer, Lars, Alexander Gallas, John Kannankulam, and Ingo Stutzle, eds. (2010). *Reading Poulantzas: On the Relevance of Marxist State Theory*. London: Merlin Press.

Brewer, Anthony. (1990). *Marxist Theories of Imperialism: A Critical Survey*. New York: Routledge.

Bridges, Amy Beth. (1973). "Nicos Poulantzas and the Marxist Theory of the State." *Politics and Society* (2): 161–190.

Buchanan, Ian. (2010). *Dictionary of Critical Theory*. Oxford: Oxford University Press.

Burnham, Peter. (2008). "Parliamentary Socialism, Labourism and Beyond." Pp. 48–63 in Paul Wetherly, Clyde W. Barrow, and Peter Burnham, eds., *Class, Power and the State in Capitalist Society: Essays on Ralph Miliband*. London: Palgrave Macmillan.

Carnoy, Martin. (1984). *The State and Political Theory*. Princeton: Princeton University Press.

Castells, Manuel. (1997). *The Information Age: Economy, Society, and Culture*, 2 vols. Oxford: Blackwell.

Castells, Manuel, ed. (2004). *The Network Society: A Cross-Cultural Perspective*. Cheltenham, UK: Elgar.

Clark, Gordon L., and Michael Dear. (1984). *State Apparatus: Structures of Language and Legitimacy*. Boston: Allen and Unwin.

Clarke, Simon. (1977). "Marxism, Sociology, and Poulantzas' Theory of the State." *Capital and Class* 2 (Summer): 1–31.

Clarke, Simon, ed. (1991). *The State Debate*. New York: St. Martin's Press.

Cleaver, Harry. (1979). *Reading Capital Politically*. Austin: University of Texas Press.

Coates, David, and Leo Panitch. (2002). "The Continuing Relevance of the Milibandian Perspective." Pp. 314–330 in David Coates, ed., *Paving the Third Way: The Critique of Parliamentary Socialism*. London: Merlin.

Commons, John R. (1965). *A Sociological View of Sovereignty*. New York: Kelley.

Comninel, George C. (1987). "Review of *Nicos Poulantzas: Marxist Theory and Political Strategy*, by Bob Jessop," *American Political Science Review* 81:616–617.

Cox, Robert. (1992). "Global Perestroika." Pp. 26–43 in Ralph Miliband and Leo Panitch, eds., *The Socialist Register, 1992*. London: Merlin Press.

Cox, Robert W. (1997). *Production, Power, and World Order*. New York: Columbia University Press.

Crick, Bernard. (1959). *The American Science of Politics*. Berkeley: University of California Press.

Crothers, Lane. (2010). *Globalization and American Popular Culture*, 2nd ed. Lanham, MD: Rowman & Littlefield.

Crotty, James. (2008). "Structural Causes of the Global Financial Crisis: A Critical Assessment of the 'New Financial Architecture'." Working paper, University of Massachusetts, Department of Economics, No. 2008–2014.

Dahl, Robert A. (1956). *A Preface to Democratic Theory*. Chicago: University of Chicago Press.

Dahl, Robert A. (1958). "A Critique of the Ruling Elite Model." *American Political Science Review* (52): 463–469.

Dahl, Robert A. (1959). *Social Science Research on Business: Product and Potential*. New York: Columbia University Press.

Dahl, Robert A. (1961). *Who Governs? Democracy and Power in an American City*. New Haven: Yale University Press.

Deleuze, Gilles, and Felix Guattari. (1987). *Thousand Plateaus: Capitalism and Schizophrenia*. London: Athlone Press.

Destanne De Bernis, Gerard. (1990). "On a Marxist Theory of Regulation." *Monthly Review*, Vol. 41, No. 8 (January): 28–37.

Dezalay, Yves, and Bryant G. Garth. (2005). *Global Prescriptions: The Production, Exploration, and Importation of New Legal Orthodoxy*. Ann Arbor: University of Michigan Press.

Domhoff, G. William. (1967). *Who Rules America?* Englewood Cliffs, NJ: Prentice-Hall.

Domhoff, G. William. (1976). "I Am Not an Instrumentalist." *Kapitalistate* (4–5): 221–224.

Domhoff, G. William. (1978). *The Powers That Be: Processes of Ruling Class Domination in America*. New York: Vintage Books.

Domhoff, G. William. (1986–1987). "Corporate-Liberal Theory and the Social Security Act: A Chapter in the Sociology of Knowledge." *Politics and Society* (15): 295–330.

Domhoff, G. William. (1990). *The Power Elite and the State: How Policy Is Made in America*. New York: de Gruyter.

Domhoff, G. William. (1998). *Who Rules America? Power and Politics in the Year 2000*, 3rd ed. Mountain View, CA: Mayfield.

Draper, Hal. (1977). *Karl Marx's Theory of Revolution*, Vol. 1. New York: Monthly Review Press.

Drucker, Peter F. (1993). *Post-Capitalist Society*. New York: HarperBusiness.

Duncan, Graeme. (1982). "The Marxist Theory of the State." Pp. 129–143 in G.H.R. Parkinson, ed., *Marx and Marxisms*. Cambridge: Cambridge University Press.

Easton, David. (1953). *The Political System: An Inquiry into the State of Political Science*. New York: Knopf.

Easton, David. (1965). *A Systems Analysis of Political Life*. Chicago: University of Chicago Press.

Easton, David. (1969). "The New Revolution in Political Science." *American Political Science Review*, Vol. 63, No. 4 (December): 1051–1061.

Easton, David. (1981). "The Political System Besieged by the State." *Political Theory* 9:303–325.

Easton, David. (1990). *The Analysis of Political Structure*. New York: Routledge.

Edelman, Maurice. (1964). *The Symbolic Uses of Politics*. Urbana: University of Illinois Press.

Editorial Collective. (1973). "An Introduction to Working Papers on the KAPITALISTATE: An International Bulletin on the Capitalist State." *Kapitalistate* (1): 1–5.

Edsall, Thomas Byrne. (1984). *The New Politics of Inequality*. New York: Norton.

Edwards, Richard C., Michael Reich, and Thomas E. Weisskopf, eds. (1978). *The Capitalist System*, 2nd ed. Englewood Cliffs, NJ: Prentice-Hall.

Ehrenreich, Barbara, and John Ehrenreich. (1977). "The Professional Managerial Class." *Radical America* 11 (March–April): 7–31.

Elliott, Gregory. (2009). *Althusser: The Detour of Theory*. Chicago: Haymarket Books.

Evans, Peter. (1997). "The Eclipse of the State? Reflections on Stateness in an Era of Globalization." *World Politics*, Vol. 50, No. 1 (October): 62–87.

Evans, Peter, Dietrich Rueschemeyer, and Theda Skocpol, eds. (1985). *Bringing the State Back In*. Cambridge: Cambridge University Press.

Ewen, Stewart. (1976). *Captains of Consciousness: Advertising and the Social Roots of the Consumer Culture*. New York: McGraw-Hill.

Ewing, Jack. (2000). "This Show of Muscle Isn't So Scary." *Businessweek Online*, January 10. www.businessweek.com:/2000/00_02/b3663186.htm?scriptFramed

Fitzhugh, George. (1960). *Cannibals All! or Slaves Without Masters*. Cambridge, MA: Belknap Press.

Flinders, Matthew. (2006). "Public/Private: The Boundaries of the State." Pp. 223–247 in Pp. 59–78 in Colin Hay, Michael Lister, and David Marsh, eds., *The State: Theories and Issues*. Houndmills, Basingstoke, Hampshire: Palgrave Macmillan.

Flinders, Matthew, and Peter John. (2013). "The Future of Political Science." *Political Studies Review*, 11:222–227.

Foster, John Bellamy. (2004). "The Commitment of an Intellectual: Paul M. Sweezy (1910-2004)." *Monthly Review*, Vol. 56, No. 5 (October): 5–39.

Foucault, Michel. (1972). *The Archaeology of Knowledge & The Discourse on Language*. New York: Harper and Row.

Foucault, Michel. (1980). *The History of Sexuality, Vol. 1: An Introduction*. New York: Vintage Books.

Freitag, Peter. (1975). "The Cabinet and Big Business." *Social Problems* (2)3:137–152.

Galbraith, John Kenneth. (1952). *American Capitalism: The Concept of Countervailing Power*. Boston: Houghton-Mifflin.

Gearey, Adam. (2005). *Globalization and Law: Trade, Rights, War*. Lanham, MD: Rowman & Littlefield.

Genovese, Eugene D. (1965). *The Political Economy of Slavery: Studies in the Economy & Society of the Slave South*. New York: Pantheon Books.

Gerstenberger, Heidi. (1978). "Class Conflict, Competition and State Functions." Pp. 148–159 in John Holloway and Sol Picciotto, eds., *State and Capital: A Marxist Debate*. Austin: University of Texas Press.

Gerstenberger, Heidi. (1992). "The Bourgeois State Form Revisited." Pp. 151–176 in Werner Bonefeld, Richard Gunn, and Kosmas Psychopedis, eds., *Open Marxism, Volume I. Dialectics and History*. London: Pluto Press.

Gestrin, Michael, and Alan M. Rugman. (1996). "The NAFTA Investment Provisions: Prototype for Multilateral Investment Rules?" Pp. 65–70 in Organization for Economic Cooperation and Development, *Market Access After the Uruguay Round: Investment, Competition and Technology Perspectives*. Paris: OECD.

Giddens, Anthony. (1984). *The Constitution of Society: Outline of the Theory of Structuration*. Cambridge: Polity Press.

Gilbert, Christopher, and David Vines. (2000). *The Work Bank: Structure and Policies*. Cambridge: Cambridge University Press.

Gill, Stephen. (1990). *American Hegemony and the Trilateral Commission*. New York: Cambridge University Press.

Gill, Stephen. (1992). "The Emerging World Order and European Change." Pp. 157–196 in Ralph Miliband and Leo Panitch, eds., *Socialist Register, 1992*. London: Merlin Press.

Gill, Stephen, and David Law. (1988). *The Global Political Economy: Perspectives, Problems, and Policies*. Baltimore: Johns Hopkins University Press.

Gilpin, Robert. (2001). *Global Political Economy: Understanding the International Economic Order*. Princeton: Princeton University Press.

Gitlin, Todd. (1987). *The Sixties: Years of Hope, Days of Rage*. New York: Bantam Books.

Global Research. (2013). "How Many People Have Lost Their Homes? US Home Foreclosures are Comparable to the Great Depression," May 17. www.globalresearch.ca/how-many-people-have-lost-their-homes-us-home-foreclosures-are-comparable-to-the-great-depression/5335430

Gold, David A., Clarence Y.H. Lo, and Erik Olin Wright. (1975a). "Recent Developments in Marxist Theories of the Capitalist State, Part I." *Monthly Review* 27:29–43.

Gold, David A., Clarence Y.H. Lo, and Erik Olin Wright. (1975b). "Recent Developments in Marxist Theories of the Capitalist State, Part II." *Monthly Review* 27:36–51.

Gorham, Bradley. (2005). "General Says Army Reserve is Becoming a 'Broken' Force." *Washington Post*, January 6, A–1.

Gottdeiner, Mark. (1987). *The Decline of Urban Politics: Political*

Theory and the Crisis of the Local State. Newbury Park, CA: Sage.

Grayson, George W. (1993). *The North American Free Trade Agreement*. New York: Foreign Policy Association.

Hall, John A., and G. John Ikenberry. (1989). *The State*. Minneapolis: University of Minnesota Press.

Hall, Rodney Bruce, and Thomas J. Biersteker. (2002). *The Emergence of Private Authority in Global Governance*. Cambridge: Cambridge University Press.

Hall, Stuart. (2000). "Introduction to the Verso Classics Edition: Nicos Poulantzas: *State, Power, Socialism*." Pp. vii–xviii in Nicos Poulantzas, *State Power, Socialism*. London: Verso.

Hamm, Bernd. (2005). "Cultural Imperialism: The Political Economy of Cultural Domination." Pp. 18–30 in Bernd Hamm and Russell Smandych, eds., *Cultural Imperialism: Essays on the Political Economy of Cultural Domination*. Sydney, Australia: Broadview Press.

Hardt, Michael, and Antonio Negri. (2000). *Empire*. Cambridge: Harvard University Press.

Harrington, Michael. (1962). *The Other America: Poverty in the United States*. New York: Macmillan.

Hartmann, Eva. (2011). "The Difficult Relation between International Law and Politics: The Legal Turn from a Critical IPE Perspective." *New Political Economy*, Vol. 16, No. 5 (November): 561–584.

Hartz, Louis. (1955). *The Liberal Tradition in America*. New York: Harcourt, Brace, and World.

Harvey, David. (1982). *The Limits to Capital*. Chicago: University of Chicago Press.

Harvey, David. (1990). *The Condition of Postmodernity*. Oxford: Blackwell.

Harvey, David. (2003). *The New Imperialism*. Oxford: Oxford University Press.

Hay, Colin. (2006). "(What's Marxist about) Marxist State Theory?" Pp. 59–78 in Colin Hay, Michael Lister, and David Marsh, eds., *The State: Theories and Issues*. Houndmills, Basingstoke, Hampshire: Palgrave Macmillan.

Henri-Levi, Bernard. (1977). *Barbarism With a Human Face*. New York: Harper and Row.

Highsaw, Robert B. (1957). "Review of *The Power Elite* by C. Wright Mills." *Journal of Politics*, Vol. 19, No. 1 (February): 144–146.

Hilferding, Rudolf. (1981). *Finance Capital: A Study of the Latest Phase of Capitalist Development*. London: Routledge & Kegan Paul.

Hillquit, Morris. (1909). *Socialism in Theory and Practice*. New York: Macmillan.

Hillquit, Morris. (1910). *History of Socialism in the United States*. New York: Funk & Wagnalls, revised and expanded (5th) ed.

Hindess, Barry, and Paul Q. Hirst. (1975). *Pre-Capitalist Modes of Production*. London: Routledge and Kegan Paul.

Hindess, Barry, and Paul Q. Hirst. (1977). *Mode of Production and Social Formation*. London: Macmillan.

Hirsch, Arthur. (1981). *The French New Left: An Intellectual History From Sartre to Gorz*. Boston: South End Press.

Hirst, Paul Q. (1979). *On Law and Ideology*. London: Macmillan.

Hirst, Paul Q., ed. (1989). *The Pluralist Theory of the State*. London: Routledge.

Holloway, John. (1994). "Global Capital and the National State." *Capital and Class* 52 (Spring): 23–49.

Holloway, John, and Sol Picciotto. (1978). "Introduction: Towards a Material Theory of the State." Pp. 1–31 in John Holloway and Sol Picciotto, eds., *State and Capital: A Marxist Debate*. Austin: University of Texas Press.

Horowitz, Irving Louis. (1983). *C. Wright Mills: An American Utopian*. New York: Free Press.

Howe, Irving. (1963). "An American Tragedy." *New York Review of Books*, Vol. 1, No. 3 (September 26).

Hufbauer, Gary Clyde, and Jeffrey J. Schott. (1993). *NAFTA: An Assessment*, rev. ed. Washington, DC: Institute for International Economics.

Jamison, Andrew, and Ron Eyerman. (1994). *Seeds of the Sixties*. Berkeley: University of California Press.

Jensen, Nathan. (2006). *Nation-States and the Multinational Corporation: A Political Economy of Foreign Direct Investment*. Princeton: Princeton University Press.

Jessop, Bob. (1977). "Recent Theories of the Capitalist State." *Cambridge Journal of Economics* 1:353–372.

Jessop, Bob. (1982). *The Capitalist State: Marxist Theories and Methods*. New York: New York University Press.

Jessop, Bob. (1985). *Nicos Poulantzas: Marxist Theory and Political Strategy*. New York: St. Martin's Press.

Jessop, Bob. (1990). *State Theory: Putting the Capitalist State in Its Place*. Cambridge, UK: Polity Press.

Jessop, Bob. (1991). "On the Originality, Legacy, and Actuality of Nicos Poulantzas." *Studies in Political Economy* 34 (Spring): 75–107.

Jessop, Bob. (1993). "Towards a Schumpeterian Workfare State? Preliminary Remarks on Post-Fordist Political Economy." *Studies in Political Economy* (40): 7–39.

Jessop, Bob. (1994). "Post-Fordism and the State." Pp. 251–279 in Ash Amin, ed., *Post-Fordism*. Oxford: Blackwell.

Jessop, Bob. (2002a). "Globalization and the National State." Pp. 185–220 in Stanley Aronowitz and Peter Bratsis, eds., *Paradigm Lost: State Theory Reconsidered*. Minneapolis: University of Minnesota Press.

Jessop, Bob. (2002b). *The Future of the Capitalist State*. Cambridge: Polity Press.

Jessop, Bob. (2008a). "Dialogue of the Deaf: Some Reflections on the Poulantzas-Miliband Debate." Pp. 132–157 in Paul Wetherly, Clyde W. Barrow, and Peter Burnham, eds., *Class, Power and the State In Capitalist Society: Essays on Ralph Miliband*. London: Palgrave Macmillan.

Jessop, Bob. (2008b). *State Power*. Cambridge: Polity Press.

Judis, John B. (2001). "Grist for Mills." *Texas Monthly*, Vol. 29, No. 3 (March): 80–90.

Kadushin, Charles. (1972). "Who Are the Elite Intellectuals?" *The Public Interest* (29): 109–125.

Kautsky, Karl. (1910). *The Social Revolution*. Chicago: Kerr.

King, Roger. (1986). *The State in Modern Society*. Chatham, NJ: Chatham House.

Konings, Martijn. (2010). "Renewing State Theory." *Politics*, Vol. 30, No. 3:174–182.

Kotz, David A. (2009). "The Financial and Economic Crisis of

2008: A Systemic Crisis of Neoliberal Capitalism." *Review of Radical Political Economics*, Vol. 41, No. 3 (Summer): 305–317.

Kovel, Joel. (1994). "Remembering Ralph Miliband." *Monthly Review* (September): 51–58.

Laclau, Ernesto. (1975). "The Specificity of the Political: The Poulantzas-Miliband Debate." *Economy and Society* (5): 87–110.

Larson, Kevin. (2009). "Nation-State." Pp. 221–238 in G. Honor Fagan and Ronaldo Munck, eds., *Globalization and Security: An Encyclopedia*. Santa Barbara, CA: Praeger Security International.

Laski, Harold J. (1935). *The State in Theory and Practice*. New York: Viking Press.

Lekachman, Robert. (1957). "Organization Men: The Erosion of Individuality." *Commentary* (March): 270–276.

Lenin, V.I. (1939). *Imperialism: The Highest Stage of Capitalism*. New York: International Publishers.

Lenin, V.I. (1974). *State and Revolution*. New York: International Publishers.

Lewis, William S. (2005). *Louis Althusser and the Traditions of French Marxism*. Oxford: Lexington Books.

Lindblom, Charles E. (1982). "The Market as Prison," *Journal of Politics*, Vol. 44, No. 2 (May): 324–332.

Lipetz, Alain. (1987). *Miracles and Mirages*. London: New Left Books.

Lowi, Theodore J. (1992). "The State in Political Science: How We Become What We Study." *American Political Science Review* Vol. 86, No. 1 (March): 1–7.

Luger, Stan. (2000). *Corporate Power, American Democracy, and the Automobile Industry* Cambridge: Cambridge University Press.

Lukacs, Georg. (1971). *History and Class Consciousness*. Cambridge, MA: MIT Press.

Lukes, Steven. (1974). *Power: A Radical View*, 1st ed. New York: Macmillan.

Lukes, Steven. (2005). *Power: A Radical View*, 2nd exp. ed. New York: Palgrave Macmillan.

Lynd, Robert S. 1968. "Power in the United States." Pp. 103–114 in G. William Domhoff and Hoyt B. Ballard, eds., *C. Wright Mills and the Power Elite*. Boston: Beacon Press.

Lyotard, Jean Francois. (1984). *The Postmodern Condition: A Report on Knowledge*; translation from the French by Geoff Bennington and Brian Massumi. Minneapolis: University of Minnesota Press.

MacLeod, Dag. (2004). *Downsizing the State: Privatization and the Limits of Neoliberal Reform in Mexico*. University Park: Pennsylvania State University Press.

Mamut, L.S. (1990). "Questions of Law in Marx's *Capital*." Pp. 95–105 in Bob Jessop, ed., *Karl Marx's Social and Political Thought: Critical Assessments*. London: Routledge, Chapman, and Hall.

Mandel, Ernest. (1971). *The Marxist Theory of the State*. New York: Pathfinder Press.

Martin, James. (2008). "Introduction." Pp. 1–24 in Nicos Poulantzas, *The Poulantzas Reader: Marxism, Law, and the State*, edited by James Martin. London and New York: Verso.

Marx, Karl. (1906). *Capital*, Vol. 1. New York: Modern Library.

Marx, Karl. (1977). *Capital*, Vol. 1. New York: Vintage Books.

Marx, Karl, and Frederick. Engels. (1970). *The German Ideology*. New York: International Publishers.

Mason, Edward S. (1964). *Economic Concentration and the Monopoly Problem*. New York: Atheneum.

Means, Gardiner C. (1939). *The Structure of the American Economy*. Washington, DC: Government Printing Office.

Meyer-Larsen, Werner. (2000). *Germany, Inc.: The New German Juggernaut and its Challenge to World Business*. New York: Wiley.

Miliband, Ralph. (1961). *Parliamentary Socialism: A Study in the Politics of Labour*. London: Allen & Unwin.

Miliband, Ralph. (1962). "C. Wright Mills." *New Left Review* (May/June 1962): 15–20.

Miliband, Ralph. (1964a). "Mills and Politics." Pp. 76–87 in Irving Louis Horowitz, ed., *The New Sociology: Essays in Social Science and Social Theory in Honor of C. Wright Mills*. Oxford: Oxford University Press.

Miliband, Ralph. (1964b). "Review of *Power, Politics, and People: The Collected Essays of C. Wright Mills.*" *British Journal of Sociology*, Vol. 15, No. 1 (March): 78–79.

Miliband, Ralph. (1965). "Marx and the State." Pp. 278–295 in *Socialist Register*, edited by R. Miliband and J. Saville. New York: Monthly Review Press.

Miliband, Ralph. (1969). *The State in Capitalist Society*. New York: Basic Books.

Miliband, Ralph. (1970a). "Lenin's *The State and Revolution*." Pp. 309–319 in Ralph Miliband and John Saville, eds., *Socialist Register*. New York: Monthly Review Press.

Miliband, Ralph. (1970b). "The Capitalist State: Reply to Poulantzas." *New Left Review* 59 (January–February): 53–60.

Miliband, Ralph. (1973). "Poulantzas and the Capitalist State." *New Left Review* 82:83–92.

Miliband, Ralph. (1977). *Marxism and Politics*. New York: Oxford University Press.

Miliband, R. (1983). "State Power and Class Interests." *New Left Review* 138 (March–April): 37–68.

Miliband, Ralph. (1989). *Divided Societies: Class Struggle in Contemporary Capitalism*. Oxford: Oxford University Press.

Miliband, Ralph. (1993). "Harold Laski: An Exemplary Public Intellectual." *New Left Review*, No. 200 (July / August): 175–181.

Miliband, Ralph. (1995). *Socialism for a Skeptical Age*. London: Polity Press.

Miliband, Ralph. (2003). *Marxism and Politics*. Pontypool, Wales: Merlin Press, reprint.

Mills, C. Wright. (1948). *The New Men of Power: America's Labor Leaders*. New York: Harcourt, Brace.

Mills, C. Wright. (1951). *White Collar*. Oxford: Oxford University Press.

Mills, C. Wright. (1956). *The Power Elite*. Oxford: Oxford University Press.

Mills, C. Wright. (1957). "Letters From Readers: To the Editor of Commentary." *Commentary* (June): 580–581.

Mills, C. Wright. (1958). "The Structure of Power in American Society." *British Journal of Sociology*, Vol. 9, No. 1 (March): 29–41.

Mills, C. Wright. (1962). *The Marxists*. New York: Dell.

Mills, C. Wright. (1963). *People, Power, and Politics: The Collected Essays of C. Wright Mills*. New York: Ballantine Books.

Mintz, Beth. (1975). "The President's Cabinet, 1897–1972: A Contribution to the Power Structure Debate." *Insurgent Sociologist* 5:131–148.

Mintz, Beth, and Michael Schwartz. (1985). *The Power Structure of American Business*. Chicago: University of Chicago Press.

Mintz, Beth. (1989). "United States of America." Pp. 207–236 in Tom Bottomore and Robert J. Brym, eds., *The Capitalist Class An International Study*. New York: New York University Press.

Mitchell, Timothy. (1991). "The Limits of the State: Beyond Statist Approaches and Their Critics." *American Political Science Review*, Vol. 85, No. 1 (March): 77–96.

Monroe, Kristen Renwick, ed. (2005). *Perestroika! The Raucous Rebellion in Political Science*. New Haven: Yale University Press.

Montag, Warren. (2013). *Althusser and His Contemporaries: Philosophy's Perpetual War*. Durham, NC: Duke University Press.

Negri, Antonio. (1989). *The Politics of Subversion: A Manifesto for the Twenty-First Century*. Cambridge: Polity Press.

Negri, Antonio. (1991). *Marx Beyond Marx: Lessons on the Grundrisse*. London: Pluto Press.

Newman, Michael. (2002). *Ralph Miliband and the Politics of the New Left*. London: Merlin Press.

O'Connor, James. (1978). *The Fiscal Crisis of the State*. New York: St. Martin's Press.

O'Connor, James. (2002). "Introduction to the Transaction Edition." Pp. xiii–xxviii in *The Fiscal Crisis of the State*. New Brunswick, NJ: Transaction Publishers.

Offe, Claus. (1975). "The Theory of the Capitalist State and the Problem of Policy Formation." Pp. 125–144 in Leon Lindberg, ed., *Stress and Contradiction in Modern Capitalism* Lexington, MA: D.C. Heath.

Offe, Claus. (1984). *Contradictions of the Welfare State*. Cambridge, MA: MIT Press.

Offe, Claus. (1996). *Modernity and the State*. Cambridge, MA: MIT Press.

Ohmae, Kenichi. (1990). *The End of the National State*. New York: Free Press.

Ollman, Bertell. (1982). *The Left Academy: Marxist Scholarship on American Campuses*. New York: McGraw-Hill.

Ollman, Bertell. (1993). *Dialectical Investigations*. New York: Routledge, Chapman, and Hall.

Organization for Economic Cooperation and Development (OECD). (1995). *México, 1995*. Paris: OECD.

Organization for Economic Cooperation and Development (OECD). (1996). *Trade Liberalisation Policies in Mexico*. Paris: OECD.

Panitch, Leo. (1994a). "Socialist Scholar." *The Nation* (June 13): 821–822.

Panitch, Leo. (1994b). "Globalisation and the State," Pp. 60–93 in Ralph Miliband and Leo Panitch, eds., *Socialist Register, 1994*. London: Merlin Press.

Panitch, Leo. (2000). "The New Imperial State." *New Left Review* 2 (March / April): 5–20.

Panitch, Leo. (2002). "The Impoverishment of State Theory." Pp. 89–104 in Stanley Aronowitz and Peter Bratsis, eds., *Paradigm Lost: Revising State Theory*. Minneapolis: University of Minnesota Press.

Panitch, Leo. (2009). "Foreword: Reading *The State in Capitalist Society*." Pp. ix–xxvii in Ralph Miliband, *The State in Capitalist Society*. Pontypool, Wales: Merlin Press.

Panitch, Leo, and Sam Gindin. (2003). "Euro-Capitalism and American Imperialism." Pp. 72–98 in Martin Beckman, Hans-Jurgen Bieling, and Frank Deppe, eds., *The Emergence of a New Euro Capitalism? Implications for Analysis and Politics*. Marburg, Germany: Forschungsgruppe Europaische Gemeinschaften (FEG).

Panitch, Leo, and Sam Gindin. (2004). "Global Capitalism and American Empire." Pp. 1–42 in Leo Panitch and Colin Leys, eds., *Socialist Register, 2004*. London: Merlin Press.

Panitch, Leo, and Sam Gindin. (2012). *The Making of Global Capitalism: The Political Economy of the American Empire*. London: Verso.

Parsons, Talcott. (1951). *The Social System*. Glencoe, IL: Free Press.

Parsons, Talcott. (1957). "The Distribution of Power in American Society." *World Politics*, Vol. 10, No. 1 (October): 123–143.

Perkmann, Markus, and Ngai-Ling Sum. (2002). *Globalization, Regionalization and Cross-Border Regions*. London: Palgrave Macmillan.

Perlo, Victor. (1950). *American Imperialism*. New York: International Publishers.

Perlo, Victor. (1957). *The Empire of High Finance*. New York: International Publishers.

Peschek, Joseph G. (1987). *Policy Planning Organizations: Elite Agendas and Rightward Turn*. Philadelphia: Temple University Press.

Picciotto, Sol. (1997). "The Internationalisation of the State." *Capital and Class* (43): 43–63.

Pierson, Christopher. (1996). *The Modern State*. London: Routledge.

Piven, Frances Fox. (1994). "Reflections on Ralph Miliband." *New Left Review* 206:23–26.

Piven, Frances F., and Richard. A. Cloward. (1977). *Poor Peoples' Movements: Why They Succeed, How They Fail*. New York: Vintage Books.

Piven, Francis Fox, and Richard A. Cloward. (1982). *The New Class War*. New York: Pantheon Books.

Poggi, Gianfranco. (1990). *The State: Its Nature, Development, and Prospects*. Stanford: Stanford University Press.

Porter, Michael E. (1990). *The Competitive Advantage of Nations*. New York: Free Press.

Porter, Michael E. (1991). *Canada at the Crossroads: The Reality of a New Competitive Environment*. Ottawa: Business Council on National Issues and Canadian Ministry of Supply and Services.

Porter, Michael E. (1998). *On Competition*. Cambridge: Harvard Business Review.

Poster, Mark. (1975). *Existential Marxism in Postwar France: From Sartre to Althusser*. Princeton: Princeton University Press.

Poulantzas, Nicos. (1967). "Marxist Political Theory in Great Britain." *New Left Review* (43): 57–74.

Poulantzas, Nicos. (1969). "The Problem of the Capitalist State." *New Left Review* 58 (November–December): 67–78.

Poulantzas, Nicos. (1973). "On Social Classes." *New Left Review* 78 (March–April): 27–54.

Poulantzas, Nicos. (1974). *Fascism and Dictatorship*. London: Verso.

Poulantzas, Nicos. (1976a). "The Capitalist State: A Reply to Miliband and Laclau." *New Left Review* 95 (January/February): 63–83.

Poulantzas, Nicos. (1976b). *Crisis of the Dictatorships*. London: Verso.

Poulantzas, Nicos. (1978a). *Political Power and Social Classes*. London: Verso.

Poulantzas, Nicos. (1978b). *Classes in Contemporary Capitalism*. London: Verso.

Poulantzas, Nicos. (1980). *State, Power, Socialism*. London: Verso.

Poulantzas, Nicos. (2000). *State Power, Socialism*, new edition with an Introduction by Stuart Hall. London: Verso.

Poulantzas, Nicos. (2008). *The Poulantzas Reader: Marxism, Law, and the State*, edited by James Martin. London and New York: Verso.

Poulantzas, Nicos. (2014). *State Power, Socialism*, new edition with an Introduction by Stuart Hall. London: Verso.

Ramirez de la O, Rogelio. (1993). "The North American Free Trade Agreement from a Mexican Perspective." Pp. 60–86 in Steven Globerman and Michael Walker, eds., *Assessing NAFTA: A Trinational Analysis*. Vancouver: Fraser Institute.

Ranciere, Jacques. (1974). "On the Theory of Ideology," *Radical Philosophy* 7:2–15.

Ranciere, Jacques. (2011). *Althusser's Lesson*. London: Continuum International Publishing.

Reissman, Leonard. (1956). "Review of *The Power Elite* by C. Wright Mills." *American Sociological Review*, Vol. 21, No. 4 (August): 513–514.

Ricci, David. (1984). *The Tragedy of Political Science*. New Haven: Yale University Press.

Rice, Condoleeza. (2000). "Campaign 2000: Promoting the National Interest." *Foreign Affairs*, Vol. 79, No. 1 (January/February): 45–62.

Riddlesperger Jr., J.W., and J.D. King. (1989). "Elitism and Presidential Appointments." *Social Science Quarterly* 70 (December): 902–910.

Robinson, Ian. (1993). *North American Free Trade As If Democracy Mattered.* Ottawa: Canadian Centre for Policy Alternatives.

Robinson, William I., and John Harris. (2000). "Towards a Global Ruling Class: Globalization and the Transnational Capitalist Class." *Science & Society* (Spring): 11–54.

Roettger, W.B. (1978). "Strata and Stability: Reputations of American Political Scientists." *PS: Political Science and Politics*, Vol. 11, No. 1 (Winter): 6–12.

Rogow, Arnold A. (1956). "Review of *The Power Elite* by C. Wright Mills." *Public Opinion Quarterly*, Vol. 20, No. 3 (Autumn): 613–615.

Ross, Gordon. (1994). "Ralph Miliband." *PS: Political Science and Politics* (27): 572.

Rossi, Peter H. (1956). "Review of *The Power Elite* by C. Wright Mills." *American Journal of Sociology*, Vol. 62, No. 2 (September): 232.

Rubio, Luis. (1999). "Mexico and NAFTA Expansion." *NAMINEWS* 23 (Summer). www.northamericaninstitute.org/naminews/issue23

Sakellaropoulos, Spyros. (2007). "Towards a Declining State? The Rise of the Headquarters State." *Science and Society*, Vol. 71, No. 1 (January): 7–32.

Sakellaropoulos, Spyros. (2009). "The Issue of Globalization through the Theory of Imperialism and the Periodization of Modes of Production." *Critical Sociology*, Vol. 35, No. 1 (January): 57–78.

Sakellaropoulos, Spyros, and Panagiotis Sotiris. (2015). "From Territorial to Nonterritorial Capitalist Imperialism: Lenin and the Possibility of a Marxist Theory of Imperialism." *Rethinking Marxism: A Journal of Economics, Culture, and Society*, Vol. 27, No. 1 (January): 85–106.

Saville, John. (1995). "Parliamentary Socialism Revisited."

Pp. 225–238 in Leo Panitch, ed., *Socialist Register.* London: Merlin Press.

Scherrer, Christoph. (2003). "Double Hegemony?: State and Class in Transatlantic Relations." Pp. 47–71 in Martin Beckman, Hans-Jurgen Bieling, and Frank Deppe, eds., *The Emergence of a New Euro Capitalism? Implications for Analysis and Politics.* Marburg, Germany: Forschungsgruppe Europaische Gemeinschaften (FEG).

Schiller, Herbert I. (1989). *Culture, Inc.: The Corporate Takeover of Public Expression.* Oxford: Oxford University Press.

Schirm, Stefan A. (2002). *Globalization and the New Regionalism.* Cambridge: Polity Press.

Schmitter, Phillipe C., ed. (1985). *Private Interest Government: Beyond Market and State.* Beverly Hills, CA: Sage.

Schneider, Eugene V. (1968). "The Sociology of C. Wright Mills." Pp. 12–21 in G. William Domhoff and Hoyt B. Ballard, eds., *C. Wright Mills and the Power Elite.* Boston: Beacon Press.

Seidelman, Raymond. (1985). *Disenchanted Realists: Political Science and the American Crisis, 1884-1984.* Albany: State University of New York Press.

Seligman, Edwin R.A. (1924). *The Economic Interpretation of History,* 2nd ed. rev. New York: Columbia University Press.

Shapiro, Ian. (2005). *The Flight from Reality in the Human Sciences.* Princeton: Princeton University Press.

Shaw, Martin. (2000). *Theory of the Global State: Globality as Unfinished Revolution.* Cambridge: Cambridge University Press.

Singer, Daniel. (1970). *Prelude to Revolution: France in May 1968.* London: Jonathan Cape.

Sklair, Leslie. (2001). *The Transnational Capitalist Class.* Oxford: Blackwell.

Skocpol, Theda. (1980). "Political Response to Capitalist Crisis: Neo-Marxist Theories of the State and the Case of the New Deal," *Politics and Society* 10:155–201.

Skocpol, Theda, and Edwin Amenta. (1986). "States and Social Policies." *Annual Review of Sociology* (12): 131–157.

Skowronek, Stephen. (1982). *Building a New American State:*

The Expansion of National Administrative Capacities, 1877–1920. Cambridge: Cambridge University Press.

Smith, David N. (1974). *Who Rules the Universities?* New York: Monthly Review Press.

Sorensen, Georg. (2006). "The Transformation of the State." Pp. 190–208 in Colin Hay, Michael Lister, and David Marsh, eds., *The State: Theories and Issues*. Houndmills, Basingstoke, Hampshire: Palgrave Macmillan.

Spring, Joel H. (1972). *Education and the Rise of the Corporate State*. Boston: Beacon Press.

Starrs, Sean. (2013). "American Economic Power Hasn't Declined—It Globalized! Summoning the Data and Taking Globalization Seriously." *International Studies Quarterly* (57): 817–830.

Steger, Manfred. (2002). *Globalism: The New Market Ideology*. Lanham, MD: Rowman & Littlefield.

Strange, Susan. (1986). *Casino Capitalism*. Oxford: Basil Blackwell.

Strange, Susan. (1996). *The Retreat of the State: The Diffusion of Power in the World Economy*. New York: Cambridge University Press.

Strange, Susan. (1998). *Mad Money: When Markets Outgrow Governments*. Ann Arbor: University of Michigan Press.

Strauss, Leo. (1959). "Political Philosophy and History." Pp. 56–77 in Leo Strauss, *What is Political Philosophy? and Other Studies*. Glencoe, IL: Free Press.

Strauss, Leo, and Joseph Cropsey, eds. (1963). *History of Political Philosophy*. Chicago: Rand McNally.

Sumner, William Graham. (1986). *What Social Classes Owe to Each Other*. Caldwell, ID: Caxton.

Surkin, Marvin, and Alan Wolfe, eds. (1970). *An End to Political Science: The Caucus Papers*. New York: Basic Books.

Sweezy, Paul. (1942). *The Theory of Capitalist Development*. New York: Monthly Review Press.

Sweezy, Paul. (1953). *The Present as History: Essays and Reviews on Capitalism and Socialism*. New York: Monthly Review Press.

Sweezy, Paul. (1968). "Power Elite or Ruling Class?" Pp.

115–132 in G. William Domhoff and Hoyt B. Ballard, eds., *C. Wright Mills and the Power Elite*. Boston: Beacon Press.

Taylor, John. (1977). *Arator: Being a Series of Agricultural Essays, Practical and Political; In Sixty-Four Numbers*. Indianapolis: Liberty Fund.

Temporary National Economic Committee. (1941a). *Investigation of Concentration of Economic Power: The Structure of Industry*. Washington, DC: Government Printing Office.

Temporary National Economic Committee. (1941b). *Investigation of Concentration of Economic Power: Final Report*. Washington, DC: Government Printing Office.

Therborn, Goran. (1976). *Science, Class, and Society: On the Formation of Sociology and Historical Materialism*. London: New Left Books.

Therborn, Goran. (1978). *What Does the Ruling Class Do When it Rules?* London: New Left Books.

Therborn, Goran. (1980). *The Ideology of Power and the Power of Ideology*. London: Verso.

Therborn, Goran. (1987). "Review of *Nicos Poulantzas: Marxist Theory and Political Strategy*, by Bob Jessop." *American Journal of Sociology* 92:1230–1231.

Thomas, Paul. (1994). *Alien Politics*. New York: Routledge.

Thomas, Paul. (2002). "Bringing Poulantzas Back In." Pp. 73–88 in Stanley Aronowitz and Peter Bratsis, eds., *Paradigm Lost: State Theory Reconsidered*. Minneapolis: University of Minnesota Press.

Thurow, Lester. (1992). *Head to Head: The Coming Economic Battle Among Japan, Europe, and America*. New York: Morrow.

Touraine, Alain. (1971). *The May Movement*. New York: Random House.

Truman, David B. (1951). *The Governmental Process: Political Interests and Public Opinion*. New York: Knopf.

United Nations. (2014). "Growth in United Nations Membership, 1945–Present." www.un.org/en/members/growth.shtml#2000

United Nations Conference on Trade and Development. (1998). *World Investment Report, 1998: Trends and Determinants*. New York and Geneva: UNCTAD.

United States Congress, House Committee on the Judiciary. (1951–1952). *Report of the Subcommittee on Study of Monopoly Power of the Committee on the Judiciary pursuant to H. Res. 95, 82nd Congress., 1st session., authorizing the Committee on the Judiciary to conduct studies and investigations relating to matters within its jurisdiction.* Washington, DC: Government Printing Office.

United States Congress. House. Committee on the Judiciary. (1952). *Bank Mergers and Concentration of Banking Facilities; a staff report to Subcommittee No. 5 of the Committee on the Judiciary, House of Representatives.* Washington, DC: Government Printing Office.

United States Congress. House. Committee on the Judiciary. (1955). *Bank Mergers. Hearings before Antitrust Subcommittee (Subcommittee No. 5) on H.R. 5948, to Amend the Clayton Act by Prohibiting the Acquisition of Assets of Other Banks by Banks, Banking Associations, or Trust Companies when the Effect May be Substantially to Lessen Competition, or to Tend to Create a Monopoly, July 5 and 6, 1955.* Washington, DC: Government Printing Office.

United States Congress. Senate. (1976). *Final Report of the Select Committee to Study Governmental Operations with Respect to Intelligence Activities, United States Senate: Together with Additional, Supplemental, and Separate Views.* Washington, DC: Government Printing Office.

United States National Advisory Commission on Civil Disorders. (1968). *Report of the National Advisory Commission on Civil Disorders.* Washington, DC: U.S. Government Printing Office.

Useem, Michael. (1984). *The Inner Circle: Large Corporations and the Rise of Business Political Activity in the U.S. and U.K.* Oxford: Oxford University Press.

Van Creveld, Martin. (1999). *The Rise and Decline of the State.* Cambridge: Cambridge University Press.

Van der Pijl, Kiels. (1984). *The Making of an Atlantic Ruling Class.* London: Verso.

Varoufakis, Yanis. (2015). "How I Became an Erratic Marxist." *The Guardian*, February 18.

Waddell, Brian. (2001). *The War Against the New Deal*. DeKalb: Northern Illinois University Press.

Wallerstein, Immanuel. (1980). *The World Capitalist System II: Mercantilism and the Consolidation of the European World Economy, 1600–1750*. New York: Academic Press.

Wallerstein, Immanuel. (2003). *The Decline of American Power*. New York: New Press.

Weber, Max. (1946). "Class, Status, and Party." Pp. 180–195 in Hans H. Gerth and C. Wright Mills, eds., *From Max Weber: Essays in Sociology*. Oxford: Oxford University Press.

Weintraub, Sydney. (1993). "The North American Free Trade Agreement as Negotiated: A US Perspective." Pp. 1–31 in Steven Globerman and Michael Walker, eds., *Assessing NAFTA: A Trinational Analysis*. Vancouver: Fraser Institute.

Weiss, Linda. (1998). *The Myth of the Powerless State*. Ithaca: Cornell University Press.

Wetherly, Paul, Clyde W. Barrow, and Peter Burnham, eds. (2007). *Class, Power, and the State in Capitalist Societies*. London: Palgrave Macmillan.

Wile, Rob. (2014). "The True Story of How McDonald's Conquered France." *Business Insider*, August 22. www.businessinsider.com/how-mcdonalds-conquered-france-2014-8

Wolfe, Alan. (1977). *The Limits of Legitimacy: Political Contradictions of Contemporary Capitalism*. New York: Free Press.

Wolfe, Alan. (1999). "The Power Elite Now." *American Prospect* (May): 90–96.

Wood, Ellen Meiksins. (1999). "Unhappy Families: Global Capitalism in a World of Nation-States." *Monthly Review*, 51 (3): 1–12.

Wood, Ellen. (2003). *Empire of Capital*. London: Verso.

World Bank. (1999). *1999 World Development Indicators*. Washington, DC: World Bank.

Wright, Erik Olin Wright. (1978). *Class, Crisis, and the State*. London: New Left Books.

Wriston, Walter. (1992). *Twilight of Sovereignty: How the Information Revolution Is Transforming the World*. New York: Scribner's.

Young, Nigel. (1977). *An Infantile Disorder? The Crisis and Decline of the New Left*. Boulder, CO: Westview Press.

Zeitlin, Maurice. (1974). "Corporate Ownership and Control: The Large Corporation and the Capitalist Class." *American Journal of Sociology* 79:1073–1119.

Zeitlin, Maurice. (1977). *American Society, Inc.: Studies of the Social Structure and Political Economy of the United States*, 2nd ed. Chicago: Rand McNally.

Zeitlin, Maurice. (1980). *Classes, Class Conflict, and the State: Empirical Studies in Class Analysis.* Cambridge, MA: Winthrop.

Zeitlin, Maurice. (1989). *The Large Corporation and Contemporary Classes.* New Brunswick: Rutgers University Press.

Zurn, Michael, and Gregor Walter. (2005). *Globalizing Interests: Pressure Groups and Denationalization.* Albany: State University of New York Press.

Zweigenhaft, Richard. (1975). "Who Represents America?" *Insurgent Sociologist* (Spring): 119–130.

INDEX